BIRKHÄUSER

Whitestein Series in Software Agent Technologies and Autonomic Computing

Series Editors:
Marius Walliser
Stefan Brantschen
Monique Calisti
Stefan Schinkinger

This series reports new developments in agent-based software technologies and agent-oriented software engineering methodologies, with particular emphasis on applications in the area of autonomic computing & communications.

The spectrum of the series includes research monographs, high quality notes resulting from research and industrial projects, outstanding Ph.D. theses, and the proceedings of carefully selected conferences. The series is targeted at promoting advanced research and facilitating know-how transfer to industrial use.

About Whitestein Technologies

Whitestein Technologies is a leading innovator in the area of software agent technologies and autonomic computing & communications. Whitestein Technologies' offering includes advanced products, solutions, and services for various applications and industries, as well as a comprehensive middleware for the development and operation of autonomous, self-managing, and self-organizing systems and networks.
Whitestein Technologies' customers and partners include innovative global enterprises, service providers, and system integrators, as well as universities, technology labs, and other research institutions.

www.whitestein.com

Issues in Multi-Agent Systems

The AgentCities.ES Experience

Antonio Moreno
Juan Pavón
Editors

Birkhäuser
Basel · Boston · Berlin

Editors:

Antonio Moreno
Universitat Rovira I Virgili Escola Tecnica
Sup. Enginyeria Dept. Eng. Informatica i
Mathematiques
Avenida Paisos Catalans 26
43008 Tarragona
Spain
amoreno@etse.urv.es

Juan Pavón
Universidad Complutense de Madrid
28040 Madrid
Spain
jpavon@fdi.ucm.es

2000 Mathematical Subject Classification: 68-02, 68T05, 68T27, 68U35

Library of Congress Control Number: 2007938079

Bibliographic information published by Die Deutsche Bibliothek
Die Deutsche Bibliothek lists this publication in the Deutsche Nationalbibliografie;
detailed bibliographic data is available in the Internet at <http://dnb.ddb.de>.

ISBN 978-3-7643-8542-2 Birkhäuser Verlag AG, Basel – Boston – Berlin

© 2008 Birkhäuser Verlag, P.O. Box 133, CH-4010 Basel, Switzerland
Part of Springer Science+Business Media
Printed on acid-free paper produced from chlorine-free pulp. TCF ∞
Printed in Germany

ISBN 978-3-7643-8542-2   e-ISBN 978-3-7643-8543-9

9 8 7 6 5 4 3 2 1   www.birkhauser.ch

Contents

Preface

The *AgentCities.NET* European network (2001-2003) was a remarkable collaborative effort of hundreds of European scientists working in many diverse aspects of agent technology. Their long-term ambition was to prove the feasibility of deploying a world-wide network of agent-based platforms to provide a variety of public available e-services. The success of the network at the European level inspired the generation of national networks in different countries such as France, the United Kingdom and Spain. The *AgentCities.ES* Spanish network has been active for over 5 years, from 2003 to 2007. It has brought together 24 research groups and more than 120 scientists. The network was organized in clusters of people working in similar topics. It helped to establish relationships among scientists from different groups with similar interests and to promote the mutual visibility and the submission of joint national research projects. The main collaboration among the different clusters took place in the form of three yearly Spring schools on agent technology, held from 2005 to 2007. As a summary, this book presents some of the research results of the AgentCities.ES network clusters. Each chapter is centered on a particular research topic in agent technology, and has been carefully edited to cope with the diversity of contributions of the different research teams.

The first chapter presents results of the *Agent-Oriented Software Engineering (AOSE)* cluster. This cluster, led by J.Pavón (UCM), tried to establish a collaboration framework for the integration of different methods and tools for the development of multi-agent systems (MAS). This has been achieved by providing an evaluation framework for agent-oriented methodologies, and by spreading the application of methods and tools among participants in the network. The chapter covers both theoretical and practical issues. With respect to theoretical works, it presents the framework for the evaluation of different agent-oriented methodologies and a discussion of the role of agent-based modeling in the software life-cycle. In the case of practical issues, readers can find the description of a tool for the analysis of massive MAS, the design of holonic manufacturing systems, and a MAS to support software management.

The second chapter was inspired by the third AgentCities.ES Spring school, held at Valencia in 2007 and coordinated by J.M.Corchado (U. of Salamanca) and J.M.Molina (UC3M), whose main topics were *ubiquitous computing* and *mobility*. The chapter describes the main technological forces behind ambient intelligence, focuses on the definition, representation and management of *contextual* information, and provides an overview on *mobile agent technology*.

It is frequently forgotten that agent technology has to apply Artificial Intelligence techniques, especially when its aim is to build autonomous entities that exhibit an intelligent behavior. The third chapter, on *cognitive abilities*, reviews the basic tasks that a smart agent should be able to perform (i.e., basic AI fields of research such as planning, reasoning, rational decision making, learning) and presents specific agent-based systems with these capabilities.

In 2006 and 2007, in conjunction with the Spring schools on agent technology, the AgentCities.ES network also organized the first two editions of the Spanish competition on *Agent Reputation and Trust* (ART, coordinated by J.Carbó (UC3M) and J.Sabater-Mir (IIIA)). This activity shows the interest that Spanish research groups have in those topics. The fourth chapter describes in detail different ways of modeling and managing trust and reputation in multi-agent systems. It also presents the testbed used in the ART competition. The final sections of the chapter cover different techniques that have been developed in the last years to improve security, especially for mobile agents.

The fifth chapter of this book changes the focus from software agents to *physical agents*. It comments in some depth on the use of a new bounded deliberative technique to implement agents capable of reacting appropriately in problems with real-time constraints. The chapter also describes two specific agent-based physical robots developed at UdG (the mobile Grill robot and the Ictineu submarine robot) and an industrial application to control a container terminal at the port of Valencia.

Artificial Social Intelligence is devoted to the study of the ways in which agents can successfully deal with the complexity of inhabiting dynamic unpredictable societies and environments. This is the topic of chapter six, which elaborates on two basic concepts: *swarm intelligence* and *electronic institutions*. Swarm intelligence refers to the way in which a complex multi-agent system can exhibit an emergent intelligent behaviour. Electronic institutions are formal tools that support the representation of the different actors within an agent-based system and the interactions in which they may engage within an institution governed by a set of rules or norms.

The importance of Tourism in the economy of countries like Spain is well known. Therefore, any improvement in this area could automatically mean greater incomes for the country. The final chapter of the book describes specific *applications of multi-agent systems in Tourism*. First of all, three systems that provide personalized touristic information and recommendations to tourists using mobile phones are described. After that, two complex problems are studied, and solutions are proposed: how to discover and use e-services dynamically in complex hierarchical environments, and how to address the issue of dynamic location tracking.

In summary, this book covers a wide range of research issues in agent technology, showing the high level of activity in this field in Spain in recent years. At the end of the book the reader can also find a brief description of the main Spanish research groups in agent technology, which have participated in the AgentCities.ES network. The research lines of each group and their main application domains have been described using the codification proposed in the AgentLink research classification.

Acknowledgment

The AgentCities.ES network has been supported by the Spanish Council for Science and Technology under grants TIC2001-5108-E, TIN2004-20447-E, and TIN2005-25869-E.

Antonio Moreno, Juan Pavón
Tarragona - Madrid
November 2007

Whitestein Series in Software Agent Technologies, 1–31
© 2007 Birkhäuser Verlag Basel/Switzerland

Agent Oriented Software Engineering

Pedro Cuesta, Alma Gómez and Juan Carlos González

Abstract. Research in Agent Oriented Software Engineering involves the integration of different disciplines, from software engineering to artificial intelligence. To demonstrate the breadth of the field, this chapter discusses a number of the research issues involved. The issues range from the definition of a framework for evaluation of agent-oriented methodologies to the integration of other software engineering practices such as the use of software components or the Model Driven Engineering approach. The works discussed involve various activities of the software life cycle: test, verification and validation of multi-agent systems, the application of multi-agent systems for software maintenance and practical multi-agent systems proposals for specific domains, such as the development of multi-agent systems applying the System Product Lines philosophy and the definition of a method based on agent-oriented methodologies for the development of Holonic Manufacturing Systems.

1. Introduction

Agent Oriented Software Engineering (AOSE) addresses the development of complex systems using the agent paradigm. Agent related concepts provide new ways to model complex, large and dynamic systems. Those concepts have been successfully used in many applications but, as pointed in [34], there is still a need to define processes, methods and tools that facilitate the development of agent-based applications in time and with quality assurance.

Development processes and methodological proposals in agent oriented development are defined by small teams of academic researchers, in contrast with the standard object oriented approach that has been driven by industry [38]. Several methodologies have been defined for developing Multi-Agent Systems (MAS); some are based on existing object oriented methodologies, while others are extensions of

---

Co-authors of this chapter: Juan Antonio Botía, Vicent Botti, Josh Dehlinger, Rubén Fuentes, Adriana Giret, Jorge Gómez, Michael Hinchey, Robyn Lutz, Joaquín Peña, Mario Piattini, Oscar Rodríguez, Antonio Ruiz-Cortés, Guillermo Vigueras, Aurora Vizcaíno.

knowledge engineering approaches or formal methods. This definition reflects the different needs and approaches of designers and supposes that each methodology uses different concepts, representations, models, etc.

The profusion of methodologies implies a lack of standardisation and makes more difficult the achievement of an integrated approach for development. An important issue, therefore, will be to reach a methodological integration in a similar way as the Unified Modelling Language (UML) de facto standard in the object oriented context. One of the most relevant attempts for accomplishing interoperability among methodologies is the identification of a shared metamodel that can be widely accepted by the AOSE community [6]. Integration and/or interoperability will constitute the foundations for future agent-oriented modelling languages and development tools, which are key aspects in industrial use of agent technology.

Agent oriented development undertakes to accomplish a huge number of activities and tasks, supported by different tools and defined using diverse methods and models. The main aim of this chapter is to share the experience of authors in the AOSE discipline, addressing the areas outlined previously. For obvious reasons not all the research areas involving AOSE can be covered, but only those related to the groups which collaborated on this chapter.

As has been pointed out before, while there have been some highly successful applications of agent technologies, there is still much to be done in research and development for the full benefits to be achieved [49]. Moreover, the impact of agent technologies has been seen in various aspects. Firstly, as a metaphor for the design of complex, distributed computational systems; secondly, as a source of technologies for such computing systems, and thirdly, as models of complex real-world systems, such as those found in biology and economics.

This chapter presents some of the new research lines in the AOSE field. To begin, the team from the Universidad de Vigo presents the results of a research project focused on the evaluation of AOSE Methodologies using a framework. The results obtained will be useful for comparing methodologies and even deciding which one should be used depending on the problem to be solved. In recent years the groups' research has evolved to the evaluation and modelling of the development process used by the analysed methodologies.

One of the conclusions of earlier research was the necessity of applying a model driven approach in support tools for agent methodologies. This is the main contribution of the second work presented. The focus of the Universidad Complutense de Madrid team is on applying model driven software engineering to INGENIAS. This work also addresses how the models contribute to the understanding of developments that use INGENIAS and are supported by the Ingenias Development Kit (IDK). Moreover the way in which models are defined in INGENIAS has inspired the work of other groups of AgentCities.ES, such as the ANEMONA proposal.

On the other hand, the industrial use of MAS requires having the capacity to test, validate and verify the developed MAS. This is the main aspect of the third contribution, from the Universidad de Murcia group, which presents a practical example of a test, verification and validation tool: ACLAnalyser. The main goal of this tool is to support and analyse FIPA multi-agent systems through monitoring and debugging tasks.

The field of Software Product Lines (SPL) is the domain selected by the Universidad de Sevilla team. Their research is focused on applying the SPL philosophy for building MAS product lines (from which concrete MAS can be quickly derived that satisfy the requirement of each customer) and for managing evolving systems (where each evolution is seen as a new product in a MAS product line). This is done using the extension of GAIA methodology due to Josh Delingher and Robyn Lutz, and extending the MaCMAS methodology developed by the Universidad de Sevilla group.

After these works that focus on generic MAS development, two particular and practical proposals for specific domains are introduced. The Universidad Politécnica de Valencia group presents ANEMONA, a specific AOSE method for the development of Holonic Manufacturing Systems (HMS). ANEMONA is based on HMS specific requirements. It incorporates software engineering principles to assist the system designer, and provides clear and unambiguous analysis and design guidelines.

Finally, the contribution of The Universidad de Castilla-La Mancha team is the design of a MAS aimed to assist software maintainers in accessing knowledge sources related to the activities they perform. The main consideration in their research was to show that software agents can be useful in addressing such problems traditionally solved by means of knowledge management systems.

2. Evaluation of agent methodologies

Research on methodological evaluation is of interest due mainly to economic reasons. The use of the most accurate methodology will lead to better results, is less time and efforts consuming and, therefore, creates money savings. This justifies the interest of researchers in the definition of a rational way to choose the most suitable methodology for a particular problem.

This section presents a framework for the comparative analysis of existing Agent Oriented Software Engineering Methodologies (AOSEM). The criteria for the comparison are taken from a software engineering point of view as well as from agent-based computing.

2.1. Previous works in the field

Some previous works in AOSE have addressed the evaluation of methodologies [75] [71]. The approach followed in those cases was to adapt frameworks applied in the field of classical software engineering. Some of the criteria defined in these works are difficult to apply in practice, while others have only subjective valuation (this means that different people will evaluate in a different way the same criterion for the same methodology).

Other important work in the field is due to Massimo Cossentino based on a previous work of Khanh Hoa Dam and Michael Winikoff [17]. The evaluation framework is implemented by means of a questionnaire which covers the following areas for the evaluation criteria: concepts or properties used by the methodology, modeling, process and pragmatics.

In this section a new framework for AOSEM evaluation is proposed. The framework defines a set of criteria which are simple (in the sense that they can be easily identified and evaluated) and objective (meaning that the evaluation can be done in a precise way). In addition, the criteria try to be exhaustive; this means that they cover all of the characteristics which are relevant in software development. This is an important difference with the frameworks introduced in the paragraphs before, because the proposed framework (detailed in the next section) includes more criteria like documentation, methodological extensions, etc. Moreover, it is much more detailed with respect to process development, allowing in this way a more precise evaluation.

2.2. Framework description

This work proposes a framework form of an AOSEM evaluation, using a tabular questionnaire. In the framework, aspects to evaluate have been classified in five areas. The first group of evaluation criteria is called the *development process* and incorporates general aspects of the methodology as well as other issues related to construction of the system. The second, *model view*, tries to reflect the methodology concepts and their representation. The third, the *agent group*, addresses all the individual agent characteristics. Finally, the points of *additional features* and *documentation* incorporate other issues of interest.

The first point of evaluation is the *development process* (see Figure 1). In this section, aspects related to the construction of the multi-agent system (how it is built) will be evaluated. These aspects can be summarised in the general questions: which are the stages proposed by the methodology? and what kind of activities must be accomplished in each stage? The particular criteria evaluated at this point are: application domain, application areas, open systems, kind of life cycle, process stages and tools support.

Model view section tries to evaluate the diagrams and techniques proposed by the methodology for defining the system. In this section, the following aspects are addressed: concepts and representation, relationships among models and deliverables.

The *agent group* of criteria takes into consideration how agent characteristics (concept of agent) and features (agent's attributes) are defined. It also introduces social aspects of agents such as: types of communication, communication protocols, co-operation and agents organisation.

The *additional features* addresses the extensions proposed by the methodologies to deal with other important aspects of MAS such as: ontological aspects, mobility features and other additional characteristics.

Aspect to be considered	Explanation	Evaluation
Application domain		Domain oriented/ Domain Independent/ Unknown
Application areas	Global Comment	
	Particular Area	Mentioned/Documented
Open systems		Yes/No/Unknown
Kind of life cycle		
Stage 1	Name	Brief Explanation of the phase and the evaluation made
Activities of	Requirements	Focused/ Partially Focused/Not Focused[1]
	Analysis	Focused/ Partially Focused/Not Focused
	Design	Focused/ Partially Focused/Not Focused
	Implementation	Focused/ Partially Focused/Not Focused
	Testing	Focused/ Partially Focused/Not Focused
	User implication	Focused/ Partially Focused/Not Focused

FIGURE 1. Part of the evaluation framework related to development process (tabular form).

Finally, an important aspect is how methodologies are documented. This aspect is evaluated taking into consideration the available *documentation* and the case studies presented by the authors. In order to have an objective evaluation of this point, the framework focuses on the number of available cases and whether they are complete or not.

The results of application of this framework are summarised in tabular form, where the value assigned for each criteria is introduced. The value can be quantitative (numerical) or qualitative (from a reduced set of possibilities; for instance Focused/ Partially Focused/Not Focused). Additional information can be introduced in the explanation column. The detailed framework for evaluation can be found in [15].

2.3. Results of the evaluation for some methodologies

Several methodologies have been evaluated taking into account all the criteria defined in the framework. The methodologies selected for evaluation were INGENIAS, Tropos, GAIA, Prometheus and MaSE, because they almost provide a full coverage of the life cycle and the development process. Other well-know methodologies, such as Passi [14] or ADEM [4], have been outside the reach of the study because they do not provide such coverage. In the case of Passi, the methodology is centred specifically in the development process; whereas ADEM is fundamentally oriented to the development activities. Finally, some modelling languages, such as

AML [4] or AUML [40], have not been studied, when considering that they do not have associated a concrete development process or life cycle.

The evaluations have been done mainly by the University of Vigo team, by means of forms available at the AOSE site (http://ma.ei.uvigo.es/isoa/). Contributions from other specialists in AOSEM were welcome and have been incorporated, after a revision, in the results. In the following paragraphs these results are briefly summarised. The complete study can be obtained at the site.

GAIA [83] is a methodology for agent-oriented analysis and design which deals with the macro-level (Society) and the micro-level (Agent) concepts. Its is domain independent, but its main disadvantage is that it can not be applied to open systems. Moreover, GAIA provides support only to analysis and design steps of the life cycle. The models proposed by methodology are complete, but some of them are not graphical and lack well-defined relationships among them. Communication is defined in some of those models, allowing the user to describe new protocols in addition to the standard ones. Finally, the methodology does not provide a way of defining ontological or mobility aspects. Nevertheless, there are extensions for adapting GAIA to open systems.

Multi-agent Systems Engineering (MaSE) [24] is a general purpose methodology for developing heterogeneous MAS. It covers the whole life cycle and is supported by a software tool, AgentTool [25]. MaSE is based on the concept of role, defined as an entity which performs some function within the system. For the authors, an agent is a specialisation of object, and may not possess intelligence. Available documentation of MaSE is composed mainly of research papers.

Prometheus is a general purpose methodology which is used to develop intelligent agent systems [55]. It is supported by some tools, such as Prometheus Design Tool (PDT) and JACK Development Environment (JDE). The methodology models the system using graphical notations but also structured textual descriptors. Nevertheless, during its evaluation some gaps between models were detected. The available documentation is mainly research papers, while the study cases presented are partial.

Tropos is considered a requirements-driven methodology based on the i* modelling framework [51]. It covers all the stages of development using the same concepts and semantics. This methodology, according to its authors is intended mainly for organisational systems. Despite the correct use of concepts in TROPOS, in analysis it uses the actor concept, while the agent concept is introduced in design without a clear explanation. In addition, the relationship among actors and agents is not detailed. Although initially there were no supporting tools for any phase of the methodology, recently, some tools have been defined, such as TAOM4E for modelling or OME for requirements [54].

INGENIAS methodology covers analysis and design of MAS, and it is intended for general use, with no restrictions on application domain [57]. It is based on UML diagrams and process (RUP), trying in this way to facilitate its use and apprenticeship. New models are added and the UML ones are enriched to introduce agent and organisational concepts. At the moment the metamodels proposed cover the whole life cycle and capture different views of the system.

In INGENIAS, agents are modelled as specific entities which are atomic, autonomous and capable of performing some function; they can be software or human. INGENIAS has a supporting tool (IDK framework [33]) that allows the construction of any of the models and their checking for completion or correctness. The available documentation of the methodology is exhaustive; in addition, several study cases have been completely developed and are available.

2.4. Conclusions

After the evaluation of methodologies, one of the objectives of the study has been achieved, that is, to obtain conclusions from the actual state of AOSEM. The most relevant ones are the importance of having methodologies which cover the whole life cycle of development (at this moment, there is not such a methodology) and the necessity of standardisation. Some groups of researchers are working to achieve both objectives in different ways. The latest works of the AOSE Agentlink group [5] defines a general standard metamodel, where every methodology may fit. On the other hand the FAME proposal of Brian Henderson [37] addresses the problem of defining a framework for integrating fragments of different methodologies and accomplishing a whole life cycle coverage.

Another important issue that must be highlighted is the necessity of quality supporting tools for aiding in the system construction. The development of such tools must be done following the latest standards in the field, namely Model Driven Architecture (MDA). Some of the methodologies presented are working in this field at the moment. Particularly the INGENIAS proposal, as it will be shown in the next section, introduces MDA for improving AOSE development and the associated IDK tool.

Finally, it is important to note the necessity of being able to establish and evaluate the process of development associated with each methodology. The first step for achieving this objective will be to model the process of development. The SPEM models can be used for defining in a standard way the process of each methodology. These models will be the basis of a subsequent evaluation using objective metrics. At the moment, the Universidad de Vigo team is focused on this aspect.

3. The relevance of modelling in AOSE

In Agent Oriented Software Engineering, most existing methodologies propose the elaboration of MAS specifications by means of models. Though methodologies can prove their capability to produce MAS, there is much work to do in order to improve the development process itself, in particular: how to create the models in an efficient way and how to transform these models into executable code. A branch of software engineering where these problems are addressed is Model Driven

Engineering (MDE). It involves the support of modelling tools, for creating models representing the system, and transformation tools, to produce code from models [72]. Adapting MDE to MAS will bring two main benefits: the access to techniques and tools developed by MDE researchers, and to clarify the MAS development process by focusing on how the models are produced instead of on coding tasks.

3.1. Towards MDE

Looking at the progress of AOSEM, one can observe a progressive increase in the relevance of models. Initial methodologies, like Vowel Engineering [26] or BDI methodology [44], were aimed at the production of a MAS, mainly. From the incorporation of MESSAGE [10] and ADELFE [7], a shift could be observed in the AOSE proposals characterised by an intensive use of meta-modelling techniques and a growing focus on obtaining the modelling terms with which a complete MAS could be obtained. MDE is based on the description of meta-models, where a meta-model is a grammar that declares how a model is to be constructed. In general, a model is made of entities connected with relationships.

Software engineering research has observed the same evolution in the development of applications [74]. As a result, a new trend, the MDE was created to capture the knowledge necessary to perform a development where the main products are models. This differs from classical software engineering where the main outcome was the software product itself. So far, the tendency seems similar to AOSE. However, there is an important difference. While the AOSE community aims to agree in one or many meta-model for MAS definition [6], MDE researchers obtain reusable tools and processes, leaving developers the burden of deciding how to use them.

The opportunity of reusing MDE results in AOSE is clear; however, there is little effort in that direction. This section presents the concrete case of INGENIAS [57] to illustrate the benefits of focusing on MDE concerns in an AOSE methodology. Namely making models the main product and increasing automation in the development process [74].

INGENIAS is the result of improvements applied by a Ph.D. thesis about MAS modelling [32]. The initial version of INGENIAS [57] already considered models, a process to produce them, and automatic code generation, all of them being elements in the spirit of MDE. INGENIAS was introduced to the MDE community as an example of how these principles were used to facilitate MAS production [58].

INGENIAS assumes a model driven approach. It is a model centric solution that can obtain an executable MAS from the specification by means of code generation facilities. The elements to be used in the models that conform to the specification come from agent research. They were obtained by surveying different areas, like theoretical models of agency, planning literature, or distributed systems. The usability of the combination of the different research terms was tested against different domains [56]: information categorisation, a game of fighting tanks, and PC assistants for document gathering. These models were processed by template based code generation facilities. Being template based, it was possible to customise the template files and adapt the generated files to the convenience of the developer.

Focusing on MDE issues, but not on MAS issues, two improvements over INGENIAS have been made. First, it has been clarified what aspects of the development process should be considered. There should be activities dedicated to verify models, for building/modifying the transformation from specification to code, and for creating quick prototypes. These activities were introduced briefly in [58]. Secondly, INGENIAS incorporates advances in automatic code generation, an important issue in MDE. Automatic code generation has an important drawback, namely, the management of changes in the generated code. Once the code is generated, if a developer modifies a file, it is not straightforward to prevent these changes from being overwritten if the code is regenerated. Aiming at the resolution of this problem, INGENIAS proposes two tools, which were presented in a Dagstuhl seminar [18]: *AppLinker* and a *template editor*. The first uploads to the specification changes made in automatically generated java interfaces. The second is an editor for modifying instances of a template and deducing which changes have to be applied to the template. Using both of them, a developer can safely modify produced code.

Currently, there is a strong effort in migrating the INGENIAS meta-models to EMF, an extended meta-model language used regularly in MDE approaches. The interest in using EMF is related with the research on MDE issues, which usually ends up in producing software working with EMF. For instance, any AOSE methodology using models has to consider and control how these models are going to evolve during the development. For these tasks, model merging [46] and model versioning are necessary. These two areas are subjects of research in MDE at the moment.

Adopting MDE brings additional benefits. First, conventional software engineers can get used to an AOSE methodology sooner if it is presented using a standardised vocabulary (e.g., expressed in terms of meta-models or transformations) and concept structure (e.g., the model construction process). Therefore, developers used to MDE, can apprehend faster a methodology, e.g., INGENIAS, if it is presented to them using terms and principles familiar to them. Second, AOSE has less experience in which activities are more meaningful for a developer when modelling is the main issue. Therefore, INGENIAS can obtain direct benefits from the experience and support tools of other MDE approaches, since the development principles are compatible. For instance, model transformation software is independent of the methodology used, as long as the meta-modeling language is compatible with the transformation engine. Therefore, INGENIAS could reuse these facilities as long as its meta-models could be expressed in the appropriate meta-modeling language. Third, making code generation mandatory makes the development more consistent. The consistency comes mainly from the adequacy of the implementation with respect to the specification. The generated system sticks to the specification as long as the code generation process implements a correct mapping. This way, developers can focus their effort on the production of the model, converting the implementation into a secondary task.

The lessons learned in INGENIAS are worth being applied in other methodologies. Mainly, the following benefits will be obtained. First, by sticking to MDE practices (expressing the definition of the MAS in form of meta-models, defining code generation processes and/or model to model transformations) the AOSE community can keep focused on the problem of obtaining an adequate set of concepts for MAS definition and still enjoying the tools provided by those working on how to facilitate MDE developments. Second, accepting that models become the main product will clarify the development process. Most activities will be dedicated to the elaboration of models. Troublesome activities such as testing or implementation will count on the support of tools that will do most of the work. Besides, this is a way of gaining technological independence. Given a set of models, it would be possible to define different code generation processes adapted to the most convenient agent platform. This is in line with the technology independence promise of the MDA [53], a concrete proposal of MDE by the Object Management Group. MDA adds to the equation the need for models to stick to different abstraction levels and transformation processes among them. Testing activities can be speeded up by deducing which tests to apply according to the elements considered in the specification as it is done in [52].

4. Testing, validation and verification of MAS software

The growing complexity of MAS is increasing the demand for better tools to test, verify and validate them during the development cycle. Complexity comes from different sources not present in conventional software engineering:

- Distribution and mobility. MAS software is concurrent and distributed, and agents may have the ability of moving from one node to another in a network. Inherent concurrency and software distribution of MAS implies that all problems common to conventional concurrent systems already exist within MAS software. Among them, two important ones are agent deadlocks and race conditions.
- Organisation. Agents are social entities. This may appear as an obvious detail, but as a matter of fact, this important feature implies having mechanisms to make assessments about the behaviour of the society. Social metaphors are required to explain why agents behave in a specific way with other agents. So it is not just a problem of analysing dialogues between agents following concrete interaction protocols, but assessing the correctness of behaviour from a social and intentional point of view.
- Autonomy. Agents themselves are not simple structures. BDI agents are autonomous entities [68], which manage goals, elaborate plans to achieve these goals, and may use several mechanisms to learn and adapt to new situations.

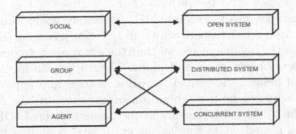

FIGURE 2. Two different perspectives for testing a multi-agent system. Also, each perspective shows a layered arrangement to cope with such a complex task.

So analysing an agent involves checking some issues: the level of fulfilment of such goals, the learning process and the consistency of belief base.

To deal with these issues many research works are being developed in the areas of MAS testing, verification and validation. Testing and debugging MAS consists of the design, application and analysis of a set of test cases for multi-agent software, with the intention of finding (for testing and debugging) and locating (for debugging) errors in the code or in the specification. Verification has the intention of checking whether a MAS possesses some properties, as for example in BDI agents, verify some mental properties defined by the tester. Validation consists of checking whether a multi-agent system fulfils its design requirements or not, i.e., to check whether the system works as is expected or not. In the next section different abstraction levels of a MAS are described, in which test, debug, verification and validation tasks are performed, depending on MAS level view.

4.1. Global perspective

Current MAS software testing, verification and validation methods could be categorised according to the six aspects that are shown in Figure 2. These aspects are organised in two columns of layers where the top layer is the most abstract and the lower layer the most concrete.

The layers on the right refer to the testing activity when the target is seen as a typical information system. It is equivalent to testing a concrete implementation. A MAS, from the system perspective, may be divided into three different layers: concurrency, distributed issues and openness in a MAS. In all these three layers, the techniques used to check them totally depend on the underlying implementation platform.

The three layers on the left side refer to check a particular MAS model specification. Hence, given a concrete model of agency, analysing a model specification might be divided into three different scopes: agent, group and social view. A deeper explanation of the three layers will be found in Sections 4.1.1, 4.1.2 and 4.1.3.

4.1.1. The agent level. The related literature includes many examples of testing single agents, all of them influenced by the BDI (*Belief, Desire, Intention*) model

of agency. For example, the Tracer Tool [47] uses beliefs, goals, intentions, actions, events, messages, and relations between them to create a concept graph. This concept graph defines the behaviour model that the agent must accomplish. Sudeikat et al. [78] considers beliefs, goals and plans. Their approach focuses on checking the consistency of beliefs, the correct adoption of goals and appropriate plan execution. This is achieved by a combination of assertions in the code and static checking to validate deliberative agents in the context of the JADEX framework.

In summary, nowadays, testing at the agent level is limited to testing single agent type specifications with respect to their implementations and using a specific BDI model of agency as the model of reference. Notice that the dependence from the concrete model of agency used is strong at this level. It will be progressively made lower in the other two levels (group and social) within the agent perspective.

4.1.2. The group level. Analysing the group level consists of the study of coordination issues derived from a type of communication activity between agents, i.e., interaction protocol (IP) based conversations, work-flows and acquaintances among agents. At the moment, very few references are found in the literature that properly address any of these tasks. Well-known works are those done in the context of Prometheus methodology [67] although they are limited to checking the correct accomplishment of conversations following clearly defined interaction protocols. A different approach is that of Alberti et al. [1]. This work follows a declarative approach and takes advantage of the semantics of communicative acts to verify some social integrity constraints. Constraints are defined in terms of expectations on interactions.

Another important source of ideas is the work of Jensen and Lesser [42]. They identify potential problems and expose them in the context of evolving agents (i.e., agents that learn and change their behaviour through time) but they are perfectly applicable for agents with incorrect behaviour specifications at design time. Jensen and Lesser define what they call *pathologies* in MAS as *a behaviour of the system where two or more agents interact in such a way that improvements in local performance do not improve the global performance of the system.* They mention four different pathologies. Thus they refer to *tragedy of the commons, lock-in, cycling, blocking*. These four pathologies (there are many more) are very interesting to help in the definition of a possible taxonomy of different kinds of potential problems which could appear in a MAS. However, they are hard to implement at the general level. A concrete instantiation of each pathology is needed for each particular kind of MAS and application domain in which it is applied.

4.1.3. The society level. To analyse a MAS as a society means checking if some given properties, restrictions and rules are accomplished by the whole MAS. Hence, the scope of such properties, restrictions, and rules is the whole system, not individual components. For instance, let us suppose a MAS of agents in an electronic market would use a global wealth measurement to track MAS evolution. According to this, in [20] a method to validate self-organisation MAS is proposed. In such a method, mathematical analysis of some MAS parameters is performed. Values for those parameters are collected from some simulations and using that collected data, are studied as to whether MAS parameters converge to desired values or not. By means of this method, the developer can determine whether the emergent agents behaviour is as expected or not.

On the other hand, to verify if some properties are accomplished in a whole MAS, model checking is a widely used technique. This technique allows one to verify concurrent issues or that agents accomplish some properties interacting with the rest of the agents in the MAS. In model checking the MAS model is expressed using some representation formalism and verified using some model checker, like SPIN and its input model language PROMELA[36].

4.2. The ACLAnalyser tool

ACLAnalyser [8] represents a prototype of a tool which helps in testing, verification and validation processes. ACLAnalyser is a set of software elements whose principal goal is to support the analysis of FIPA multi-agent systems through monitoring and debugging tasks.

Taking as reference the notion of MAS testing that is depicted in Figure 2 and explained in Section 4.1, the ACLAnalyser supports MAS analysis at group and social levels. At group level the performed analysis consists of: interaction protocol analysis, acquaintances view between agents and groups, causality relationship representation and social pathologies detection by searching unfinished tasks. At the social level the tool allows to measure MAS parameters and analyse its evolution when stressing the MAS.

The ACLAnalyser tool has been designed to analyse runs on any FIPA compliant platform. It has been implemented, as a proof of concept, for the JADE platform, although versions for 3APL, Jason, JADEX and Agent Factory are being considered. The tool consists of three elements: the sniffer agent (different from the JADE sniffer agent), a relational database with the associated data management software from the tool, and the analysis components.

The sniffer agent receives a copy of all messages sent through JADE in a MAS run. It also stores, in a convenient format, all messages for further analysis, calling the database API. The relational database management system (RDMS) is designed for storing sessions, conversations, messages, senders and receivers. More details about the schema defined to represent all the logged data inside the database can be found in [8].

The component in charge of all tasks related with the analysis of the stored data on a MAS run, is the analyser. While the other two elements of the ACLAnalyser work on-line at run time, this third component works off-line once the MAS has finished an execution (usually it is finished by the developer). Its source of data for analysis consists in all the information, including messages exchanged, related to the last MAS execution.

4.3. Conclusions

As explained in the introduction, MAS have special issues that differentiate them from conventional software. Those issues increase development complexity and motivate researchers to develop methods to test, verify and validate a MAS. These methods have been structured according to two views of a MAS: one logical dealing with agent concepts and metaphors, and another more related with implementation specific concerns. As a practical example of MAS analysis, is described the ACLAnalyser tool. This tool is platform independent and allow to analyse a MAS at group and society level.

5. Current research in multi-agent systems product lines

AOSE methodologies provide powerful techniques and tools with which software engineers can understand, model and develop MAS using high-level abstractions. However, current AOSE methodologies provide only limited accommodations for handling the complexity of evolving MAS and lack adequate mechanisms for reuse. These limitations impede the adoption of AOSE as a software development paradigm in industry.

The agents comprising a MAS are typically autonomous, proactive and highly dynamic in nature [82]. In order to adapt to the challenges of its environment, a MAS may be required to self-adapt and self-configure as an evolving system. As the MAS evolves, it essentially represents multiple instances of the originally developed system as variations and changes are incorporated. However, current AOSE methodologies fail to gracefully provide developers with the requirements, design and architectural techniques and tools to handle the complexity of evolving MAS.

From the beginning, one of the goals of AOSE was to provide methodologies for reusing and maintaining MAS [82]. The realisation of a reuse-oriented AOSE methodology that defines and identifies reusable assets at an early stage in the development life cycle can promote reductions in development time and cost in building MAS. Since many MAS will be developed utilising techniques, adaptations and approaches similar to previously built MAS, the opportunity for reuse is great.

Current AOSE methodologies are solely designed for the development of a single MAS. A few techniques (e.g., [27] and [35]), have been proposed as reuse mechanisms for MAS. However, these techniques fail to capture the reuse potential of MAS development, since they focus on the later stages of development for specific MAS applications.

Product-line engineering emphasises the construction of a family of products instead of a single system [13], [64], [81]. Multiagent Systems Product Lines (MAS-PL) is a field that incorporates product-line research into AOSE [23], [21], [60]. In this paper we discuss current research in this area, whose main contribution is providing valuable tools and techniques to ease the adoption of AOSE in industry.

5.1. SPL and AOSE

The software product line field tries to provide all the engineering tools and techniques needed for building a family of systems from which concrete systems demanded by customers are derived rapidly. Thus, SPL helps to develop the products required by customers by reducing time-to-market and costs, and simultaneously improving quality, by making greater effort in design, implementation and testing more financially viable, as this effort can be amortised over several products [13]. For example, the SPL requirements engineering phase identifies for a specific application domain the commonalities (the requirements shared by all systems of the SPL) and the variabilities (requirements for only some systems of the SPL).

The software development process proposed in AOSE presents many similarities with the process followed in SPL for the activities of the *domain engineering phase*, which provides the reusable core assets that are exploited in the derivation of products, done during the *application engineering phase* [64].

As described in [64], the activities, usually performed iteratively and in parallel, of domain engineering that present a correlation with AOSE are:

Domain requirements engineering phase. Both approaches use models based on similar concepts: features in the case of SPLs, and system-goals in the case of AOSE [9, 16]. Both represent requirements observable by the end user in a hierarchical structure. However, SPL emphasises the analysis of the scope of the SPL, i.e., the products inside it, and the analysis of common and variable features across the SPL, which are not carried out by AOSE. In [21, 62], the first steps toward adapting system-goals to MAS-PL and documenting variability are shown.

Domain engineering design phase. Both approaches develop architecture-independent models that attempt to analyse how features and variability can be built. In AOSE, role models are used with this purpose [82], and some approaches in SPL also propose the same approach [41, 77]. However, agent-focused models show additional information that is not needed in SPL-role models, such as the goals of the agents, or whether they are used to abstract AI techniques, while not showing how these role models can be reused for different products.

Domain realisation phase. Both approaches focus on designing a detailed architecture. In the case of SPL, a common architecture for all products and a set of reusable assets are developed. In the case of AOSE, a single architecture that fulfils all of the system-goals of the MAS is developed. Some approaches in both fields base the construction of the architecture on role model composition [41, 77].

This, along with the first research papers discussed in the next section, shows that the benefits from enabling MAS-PL are reachable.

5.2. Current research

In this section the main approaches published in the MAS-PL field are covered.

5.2.1. GAIA and MAS-PL.
In [23] and [21], Dehlinger and Lutz present an adaptation of the GAIA AOSE methodology [82] incorporating software product-line

engineering concepts from Weiss and Lai's FAST approach [81]. The product-line engineering adaptation of GAIA uses this approach to define the core assets (requirements, specifications, etc.) of a MAS in a Commonality and Variability Analysis (CVA) as well as in several modified GAIA templates during domain engineering. It then reuses these assets during application engineering by defining an agent in a modified GAIA template. Dehlinger and Lutz found that using this approach helped manage the complexity of a MAS by systematically capturing the shifting configurations of agents and roles during the requirements analysis, design and detailed design phases of GAIA. In addition, it was found that reuse is possible during initial MAS development as well as during MAS evolution.

In order to integrate product-line engineering concepts into GAIA, the notion of an agent having different possible levels of intelligence for a given role was used as a variation point. In a MAS, variation points for a specific role of an agent are the differing protocols, activities, permissions and responsibilities available to that role. For example, a role in a distributed system of nodes, depending on its environment and context, may have differing intelligence levels [12], [23] and [21]; may be delegated as a hot-spare, warm-spare or cold-spare; or may be assigned to be active or passive.

For MAS that are safety-critical, Dehlinger and Lutz developed safety analysis techniques for the product-line engineering adaptation of GAIA [21], [22]. These safety analyses provide some assurance that core assets defined in the domain engineering phase are being safely reused during the application engineering phase. In [21], a tool-supported product-line software fault tree analysis technique illustrates how the causes of a safety hazard for a MAS constructed using the product-line GAIA methodology can be identified and how additional safety requirements can be derived. In [22], a software failure mode, effects and criticality analysis (SFMECA) technique specifically for the product-line GAIA methodology, was provided to give developers a structured process by which to identify and document failures of an agent.

5.2.2. MaCMAS and MAS-PL.

The Methodology for analysing Complex Multi-Agent Systems[1] (MaCMAS), developed by Peña, is an AOSE methodology focused on dealing with complexity, which uses UML as a modelling language and builds on the current research and development experience of authors in the field of SPLs[59]. MaCMAS provides support for building the core architecture of a MAS-PL and for modelling evolving systems.

For enabling a product line, one of the important activities to be performed is to identify a core architecture for the family of software products. The only MAS-oriented work known in this direction is [62]. In the paper, Peña, Hinchey, Ruiz-Cortés and Trinidad present how to build the core architecture of a MAS-PL using MaCMAS and exemplify it with a case study based on a future NASA mission for space exploration.

---

[1]http://james.eii.us.es/MaCMAS/

This approach consists of using goal-oriented requirement documents, role models, and traceability diagrams in order to build a first model of the system, and later using information on variability and commonalities throughout the products to propose a transformation of the former models that represent the core architecture of the family.

Peña et al. introduce a mapping between feature models and role models used to document the architecture. The feature model is automatically analysed using an algorithm for performing commonality analysis (that is to say, to automatically analyse the probability that a feature appears in a product). Later, having these probabilities, the authors propose an operation to compose the role models corresponding to each feature which is automated in the case tool ArgoUML following an MDE approach [63]. This operation allows the authors to semi-automatically build the core architecture including those features whose probability of appearing is above a given threshold.

MaCMAS has also used an MAS-PL approach to build evolutionary systems [61]. In this paper, Peña, Hinchey et al. view an evolutionary system as being a software product line, exemplifying it also by a NASA case study. The core architecture is seen as the the unchanging part of the system and each version of the system is viewed as a product from the product line. Each "product" is described as the core architecture with some agent-based additions.

The paper provides a state-based notation using UML to represent the evolution of the system. In this notation, each state represents a product and each transition is built by a guard, representing the condition to evolve from one product to another, and the features added/deleted. It also shows how to add features by composing/decomposing the role models that represents these features.

5.3. Conclusions and future challenges

For MAS-PL to be adopted as a development paradigm in industry, additional tool-support as well as additional reuse mechanisms may be needed. Further, along with providing developers with the ability for reuse, MAS-PL must also provide techniques to ensure that the reuse is safe for a MAS when safety is required.

Another promising research area for MAS-PL is MDE (see Section 3). Building MAS-PL involves transformations of models (e.g., for adding / deleting features) and automated analysis of models (e.g., for ensuring safe reuse). Automated tools implementing model-based techniques can provide additional support for building and evolving MAS-PL.

6. Using AOSE for engineering holonic manufacturing systems

Holonic Manufacturing Systems (HMS) was first proposed as a new manufacturing paradigm in the beginning of the 1990s [39] and has since then received a lot of attention in academic and industrial research. The application of holonic concepts to manufacturing was initially motivated by the inability of existing manufacturing systems (i) to deal with the evolution of products within an existing production facility and (ii) to maintain a satisfactory performance outside normal operating conditions. Due to the manufacturing specific requirements, the holonic fundamental characteristics, and the complexity of real life manufacturing systems, the development process of such systems needs to be directed by flexible, scalable and complete software engineering methods [50]. In this section a specific AOSE method for the development of HMS, named ANEMONA, is presented. ANEMONA is based on HMS specific requirements; it incorporates software engineering principles to assist the system designer, and provides clear and unambiguous analysis and design guidelines. Section 6.1, overviews the HMS background, and the state of the art of this field. Section 6.2, describes the HMS modelling requirements. Section 6.3, illustrates the relationships among holons and agents. Section 6.4, describes the ANEMONA methodological approach. Section 6.5, summarises some conclusions.

6.1. HMS

The holonic concept was developed by the philosopher Arthur Koestler [45] in order to explain the evolution of biological and social systems. These observations led Koestler to propose the word "*holon*" which is a combination of the Greek word 'holos' meaning whole and the Greek suffix "*on*" meaning particle or part as in proton or neutron. The strength of holonic organisation, or *holarchy*, is that it enables the construction of very complex systems that are nonetheless efficient in the use of resources, highly resilient to disturbance (both internal and external), and adaptable to changes in the environment in which they exist.

The HMS is a research initiative for advanced manufacturing systems inspired by the concepts proposed by Koestler. The goal of the HMS is to attain in manufacturing the benefits that holarchies provide to living organisms and societies. Holons in a HMS assist the operator to control the system: holons autonomously select appropriate parameter settings, find their own strategies and build their own structure. In the last ten years, an increasing amount of research has been devoted to HMS over a broad range of both theoretical issues and industrial applications. These research efforts can be divided into three groups [50]: (i) holonic control architectures, (ii) holonic control algorithms and (iii) methodologies for HMS. For an extensive review of the state of the art see [76].

6.2. Requirements of a methodology for HMS

Manufacturing requirements impose important properties on HMS [39]. A methodology requirements list based on the developments reported in HMS, and authors' experience with software methods have been defined: (1) Manufacturing control systems require autonomous entities organised in holarchy structures. (2) Manufacturing control units need a routine based behaviour which is both effective and timely. (3) A HMS method should lead straight forwardly from the control task to autonomous entities. (4) A HMS method should define a development process guided by abstraction levels with modelling artefacts and guidelines to manage it. (5) A HMS method should define a mixed top-down and bottom-up development

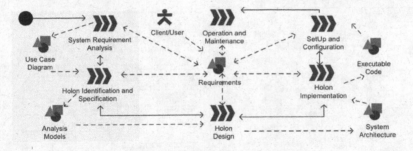

FIGURE 3. Phases of ANEMONA.

process. (6) A HMS method should integrate the entire range of manufacturing activities.

6.3. Agents and holons

Holons and agents are very similar concepts (for a detailed comparison of these two notions see [28]). The recursive structure is the only holon property which is not presented, as such, in the agent definition. To cope with this limitation in [30] the authors propose the Abstract Agent notion (A-Agent) as a modelling artefact for autonomous entities with recursive structures. The A-Agent extends the traditional agent definition adding a structural perspective to the agent concept: "... *an A-Agent can be an agent; or it can be a MAS made up of A-Agent...*". The A-Agent is an attempt to unify the concepts of holons and agents and to simplify and close the gap between holons and agents in analysis and design steps. In this way, it will be easier to translate modelling products obtained from HMS methods into coding elements for the implementation of the HMS.

6.4. ANEMONA

In this section ANEMONA, its foundations and its usage[2] are presented. In this method, the HMS is specified by dividing it into more specific characteristics that form different *views* of the system. These views are defined in terms of MAS technology; therefore, talking about agents, roles, goals, beliefs, organisations, etc. A-Agent and holon are used as similar notions [28]. The views can be considered as general MAS models that can also be applied to other domains. The way in which the views (models) are defined [29] is inspired by the INGENIAS methodology [56]. The extensions made to the INGENIAS meta-models deal with: the addition of the A-Agent notion and the properties to model real-time behaviours [43], the redefinition of some relations to conform to the new modelling entities and the

---

[2]The modelling diagrams were obtained from a real manufacturing case study from a ceramic tile factory. The tile factory is divided into departments. The tile production process is as follows: the clay is obtained, mixed, refined, dried, pressed or extruded, decorated/glazed and baked in ovens known as kilns. The HMS for the Tile Factory must: (i) integrate the different departments of the company, (ii) arrange factory resources for both on-demand and stock production orders, and (iii) automate resources and processes controls at different levels in the company.

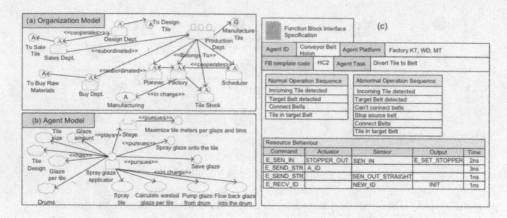

FIGURE 4. (a) An Organisation Diagram from the analysis phase.
(b) An Agent Diagram of the Spray Glaze Applicator Agent of the
Ceramic Tile Factory. (c) A Function Block Interface Specification
of the Conveyor Belt Holon from the design phase.

dependencies between them. These extensions are motivated by requirements 1
and 2 of Section 6.2.

The development process of ANEMONA (Figure 3) provides HMS specific
modelling guidelines [31]. It is motivated by requirements 3 to 6 of Section 6.2. In
the **analysis phase** the HMS is specified in terms of the five models and UML *use
case diagrams*. This is a top-down, recursive and incremental process. The main
goal of the analysis step is to identify the system holons and to provide an initial holons specification. From the *requirements set* and the *domain definition* the
designer has to produce the *analysis models* (Figure 4(a),(b)). Each iteration of
the analysis phase identifies and specifies holarchies of different levels of recursion
(holons made up of holons). The first iteration identifies an initial holarchy, made
up of holons which co-operate to fulfil the global system requirements. At the end
of every iteration the designer has to analyse every holon trying to figure out the
advantages of decomposing it into a new holarchy. In this way, each new iteration will have as many concurrent processes as constituent holons of the previous
iteration that it was decided to decompose. This process is repeated until every
holon is completely defined and there is no need for further decompositions. In
this phase the designer may use [31]: (i) *HMS UC Guidelines* to identify domains
co-operation and system goals as use cases; and (ii) *PROSA Guidelines* to identify
A-Agents and to categorise them as PROSA types of holons [79].

The *analysis model* is an initial system architecture, which has to be completed with details of the target implementation platform in the **design phase**. For
intra-holon information processing and for inter-holon co-operation ANEMONA
provides design guidelines for JADE. Whereas for the low level control, that is for
physical operations, it provides design guidelines for function blocks (FB - IEC

61499 series of standards). From the *system architecture* (Figure 4(c) presents a FB template example for a conveyor belt holon) the **holons implementation phase** produce the *executable code* for the HMS. Configuration activities are carried out in the **set-up and configuration phase** to deploy the HMS at the target destination. Finally in the **operation and maintenance phase** maintenance activities are performed. In case of new requirements a new development process has to be initiated.

6.5. Conclusions

ANEMONA is an AOSE method for HMS, based on the A-Agent notion and six HMS modelling requirements. The ANEMONA process is a mixed top-down and bottom-up approach. It provides the HMS designer with HMS-specific modelling guidelines, and complete development phases for the HMS life cycle.

7. A multi-agent system to manage knowledge sources in software maintenance environments

As a software process, maintenance is knowledge intensive. Moreover, maintenance may be even more knowledge intensive, and consequently a more demanding job than software development [11]. This is because maintainers also must know and understand the structure and functionality of the software they are modifying, as well as the possible secondary effects of the modifications in the entire system. Many of the main problems in software maintenance can be considered as knowledge management problems [2], such as unused knowledge because its sources are unknown, inaccessible, difficult to locate, or because maintainers do not know what knowledge can be obtained from them [73].

Considering that maintenance is the most expensive stage of the software life cycle, since it consumes most of the resources of software organisations [65], it is clear that providing means to solve knowledge related problems in software maintenance environments is important. Knowledge management (KM) is a discipline that studies how to provide methods, techniques, technologies, or strategies to help organisations to use their knowledge better; avoiding its loss, and augmenting and improving its use [19]. Therefore, many software organisations have applied KM to improve their processes [3]. Little work exists in the literature, however, that explicitly explores how KM can be applied to software maintenance. In addition, most of the KM strategies or systems implemented in software organisations fail because of situations such as employees having no time even for searching knowledge [48], perhaps because they do not know what to search for, or how to search for it. Researches have shown that software agents can be useful in solving such problems when presented with traditional KM systems in other domains [80].

Based on the above, a multi-agent based system aimed to help software maintainers to access knowledge sources that could be related to the activities they must perform has been designed.

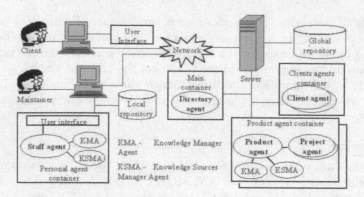

FIGURE 5. Agent based architecture for a software maintenance KM system.

7.1. A multi-agent architecture to support KM in software maintenance

Before explaining the multi-agent architecture it is convenient to clarify some aspects of software maintenance which motivated us to design the different types of agents that will be described in this section. In the software maintenance domain projects frequently involve an interaction between two organisations, the client and the staff, where the client is the organisation in charge of requesting a modification, and the staff is the people in charge of accomplishing the request [66]. Commonly, a maintenance request generates a maintenance project, which consists of a set of tasks or activities that must be done by the staff. In those projects different sources of information or knowledge are created. At the same time, the sets of sources generated during each maintenance project, jointly with those generated at the initial development of a software product, constitute the sources of knowledge of such product. They contain important information about how the software product has evolved and how it has been modified. In order to help manage the sources of knowledge involved in a maintenance environment, we have designed a multi-agent architecture where the agents are based on the different elements just exposed. Therefore, the architecture has five main types of agents: staff, product, client, project and directory agents (Figure 5).

The *staff agent* is a mediator between the maintainer and the system. It acts like an assistant to the maintainer. The staff agent monitors the maintainer's activities and requests to the Knowledge Manager Agent (KMA) to search for knowledge sources that can help the maintainer to perform his/her job. This agent has information that could be used to identify the maintainer's profile, such as which kinds of knowledge or expertise s/he has or which kinds of sources s/he often consults.

The *product agent* manages information related to a product, including its maintenance requests and the main elements that integrate the product (documentation, source code, databases, etc.). The main role of this agent is to have updated information about the modifications carried out in a product and the people that were involved in it. When the product agent receives a maintenance request, it creates a new project and proposes the tasks that must be done in order to fulfil the request. The agent also proposes the most suitable people to perform those tasks and sends the proposal to the staff agent in charge of assisting the maintenance engineer who plays the role of project manager. The staff agent informs the maintainer of these proposals, and s/he decides if the proposal is accepted or modified. Once the proposal has been accepted, the project agent starts working.

Each project is managed by a *project agent*, who is in charge of informing the maintainers involved in a project about the tasks that they should perform. To do this, the project agents communicate with the staff agents. The project agents also control the evolution of the projects.

The *client agent* manages information related to the maintenance requests or error reports performed by a client. There is one agent of this kind per client. Its main role is to assist them when they send a maintenance request, directing it to the corresponding product agent.

The *directory agent* manages information required by agents to know how to communicate with other agents that are active in the system. This agent knows the type, name, and electronic address of all active agents. Its main role is to control the different agents that are active in the system at each moment.

Two auxiliary types of agents are considered in the architecture, the *Knowledge Manager Agent* (KMA) and the *Knowledge Source Manager Agent* (KSMA). The KMA is in charge of providing support in the generation of knowledge and the search of knowledge sources. This kind of agent is in charge of managing the knowledge base. The staff's KMA generates new knowledge from the information obtained from the maintenance engineers in their daily work. For example, if a maintainer is modifying a program developed in the Java language, the KMA can infer that he has knowledge of this language and add his/her name to the knowledge base as a possible source of knowledge about Java. On the other hand, the product KMA generates knowledge related to the activities performed on the product. It could identify patterns on the modifications done to the different modules. For example, it could detect that there are modules or documents that should be modified or consulted when a specific module is modified, and in this way, it could indicate which modules or programs can be affected by the changes done on others. Finally, the KSMA has control over the knowledge sources, such as electronic documents. It knows the physical location of those sources, as well as the mechanisms used to consult them. Its main role is to control access to the sources.

7.2. Implementation of the architecture

To evaluate the feasibility of the implementation of the architecture, a prototype has been developed. The requirements were obtained from the scenarios identified in two case studies [70]. The information managed by the prototype was obtained from one of the organisations where the case studies were done. The prototype was tested specifically following the scenario described next.

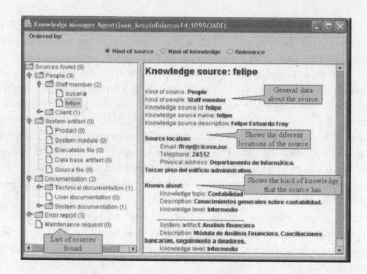

FIGURE 6. Screen shot of the knowledge sources list.

First, the maintainer looks at a list of the projects s/he has assigned. These are shown by the *staff agent* through its screen. When the maintainer selects one project, an event is triggered and captured by the *staff agent*, which obtains the information of the project, identifies knowledge topics (system and module where the problem appeared, kind of problem, etc.) and generates some rules to request the KMA to search· for knowledge sources. To create the rules, the *staff agent* tries to identify the knowledge that the engineer would need to do the assignment. Also the agent considers the types of sources the engineer consults, assigning more relevance to the sources that he consults most frequently. When the search has finished, the *KMA* sends a message to the *staff agent* informing it about the sources found. The *staff agent* displays a message with the number of knowledge sources found in order to inform the maintainer of their availability. Finally, if the engineer wants to look for the sources, s/he chooses a button in the *staff agent* screen, and the agent will display a window with the list of sources grouped by categories (see Figure 6). When the maintainer selects one source from the list, the window shows information related to that source such as: location, the knowledge that it has, etc.

The system helps to find and locate sources of information that can be relevant to the activities performed for maintainers. In this way, sources that could not be consulted for ignorance of their existence or location could now be consulted thanks to the automatic search the system does, informing the maintainer about those sources, so that they can determine if they could help them to complete their jobs.

7.3. Concluding remarks

The architecture of a system to support KM in a software maintenance environment has been presented. This architecture was designed as a multi-agent system, where each agent has specific roles, and can collaborate with each other to provide KM support to the users of the system. Particularly, the system facilitates access to knowledge sources that may be useful to the users in the accomplishment of their jobs. The use of agents as a basis of the system has several advantages. First, frequently, users of KM systems do not search for knowledge sources because they do not know that they exist, or how or where to search for them. Since agents are proactive, they can monitor the users' activities and start searching for knowledge sources useful for such activities. This can enable users to consult sources that they don't know existed. Therefore, this fact can assist the users to increase the use of the knowledge they may have at hand.

8. Conclusions

This chapter presents some of the main research and experience of authors in the AOSE discipline. From the AOSE evaluation perspective, several conclusions can be drawn, but the most important one is the necessity of a standard model which covers the whole life cycle of development. This may be done by defining a general metamodel and adopting MDA, as proposed in the second section. The latest works of AOSE Agentlink group [5] and the FAME proposal of Brian Henderson [37] address this issue.

The third section presents a practical example of a tool for the analysis of massive MAS: ACLAnalyser. This tool assists in the test, verification and validation of MAS developments. After, MAS-PL is suggested as a promising paradigm for MAS development to be applied in industry, when integrated with specific tools based on the MDE approach proposed previously.

Following the industrial interest, the ANEMONA process to help in the design and implementation of HMS is introduced. As software maintenance is a key field for complex and distributed systems, the use of MAS architecture to support KM in the software maintenance environment is presented as a main activity that could contribute to increase the use of background knowledge to facilitate software maintenance.

The works in the chapter show the individual line of each group research. As can be easily seen, there are some points in common among them. This allows the groups to work jointly in order to solve concrete open issues. For instance, at the moment the Universidad de Vigo, Complutense and Murcia are working jointly to apply the MDE to develop a new support tool for INGENIAS methodology using the conclusions of methodological evaluation and the ideas underlying ACLAnalyser. In addition, the basic model of INGENIAS methodology is being used by the Universidad de Valencia group and also by the Universidad de Castilla-La Mancha team, for defining new methods and tools in their particular domain of research.

References

[1] M. Alberti, M. Gavanelli, E. Lamma, P. Mello, and P. Torroni. Specification and verification of agent interaction using social integrity constraints. *Electronic Notes in Theoretical Computer Science*, 85(2), 2004.

[2] N. Anquetil, K. M. de Oliveira, K. D. de Sousa, and M. G. Batista Dias. Software maintenance seen as a knowledge management issue. *Information and Software Technology*, page In press, 2006.

[3] A. Aurum, R. Jeffery, C. Wohlin, and M. Handzic, editors. *Managing Software Engineering Knowledge*. Springer, 2003.

[4] Birkhäuser Basel, editor. *The Agent Modeling Language - AML*. Springer-verlag, 2007.

[5] C. Bernon, M. Cossentino, and J. Pavón. Agent-oriented software engineering. *Knowl. Eng. Rev.*, 20(2):99–116, 2005.

[6] C. Bernon, M. Cossentino, and J. Pavón. Agent-oriented software engineering. *The Knowledge Engineering Review*, 20(02):99–116, 2006.

[7] C. Bernon, M. P. Gleizes, S. Peyruqueou, and G. Picard. Adelfe: A methodology for adaptive multi-agent systems engineering. In P. Petta, R. Tolksdorf, and F. Zambonelli, editors, *ESAW*, volume 2577 of *Lecture Notes in Computer Science*, pages 156–169. Springer, 2002.

[8] J. A. Botía, J. M. Hernansáez, and A. F. Gómez-Skarmeta. Towards an approach for debugging mas through the analysis of acl messages. *Computer Systems Science and Engineering*, 20, July 2005.

[9] P. Bresciani, A. Perini, P. Giorgini, F. Giunchiglia, and J. Mylopoulos. Tropos: an agent-oriented software development methodology. *Journal of Autonomous agents and Multiagent Systems*, 8(3), 2004.

[10] W. Caire, G.and Coulier, F. J. Garijo, J. J. Gómez-Sánz, J. Pavón, F. Leal, P. Chainho, P. E. Kearney, J. Stark, R. Evans, and P. Massonet. Agent oriented analysis using message/uml. In *Agent-Oriented Software Engineering II*, volume 2222 of *Lecture Notes in Computer Science*, pages 119–135. Springer, 2002.

[11] N. Chapin. The job of software maintenance. In *Proc. of the Conf. on Software Maintenance-1987*, pages 4–12. IEEE Computer Society Press, 1987.

[12] S. Chien, R. Sherwood, G. Rabideau, R. Castano, A. Davies, M. Burl, R. Knight, T. Stough, J. Roden, P. Zetocha, R. Wainwright, P. Klupar, J. Van Gaasbeck, P. Cappelaere, and D. Oswald. The techsat-21 autonomous space science agent. In *AAMAS '02: Proceedings of the first international joint conference on Autonomous agents and multiagent systems*, pages 570–577, New York, NY, USA, 2002. ACM Press.

[13] P. Clements and L. Northrop. *Software Product Lines: Practices and Patterns*. SEI Series in Software Engineering. Addison–Wesley, August 2001.

[14] Massimo Cossentino. *Agent Oriented Methodologies*, chapter From Requirements to Code with the PASSI Methodology, pages 79–106. Idea Group, 2005.

[15] P. Cuesta, A. Gómez, J. C. González-Moreno, and F. J. Rodríguez. A framework for evaluation of agent oriented methodologies. Technical report, Universidade de Vigo, 2003.

[16] K. Czarnecki and U. Eisenecker. *Generative Programming: Methods, Tools, and Applications.* Addison–Wesley, 2000.

[17] K. H. Dam and M. Winikoff. Comparing agent-oriented methodologies. In *Agent-Oriented Information Systems: AOIS*, pages 78–93, Berlin / Heidelberg, 2003. Springer.

[18] M. Dastani, John-J. Ch. Meyer, and R. H. Bordini. 06261 abstracts collection: Foundations and practice of programming multi-agent systems. In Rafael H. Bordini, Mehdi Dastani, and John-Jules Ch. Meyer, editors, *Foundations and Practice of Programming Multi-Agent Systems*, number 06261 in Dagstuhl Seminar Proceedings. Internationales Begegnungs- und Forschungszentrum fuer Informatik (IBFI), Schloss Dagstuhl, Germany, 2007.

[19] T. H. Davenport and L. Prusak. *Working Knowledge: How Organizations Manage What they Know.* Harvard Business School Press, 2000.

[20] T. De Wolf and T. Holvoet. Towards a methodology for engineering self-organising emergent systems. *Self-Organization and Autonomic Informatics*, 135:18–34, 2005.

[21] J. Dehlinger and R. R. Lutz. A product-line requirements approach to safe reuse in multi-agent systems. In *SELMAS '05: Proceedings of the fourth international workshop on Software engineering for large-scale multi-agent systems*, pages 1–7, New York, NY, USA, 2005. ACM Press.

[22] J. Dehlinger and R. R. Lutz. Bi-directional safety analysis for product-line, multi-agent systems. SIGBED Review: Special Issues on Workshop on Innovative Techniques for Certification of Embedded Systems, 3(4), 2006.

[23] J. Dehlinger and R. R. Lutz. A product-line approach to promote asset reuse in multi-agent systems. In A. F. Garcia, R. Choren, C. J. Pereira de Lucena, P. Giorgini, T. Holvoet, and A. B. Romanovsky, editors, *Software Engineering for Multi-Agent Systems IV, Research Issues and Practical Applications*, volume 3914 of *Lecture Notes in Computer Science*, pages 161–178. Springer, 2006.

[24] S. A. DeLoach. Multiagent systems engineering of organization-based multiagent systems. *SIGSOFT Softw. Eng. Notes*, 30(4):1–7, 2005.

[25] S. A. DeLoach and M. Wood. Developing multiagent systems with agenttool. In C. Castelfranchi and Y. Lesperance, editors, *Intelligent Agents VII. Agent Theories Architectures and Languages, 7th International Workshop (ATAL 2000)*, volume 1986 of *Lecture Notes in Computer Science*. Springer-Verlag, 2001.

[26] Y. Demazeau. From interactions to collective behaviour in agent-based systems. In *Proceedings of the 1st. European Conference on Cognitive Science*, 1995.

[27] R. Girardi. Reuse in agent-based application development. In *First International Workshop on Software Engineering for Large-Scale Multi-Agent Systems*, pages 1–7, Orlando, FL, USA, 2000.

[28] A. Giret and V. Botti. Holons and Agents. *Journal of Intelligent Manufacturing*, 15:645–659, 2004.

[29] A. Giret and V. Botti. *Multiagent System Technologies*, chapter On the definition of meta-models for analysis of large-scale MAS, pages 273–286. LNAI 3187, 2004.

[30] A. Giret and V. Botti. Towards an Abstract Recursive Agent. *Integrated Computer-Aided Engineering*, 11(2):165–177, 2004.

[31] A. Giret and V. Botti. From system requirements to holonic manufacturing system analysis. *International Journal of Production Research*, 44:3917–3928, 2006.

[32] J. J. Gómez-Sánz. *Modelado de Sistemas Multi-Agente*. PhD thesis, Universidad Complutense de Madrid, 2003.

[33] J. J. Gómez-Sánz and J. Pavón. *IDK MANUAL*, 2005.

[34] Z. Guessoum, M. Cossentino, and J. Pavón. *Methodologies and Software Engineering for Agent Systems*, chapter Roadmap of Agent-Oriented Software Engineering, pages 431–451. Kluwer, 2004.

[35] H. Hara, S. Fujita, and K. Sugawara. Reusable software components based on an agent model. In *ICPADS '00: Proceedings of the Seventh International Conference on Parallel and Distributed Systems: Workshops*, page 447, Washington, DC, USA, 2000. IEEE Computer Society.

[36] K. Havelund, M. Lowry, and J. Penix. Formal analysis of a space-craft controller using spin. *IEEE Trans. Softw. Eng.*, 27(8):749–765, 2001.

[37] I. Hawryszkiewycz, B. Henderson-Sellers, and Quynh-Nhu Numi Tran. Fragments for composing collaborative systems. In *ISTA*, pages 95–106, 2006.

[38] B. Henderson-Sellers and P. Giorgini. *Agent-Oriented Methodologies*. Idea Group Inc., 2005.

[39] Press Release HMS. *HMS Requirements*. HMS Server, http://hms.ifw.uni-hannover.de/, 1994.

[40] Marc-Philippe Huget. Agent uml notation for multiagent system design. *IEEE Internet Computing*, 8(4):63–71, 2004.

[41] A. Jansen, R. Smedinga, J. Gurp, and J. Bosch. First class feature abstractions for product derivation. *IEE Proceedings - Software*, 151(4):187–198, 2004.

[42] D. Jensen and V. Lesser. Social pathologies of adaptive agents. *Safe Learning Agents: Papers from the 2002 AAAI Spring Symposium*, TR SS-02-07, August 2002.

[43] V. Julian and V. Botti. Developing real-time multiagent systems. *Integrated Computer-Aided Engineering*, 11:135–149, 2004.

[44] D. Kinny, M. Georgeff, and A. Rao. A methodology and modelling technique for systems of BDI agents. In Walter Van de Velde and John W. Perram, editors, *Agents Breaking Away: Proceedings of the Seventh European Workshop on Modelling Autonomous Agents in a Multi-Agent World*, volume 1038 of *Lecture Notes in Computer Science*, pages 56–71. Springer, 1996.

[45] A. Koestler. *The Ghost in the Machine*. Arkana Books, 1971.

[46] D. S. Kolovos, R. F. Paige, and F. Polack. The epsilon object language (eol). In Rensink and Warmer [69], pages 128–142.

[47] D. N. Lam and K. S. Barber. Comprehending agent software. In *AAMAS '05: Proceedings of the fourth international joint conference on Autonomous agents and multiagent systems*, pages 586–593, New York, NY, USA, 2005. ACM Press.

[48] M. Lindvall and I. Rus. *Managing Software Engineering Knowledge*, chapter Knowledge Management for Software Organizations, pages 73–94. Springer, 2003.

[49] M. Luck and P. McBurney. Challenges for Agent Technology Moving towards 2010. *Upgrade*, V(4), 2004.

[50] D. C. McFarlane and S. Bussmann. *Agent-Based Manufacturing. Advances in the Holonic Approach*, chapter Holonic Manufacturing Control: Rationales, Developments and Open Issues, pages 301–326. Springer-Verlag, 2003.

[51] J. Mylopoulos, M. Kolp, and J. Castro. Uml for agent-oriented software development: The tropos proposal. *Lecture Notes in Computer Science*, 2185:422–441, 2001.

[52] A. J. Offutt and A. Abdurazik. Generating tests from uml specifications. In R. B. France and B. Rumpe, editors, *UML*, volume 1723 of *Lecture Notes in Computer Science*, pages 416–429. Springer, 1999.

[53] OMG. Mda foundation model. http://www.omg.org/cgi-bin/doc?ormsc/05-04-01, 2007.

[54] L. Padgham, J. Thangarajah, and M. Winikoff. Tool support for agent development using the prometheus methodology. In *Fifth International Conference on Quality Software (QSIC 2005)*, pages 383–388. IEEE Computer Society, 2005.

[55] L. Padgham and M. Winikoff. *Prometheus: A Practical Agent-Oriented Methodology*, chapter Chapter 5 in Agent-Oriented Methodologies, pages 107–135. Idea Group, 2005.

[56] J. Pavón and J. J. Gómez-Sánz. Agent Oriented Software Engineering with INGE-NIAS. *3rd International Central and Eastern European Conference on Multi-Agent Systems (CEEMAS 2003) : V. Marik, J. Müller, M. Pechoucek:Multi-Agent Systems and Applications II, LNAI 2691*, pages 394–403, 2003.

[57] J. Pavon, J. J. Gómez-Sánz, and R. Fuentes. *Agent-Oriented Methodologies*, chapter The INGENIAS Methodology and Tools, pages 236–276. Idea Group Publishing, 2005.

[58] J. Pavón, J. J. Gómez-Sánz, and R. Fuentes. Model driven development of multi-agent systems. In Rensink and Warmer [69], pages 284–298.

[59] J. Peña. *On Improving The Modelling Of Complex Acquaintance Organisations Of Agents. A Method Fragment For The Analysis Phase*. PhD thesis, University of Seville, 2005.

[60] J. Peña and M. G. Hinchey. Multiagent system product lines: Challenges and benefits. *Communications of the ACM*, 49(12), December 2006.

[61] J. Peña, M. G. Hinchey, M. Resinas, R. Sterritt, and J. L. Rash. Designing and managing evolving systems using a mas-product-line approach. *Journal of Science of Computer Programming*, 2006.

[62] J. Peña, M. G. Hinchey, A. Ruiz-Cortés, and P. Trinidad. Building the core architecture of a nasa multiagent system product line. In *7th International Workshop on Agent Oriented Software Engineering 2006*, volume 4405, pages 208–224, Hakodate, Japan, May, 2006. LNCS.

[63] J. Peña, M. G. Hinchey, R. Sterritt, A. Ruiz-Cortés, and M. Resinas. A model-driven architecture approach for modeling, specifying and deploying policies in autonomous and autonomic systems. In *Second International Symposium on Dependable Autonomic and Secure Computing (DASC 2006), 29 September - 1 October 2006, Indianapolis, Indiana, USA*, pages 19–30. IEEE Computer Society, 2006.

[64] K. Pohl, G. Böckle, and F. van der Linden. *Software Product Line Engineering : Foundations, Principles and Techniques*. Springer, September 2005.

[65] M. Polo, M. Piattini, and F. Ruiz, editors. *Advances in Software Maintenance Management: Technologies and Solutions*. Idea Group Inc., 2003.

[66] M. Polo, M. Piattini, F. Ruíz, and C. Calero. Roles in the maintenance process. *SIGSOFT Softw. Eng. Notes*, 24(4):84–86, 1999.

[67] D. Poutakidis, L. Padgham, and M. Winikoff. Debugging multi-agent systems using design artifacts: The case of interaction protocols. In *AAMAS'02*, Bologna, Italy, July 2002.

[68] A. S. Rao and M. P. Georgeff. BDI-agents: from theory to practice. In *Proceedings of the First Intl. Conference on Multiagent Systems*, San Francisco, 1995.

[69] A. Rensink and J. Warmer, editors. *Model Driven Architecture - Foundations and Applications, Second European Conference, ECMDA-FA 2006, Bilbao, Spain, July 10-13, 2006, Proceedings*, volume 4066 of *Lecture Notes in Computer Science*. Springer, 2006.

[70] O. M. Rodríguez, A. I. Martínez, J. Favela, A. Vizcaíno, and M. Piattini. Understanding and supporting knowledge flows in a community of software developers. *Lecture Notes in Computer Science*, 3198:52–66, 2004.

[71] A. Sabas, M. Badri, and S. Delisle. A comparative analysis of multiagent system development: Towards a unified approach. In *Proceedings of Third Interanational Symposium "From Agent Theory to Agent Implementation" AT2AI-3*, pages 624–631, 2002.

[72] D. C. Schmidt. Model Driven Engineering. *IEEE Computer*, 39(2):25–31, 2006.

[73] C. Seaman. The information gathering strategies of software maintainers. In *Proc. of the Intl. Conf. on Software Maintenance (ICSM'2002)*, pages 141–149. IEEE Computer Society Press, 2002.

[74] B. Selic. The pragmatics of model-driven development. *IEEE Software*, 20(5):19–25, 2003.

[75] O. Shehory and A. Sturm. Evaluation of modeling techniques for agent-based systems. In *AGENTS '01: Proceedings of the fifth international conference on Autonomous agents*, pages 624–631, New York, NY, USA, 2001. ACM Press.

[76] W. Shen and D. H. Norrie. Agent-Based Systems for Intelligent Manufacturing: A State-of-the-Art Survey. *Knowledge and Information Systems, an Internatinal Journal*, 1(2):129–156, 1999.

[77] Y. Smaragdakis and D. Batory. Mixin layers: an object–oriented implementation technique for refinements and collaboration-based designs. *ACM Trans. Softw. Eng. Methodol.*, 11(2):215–255, 2002.

[78] J. Sudeikat, L. Braubach, A. Pokahr, W. Lamersdorf, and W. Renz. On the validation of belief-desire-intention agents. In R. Bordini, M. Dastani, J. Dix, and A. El Fallah, editors, *Programming Multi-Agent Systems Workshop at AAMAS 2006*, 2006.

[79] H. Van Brussel, J. Wyns, P. Valckenaers, L. Bongaerts, and P. Peeters. Reference Architecture for Holonic Manufacturing Systems: PROSA. *Computers In Industry*, 37:255–274, 1998.

[80] L. van Elst, V. Dignum, and A. Abecker. Towards agent-mediated knowledge management. *Lecture Notes in Artificial Intelligence*, 2926:1–30, 2003.

[81] D. M. Weiss and C. T. R. Lai. *Software Product-Line Engineering*. Addison Wesley, 1999.

[82] F. Zambonelli, N. Jennings, and M. Wooldridge. Developing multiagent systems: the GAIA methodology. *ACM Transactions on Software Engineering and Methodology*, 12(3):317–370, July 2003.

[83] F. Zambonelli, N. R. Jennings, and M. Wooldridge. Developing multiagent systems: The Gaia methodology. *ACM Transactions on Software Engineering and Methodology (TOSEM)*, 12(3):317–370, 2003.

Pedro Cuesta
Departamento de Informática - Universidade de Vigo
Escola Superior de Enxeñería Informática
Campus Universitario As Lagoas S/N
32004 - Ourense. Spain
e-mail: pcuesta@uvigo.es

Alma Gómez
Departamento de Informática - Universidade de Vigo
Escola Superior de Enxeñería Informática
Campus Universitario As Lagoas S/N
32004 - Ourense. Spain
e-mail: alma@uvigo.es

Juan Carlos González
Departamento de Informática - Universidade de Vigo
Escola Superior de Enxeñería Informática
Campus Universitario As Lagoas S/N
32004 - Ourense. Spain
e-mail: jcmoreno@uvigo.es

Whitestein Series in Software Agent Technologies, 33–57
© 2007 Birkhäuser Verlag Basel/Switzerland

Ubiquitous Computing for Mobile Environments

José M. Molina, Juan M. Corchado and Javier Bajo

Abstract. The increasing role and importance of ubiquitous computing and mobile environments in our daily lives implies the need for new solutions. The characteristics of agents and multi-agent systems make them very appropriate for constructing ubiquitous and mobile systems. This chapter presents some of the advances in practical and theoretical applications of multi-agent systems in the fields of ubiquitous computing and mobile environments carried out by several AgentCities.ES research groups.

1. Introduction

Intelligent environments, also known as Ambient Intelligence, have became increasingly important in recent years. These environments are characterized by certain capacities (all or some of them) such as ubiquity, transparency and intelligence. The multi-agent systems (MAS) have become increasingly relevant for developing distributed and dynamic intelligent environments. One of the advantages of the agents is their adaptability to work in mobile devices, so they support wireless communication (Wi-Fi, Bluetooth,WiMAX, UMTS, etc.) which facilitates their portability to a wide range of mobile devices. This advantage makes the agents and multi-agent systems very appropriate to be applied to the development of ubiquitous and mobile environments.

Agents can be characterized through their capacities in areas such as autonomy, reactivity, pro-activity, social abilities, reasoning, learning and mobility [78]. These capacities make the multi-agent systems very appropriate for constructing intelligent environments. An agent can act as an interface between the user and the rest of the elements in the intelligent environment. Furthermore, given the adaptability of agents to mobile devices (with low memory and processing resources), it is possible to provide an ubiquitous and transparent interaction, even personalizing

Co-authors of this chapter: Estefanía Argente, Juan A. Botía, Sergio Ilarri, Vicente Botti, Emilio S. Corchado, Virginia Fuentes, Manuel González, Arantza Illarramendi, Vicente Julián, Eduardo Mena and Nayat Sánchez.

the user access. An intelligent agent can adapt itself to environmental changes or make predictions based on previous knowledge or experience. In this sense an agent is context-sensitive and can take decisions allowing it to automatically adapt itself to the changes in its surroundings. An agent usually integrates within a multi-agent system, or agent society, exchanging information and resolving problems in a distributed way. It requires an organization-oriented perspective to model this kind of problems, identifying the roles that every agent plays in the society or organization. These characteristics facilitate both ubiquitous communication and computation.

This chapter presents some advances in practical and theoretical applications of multi-agent systems in the fields of ubiquitous computing and mobile environments, and is structured as follows. In the next section a brief summary of the technologies used to construct intelligent environments is presented. Then, some real developments in ambient intelligence using agent technology are enumerated. In the third section the importance of the context definition for ubiquitous computing is emphasized. The main strategies for both representation and managing of context information are presented. Section four carries on with the importance of context information and focuses on ontology definition of context-based applications based on agents. The deployment of an ontology for environment definition is explained. Then ontology definition for agent communication and ontology definition for agent interaction are presented. The fifth section focuses on the need for social organization in ubiquitous systems. In this sense this section reviews the organizational model in agent societies and presents a new organization oriented multi-agent platform, which can be used in mobile devices. Finally, the last section of this chapter focuses on mobile agents. The advantages and benefits of mobile agents are discussed, the existing mobile agent platforms are studied and, as a conclusion, the possibilities for mobile agents in the future are shown.

2. Ambient Intelligence

2.1. Technology for Ambient Intelligence

Ambient Intelligence proposes a new way to interact between people and technology, where the technology is adapted to individuals and their context within which they live. This new way has the following goals:

- Promote a vision of people surrounded by intelligent interfaces that merge into daily life;
- Foster a computer-literate environment of intelligent data processing and communication by creating a simple, natural and effortless human-system interface;
- Develop an array of intelligent and intuitive systems and interfaces;
- Develop the capability to recognize and respond to individual user's requirements in a comprehensive manner;

- Create technologically complex environments in numerous contexts, such as medicine, academia, social structures, etc.

From this perspective, agents must be able to respond to events, take the initiative according to their goals, communicate with other agents, interact with users, represent and manage context information and make use of reasoning mechanisms to find the best solutions to achieve goals.

New approaches for Ambient Intelligence agent-based systems propose the use of context aware agents that handle a set of technologies and the incorporate mechanisms for representing and managing context information that provide the agents with the flexibility and adaptation to survive on dynamic environments and accomplish the Ambient Intelligence vision. The growing use of wireless devices (especially hand-held devices) in recent years has led to new requirements as well as to a great opportunity to extend traditional wired communication techniques. In this section, the main wireless technologies used to construct intelligent environments are presented. In Sections 3 and 4 the context aware middleware and ontologies are studied in detail.

The aim of ambient intelligence (AmI) is to construct intelligent environments that facilitate a ubiquitous access with independence of the physical location [19]. Wireless networks are location-independent (in the sense that wires are not needed) and provide a wide range of coverage. Protocols used to communicate in wireless technologies are mainly classified in the 802.1x.x protocol family for Bluetooth, infrared and Wi-Fi, and protocols used in mobile phones within the GPRS or UMTS technologies. Other wireless technologies that must be taken into account are GSM, GPS, RFID or ZigBee. Wireless LANs, also known as Wi-Fi (Wireless Fidelity) networks can be used as a replacement or as an extension of wired LANs [36]. They provide reduced infrastructure and low installation cost, and also give more mobility and flexibility by allowing workers to stay connected to the network as they roam among covered areas, increasing efficiency by allowing data to be entered and accessed on site [36]. Infrared connections require optic signals and the principal inconvenience is the need of direct-vision between devices. Bluetooth is a wireless technology that utilizes a short-range radio link and operates in the 2.4 - 2.48 GHz frequency band. Bluetooth is a technology that facilitates the interaction between near devices providing a high reliability and low energy consumption. GPRS uses a packet-switched system which provides data transfer services on mobile phone networks. UMTS is a universal mobile telecommunications system that operates in the 2 GHz frequency band and emphasizes the compatibility. This great amount of technologies, requires compatibility solutions. Some works, like the RASCAL system [41], allow mobile devices to autonomically self-manage connection endpoints and data transmission over available network technologies, providing a contingency manager system with autonomic capabilities which enables collaboration among a set of ubiquitous services deployed in the infrastructure and/or in the ad-hoc network. Other works, like ASAM [9], Adaptive Service Access Management, enables effective delivery of next generation ubiquitous services by dynamically combining end user requirements and service provisioning policies with network-facing management and control functionality.

RFID technology is used to identify and receive information about humans, animals and objects on the move. An RFID system contains basically four components: tags, readers, antennas and middleware [71]. Tags with no power system (batteries) integrated are called passive tags or *transponders*. The reader is a device that interrogates or sends electromagnetic waves. RFID systems typically operate in three different frequency ranges: low frequency (30KHz - 500 KHz) and ultra high frequency (850 MHz - 950 MHz and 2.4 GHz - 2.5 GHz). Systems operating on low frequency are less costly, but have a shorter reading range. The middleware consists of processing software and hardware required to convert the tag signals into valid data [71]. The tag or transponder is placed on the object itself. As this object moves into the reader's capture area, the reader is activated and begins signaling via electromagnetic waves (radio frequency). The transponder subsequently transmits its unique ID information number to the reader, which transmit it to a device or a central computer where the information is processed and displayed. This information is not restricted to the location of the object, and can include specific detailed information.

One of the most important issues using wireless Technologies is to provide security guarantees when a communication between mobile devices is established. At the moment some services are provided: authentication services (WPA, WPA2, CCKM), data encoding services (RSN, TKIP, WEP, CKIP, CMIC), access control services (PEAP, smart card) or private virtual network services (IP-SEC or SSL) [45].

2.2. Agent Technology and Real Developments in Ambient Intelligence

In this section a brief summary of real developments in ambient intelligence using agent technology is presented. The incorporation of artificial intelligence techniques has led to further studies and to the modeling of shopping and leisure time in shopping malls in terms of multi-agent systems [4, 5, 15]. These authors focus on the shopping problem and on the recommendations that can be made to users. The growing use of hand-held devices in recent years has led to new requirements as well as to a great opportunity to extend traditional commerce techniques and apply new techniques. These new devices facilitate the use of new interaction techniques, for instance, some systems focus on facilitating users with guidance or location systems [15] by means of their wireless devices. The application of intelligent environments to health care and elderly care is one of the priorities in ambient intelligence. In this way different agent-based applications have been developed [16]. These applications make important contributions to traditional care techniques and improve the patient's quality of life. Another important field of application for ambient intelligence is housing. Nowadays it is usual to find services based on home automation in our homes. There are some agent-based home automation intelligent environments [60] which facilitate daily life at home. Ambient intelligence has also been highly accepted in mobility and transportation problems. As a good example we can cite the navigation systems installed in our cars. Some examples of agents applied to the development of intelligent environments are navigation, delivery or route optimization [7, 11, 15, 80]. Finally, another important field where the application of ambient intelligence has been successful is education and learning [38], as well as culture, leisure and entertainment [4, 5, 12]. All these real developments have obtained promising results and demonstrate the importance of agents and multi-agent systems in the construction of intelligent environments. Agent technologies applied to ambient intelligence open a new research line which offers new interesting possibilities.

3. Context Definition

3.1. Context aware applications

A generic definition of context could be the following:

Context information is the set of useful data that, in a concrete instant of time, describe the elements which surround the user and some interesting aspects of the user itself.

Figure 1 represents all the typical elements which might be part of user context in a conventional ubiquitous computing system (which includes those based on agents software).

This information has static and dynamic components. Static information embraces all details related to the user that do not change through time, or at least do not frequently vary. User profile is an example of such information. In the profile, the birth date does not change but preferences in music, for example, may change through time. Dynamic information constantly changes and provides a description of an up-to-date snapshot of the user and his surroundings. For example, the location of the user in a building is a good example of such kind of information.

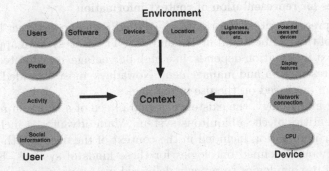

FIGURE 1. Information composition for the user context in a conventional ubiquitous computing system.

But, what is actually a context-aware service? We define a context-aware service as the kind of service which modifies its behavior according to information it has, related to user context. Hence, a music search service which implicitly takes into account user profile could be a context-aware service. Another example is a service which looks for restaurants for a user, taking into account his proximity to the possible options. An interesting concept related to this kind of service is context-aware service provisioning. It consists of the necessary mechanisms to dynamically provide users or software with services. The set of offered services will depend on time and context information for their selection. Think, for example, of an application in which, depending on the direction you take in a cross road of a highway, the software which interacts with the user through a hand held device offers a Theaters search service if going downtown or a sports facility booking menu if going to the suburbs.

Why should context be incorporated into ubiquitous computing information systems? Context information is crucial to guarantee that services can be personalized depending on user profile, user location, user state (i.e., working, not to be disturbed, out of office) and user's device. These elements compose a set of contextual information whose availability at any time and anywhere will allow the development of flexible services in such systems. Typical advantages obtained by incorporating context into a system are the following:

- increasing user satisfaction as services are more adapted to his preferences and profile;
- automating some functions: by means of behavior rules defined by the user, some activities can be automated;
- right information, in the right time and at the right place: a semantic model of context information makes it possible to filter incoming information, depending on the user situation;
- low obtrusive software: as it is capable of deciding when is more appropriate, and how, to interact with the user and
- increased personalization.

3.2. Strategies for representation of context information

In order to represent context information, we need to define a correct life cycle for it. Examples of this can be found in [76] and [57]. The success of an application relying on context information depends, in a high percentage, on what technology we use for its representation and management. Nowadays, most extended approaches to this problem are based on the use of ontologies.

By using an ontology, the existence is guaranteed of a common model for all the software entities of the ubiquitous system. Main advantages include a common model for information included in the context of the user and the possibility of reusing previously defined ontologies for these kinds of systems. Examples of systems which use ontologies to process delivered information in ubiquitous computing systems are [75, 33]. Its basic functioning is based on OWL [64] language and related technologies.

The first work which used OWL to describe information entities in a context-awareness based information system can be found in the CoBrA system [13]. Within this work, a first standard ontology to model ubiquitous computing information was proposed, Cobra-Ont. This ontology reused SOUPA [1] (Standard Ontology for Ubiquitous and Pervasive Applications) [14]. SOUPA is a shared ontology for ubiquitous computing applications. SOUPA delivers a common vocabulary for pervasive computing application developers. It combines a number of different basic vocabularies whose origins are found in commonly accepted ontologies. This ontology is divided into two different but related groups of vocabularies: the kernel or nucleus, the SOUPA core and extensions to the core. SOUPA reuses other more or less standard ontologies like, for example DAML-time and others. In the CoBrA system, as it could be expected, we already find an element which performs reasoning on contextual information using the advantages offered by ontologies. However, there are no explicit rules to identify interesting events like that cited above [75]. Another interesting detail about this architecture is that it is based on the agent metaphor [79], as it uses concepts like role, belief, desire and intention which belong to the BDI model of agency.

3.3. Managing context information

Managing context information includes operations for register, search, delete and update context information. These are basic operations, although other less direct operations include delivery, reasoning and aggregation. In order to have an up to date context information registry, a repository of context information is needed. And this repository should allow for registry, search, delete and update operations with pieces of context for a single user or a group of them.

Context delivery (i.e., the process of making context available and up to date for interested users, services and/or applications) might be a delicate task, depending on the kind of system architecture we have (i.e., if it is distributed, with a centralized directory or with no central directory at all). Moreover, the coordination model for delivery must be taken into account (i.e., if we use a blackboard model or a publish/subscribe notification strategy and so on.). A review is out of the scope of this chapter but more details on this issue might be found in [54].

Context reasoning and aggregation are two tasks which are strongly interrelated. Reasoning on context is the process of using a deductive process to infer new interesting situations from a basic context definition. For this, a logic theory with foundational facts and axioms is needed. In most of the cases, descriptive logic and user defined `if-then` rules are used for concrete implementations. Context aggregation is the process of defining mechanisms for dealing with the same representation of context but seen at different levels of abstraction. Aggregation is used to get more convenient representations depending on the application.

---

[1] http://ebiquity.umbc.edu/paper/html/id/165/The-SOUPA-Ontology-for-Pervasive-Computing

4. Ontology definition of context-based applications based on agents

Nowadays, communication between software systems, organizations, and persons causes difficulties of interoperability, re-use and communication, due to the existing differences of each one, with respect to concepts, models and structures. Defining ontologies help to solve these problems, since the main motivation relies on integrating different domains into a coherent framework, providing a common vocabulary definition and interoperability between heterogeneous systems [70].

Originally, the term *ontology* comes from the existence concept defined by philosophers, but it has been adopted by Artificial Intelligence with the idea of representing the real world, viewed as a set of concepts (entities, attributes, and processes), their definitions and relationships between them. This representation is achieved by the ontology conceptualization mechanism [70].

Applying the ontology definition to the context of a multi-agent system, ontologies are defined as a common vocabulary to share information in the exchanged queries and assertions messages between participating agents [34]. The ontology role in a communication process is to avoid ambiguous definitions of terms for facilitating agents to share knowledge between them inside a domain.

The main reasons for using an ontology in a context- aware multi-agent system are the following [59]: the ontology development allows sharing knowledge, ontology universe allows context reasoning, for composing complex contextual information and reasoning about it, and finally, ontologies detect inconsistencies in contextual information, since it can be highly imperfect.

Normally, ontology represents a conceptualization of particular domains. However in case of context-aware applications, the context is not limited to a specific environment, since it can be whatever domain (airport, fairground, university, shopping center etc.)[26]

Following the categorization defined by Schilit [62] that divided contextual information in: computing context (network, devices, etc.), user context (preferences, location, and social situation) and physical context (temperature, traffic, etc.), a contextual information of a context-aware system for dynamical environments can be defined by ontologies. The ontology definition must gather all concepts and their properties and relationships for accomplishing this contextual definition.

For building ontologies, Noy and McGuiness propose an iterative process based on the methodology proposed by Gruninger and Fox [35] who defined the competency questions used in the scope and goal step, and the development of the classes hierarchy based on Top-Down and Bottom-Up strategies. The steps for developing an ontology are described as follows [55]:

1. Determine ontology goal: it is important to have clear requirements and the intention of the ontology use. The scope of the ontology can be limited by a question-answer iterative process, making several questions about the domain that ontology may cover, what is the use of ontology, etc.

2. Consider the integration of existing ontologies: reusing ontologies is a requirement in order to interact with other applications that base on particular ontologies or controlled vocabularies. In the case that no relevant ontology can be reused, the better option is to develop a new ontology from scratch.

3. Ontological acquisition: defining the ontology implies a process of ontological acquisition, which consists of the identification of the key concepts and relationships of interest domain. A Top-Down strategy or a Bottom-Up strategy or a combination of both of them can be used for the ontological acquisition step.

4. Codification process: it consists of specific and formal representation of the conceptualization gathered in the capture phase and it allows selecting representation language. In this step the ontology could be created using the Protege tool [58]

The proposed steps set up the basis of the ontology development. However there are other alternatives of methodologies for ontology development as Gomez-Perez [31] and Uschold [70] present alternative ontology-development methodologies. The Ontolingua tutorial [23] discusses some formal aspects of knowledge modeling and Ontolingua for portable ontologies defined by Gruber presents a system for describing ontologies using multiple representation languages.[34]

4.1. Developing an ontology for environment definition

Following defined steps, there is a proposal of a meta-ontology [25] that focuses mainly on the definition of all the concepts in order to be valid for any environment or domain. These ontological high level concepts (Figure 2) are considered to be meta-concept or meta-object for composing the environmental model in context-aware systems, and can be described as follows:

- Framework is the general application concept which includes high level system concepts and defines what is the current environment or domain of the system. It has two slots: Sector and Event, that represents, system sector (technology, entertainment, market etc.) and the current event (fairground, conference, congress, exhibition etc.), respectively. These slots are properties of whole subclasses of Framework. Sector can take *mobile* value and Event can take *fairground* value in mobile fairground domain, for instance.

- Location represents the (x, y) coordinates of any place, participant or object.

- Spatial region and temporal region concepts define the environment area and temporal system information about users in any location in spatial region, respectively. Spatial region represents the map or NxM area, and it is composed of segments with a range of positions for each one. For example, segment1 is a segment with the range of positions: (3, 5) (3, 6). Temporal region represents user date (dd/mm/yyyy) and hour (hh:mm) when he is in a specific position inside the map. This spatial and temporal representation is shared for all system domains.

- Place concept represents interest points in the environment. Places can be participant company's expositors like Nokia, Siemens etc. in a fairground domain, for instance.
- Participant concept refers to people or companies that play a role in the system. In mobile fairground domain, participants can be visitors and companies (Nokia, Siemens, Motorola etc). A preference is a Participant's subclass, and it gathers preferential product, firm, price, model etc.
- Service concept can be any kind of system provision offered to users referred to contextual information. A service could be a notification in a user device about preferential user product.
- Product represents any kinds of information or object that users require to be informed. A product in the fairground domain is a mobile, for instance.
- Device concept gathers information about different user's devices in which the system works. An example of a user device is a PDA or a smart phone.

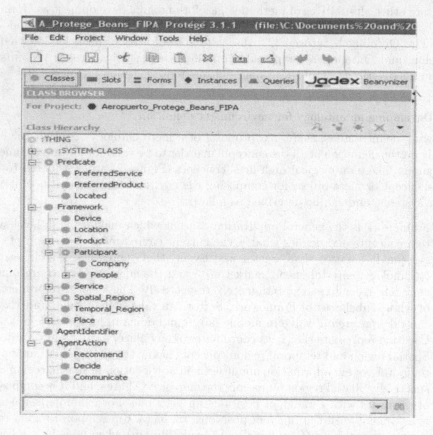

FIGURE 2. Ontology High Level Conceptualization.

4.2. Ontology definition for agent communication

The use of domain ontology [34] is one of the most promising approaches to model the distributed agents' knowledge, constituting the common ground of an entire multi-agent system. This ontology describes, in a natural way, ontological commitments for a set of agents so that they might be able to communicate about a domain of discourse without a necessary operation of a globally shared theory.

When an agent A communicates with another agent B, a certain amount of information I is transferred from A to B by means of an ACL (Agents Communication Languages) Message. Inside the ACL Message, I is represented as a content expression consistent with a proper content language and encoded in a proper format [8].

Ontology application to a multi-agent system describes agents knowledge in communication process and this communication is achieved by FIPA-ACL using ontological concepts for messages [8]. The model of communication FIPA [69] is based on the assumption that two agents share a common ontology for the domain of discourse. It ensures an agents mutual understanding because they describe the same meaning for the symbols used in the messages. In order to perform the proper semantic checks on a given content expression it is necessary to classify all possible elements in the domain of discourse according to their generic semantic characteristics. This classification is derived from the ACL language defined in FIPA that requires the content of each ACL Message to have a proper semantics according to the performative of the ACL Message. To satisfy the content of FIPA-ACL messages, ontology should define a set of different type of schemes: predicates, concepts and actions. Predicates are expressions that say something about the status of the world and can be true or false, e.g.,

(Belongs-to (Mobile: model NOKIA 6230)(Company: NOKIA))

stating that *the Mobile NOKIA 6230 belongs to the company NOKIA*. Agent actions, i.e., special concepts that indicate actions that can be performed by some agents, e.g.,

(Sell (Mobile: model NOKIA 6230)(Person: name Anne))

Concepts are expressions that indicate entities with a complex structure that can be defined in terms of slots, e.g.,

(Person: name Anne: age: 30)

Concepts typically make no sense if used directly as the content of an ACL message. They are generally referenced inside predicates and other concepts such as in

(Mobile: model NOKIA 6230: Belongs-to(Person: name Anne))

A fully expressive content language should be able to represent and distinguish between all the above types of elements. An ontology for a given domain is a set of schemes defining the structure of the predicates, agent actions and concepts that are pertinent to that domain.

4.3. Ontology definition for agent interaction

Ontology must define predicates, agent actions etc., for gathering the appropriated semantic according to ACL messages, so these ontology concepts are related with the different kinds of message in FIPA. Predicates can be used as the content of an INFORM or QUERY-IF message and Agent Actions can be used in REQUEST ACL message [8].

The interaction model is used to represent the dependencies and relationships between agent roles in the multi-agent system, according to the protocol definitions, that are actions that involve interaction between two roles played by agents in a multi-agent system. In [27] an interaction model is proposed as a phase of the analysis and design process, according to Gaia methodology. Some protocols between agents are defined for the goals of providing context-based services in any environment, for instance:

- Receive-Registry-Profile: an agent receives a REQUEST message of registry from another agent, and its profile.
- Agree-Registry: Send an AGREE message to confirm the agent registry.
- Warn-provider: Send an INFORM message to the closer provider role for alerting the presence of other agent.
- Offer-Service: Send a PROPOSE message for offering contextual-information services to other agents.

5. Social Networks

5.1. Agent Societies

Ubiquitous systems need methodologies, frameworks and software that take care of situatedness, openness, locality in control and locality in interactions [81]. Situatedness implies that software components execute in the context of an environment and can influence it or be influenced by it. Moreover, systems can dynamically change their structure, so its elements can enter and leave the system through time. Furthermore, there is locality both in control (with autonomous and proactive control) and interaction (components interact with each other according to local, geographical or logical, patterns). Finally, emerging societies can be formed in which teams, coalitions or other organizational structures are needed. For example, in mobile-commerce settings, personalized information agents, each representing a potential business partner, might dynamically form temporary profit-oriented coalitions to enhance a customer's purchasing and negotiating strategies in multiple electronic marketplaces [46]. Thus, ubiquitous systems will need to be modeled and designed in terms of social systems, following an organizational point of view.

An organization provides a framework for activity and interaction through the definition of roles, behavioral expectations and authority relationships [29]. Thus, an *agent organization* is a social entity composed of a specific number of members that accomplish several distinct tasks or functions and that are structured following some specific topology and communication interrelationship in order to achieve the main goal of the organization.

Dynamic agent organizations that self-adjust for making the most of their current environment are more and more important. These organizations could appear in dynamic or emerging societies of agents such as Grid domains, peer-to-peer networks, or other environments in which the agents coordinate in a dynamic way for offering combined services. So, it can be an appropriate approach to solve problems related with mobile ad-hoc networks. For example, agent-based virtual organisations for the Grid have been employed in the CONOISE-G project [65], in which an infrastructure to support robust and resilient virtual organisation formation and operation is developed. The social factors in the organization of multi-agent systems are also more and more important for structuring interactions in dynamic open environments.

5.2. Towards an organization oriented open MAS

Organizational models have been recently used in agent theory for modeling coordination in open systems and to ensure social order in MAS applications [17, 63].

Three dimensions can be used to describe the MAS from an organizational point of view [3]: its structure; its functionality; and its norms. In [2], a survey of MAS organization-oriented methodologies is detailed. Many MAS methodologies and frameworks, such as Agent-Group-Role [24] or INGENIAS [32], only take into account the structure and functionality view, specially detailing the organization roles, groups and role relationships.

Other methods, such as Tropos [30], go further on detailing more complex and elaborated organizational structures, such as hierarchies, matrices, congregations, federations and so on. They also propose using those organizational structures in the analysis and design phases. A deeper explanation of all those complex structures can be found in [37] [1].

Finally, other approaches are focused on the social norms (SODA [56], Electronic Institutions [22] or OMNI [73], for example). They explicitly define control policies to establish and reinforce them, taking into account the organizational dynamics of the system, but they hardly take advantage of the topological structure of the system and intrinsic relationships of its members.

Regarding agent platforms, the most well-known agent platforms [2] offer generic agents with basic functionalities, which users should extend; and an execution environment that facilitates agent communication at execution time. However, very few agent platforms support agent organizational features, such as AMELI [21], JACK Teams [39] and MOISE+ [40], which do take into account some of the concepts proposed in the organizational approach. More specifically, AMELI and MOISE help designers to control obligations and norms of agents; whereas JACK Teams provide team behaviors.

5.2.1. Organizations in Ubiquitous systems.
Over the last few years, only a few testbeds and real applications have been developed and reported in this area. The Universidad Politecnica de Valencia has developed an organization oriented multi-agent platform, called SPADE, which can be employed too in mobile devices.

SPADE (a Smart Python multi-agent Development Environment) [20] is a new agent platform, fully FIPA compliant, that supports a new communication protocol between agents, based on Instant Messaging systems, that uses a distributed network to route messages from one agent to another. It also supports agent mobility, presence notification between components (this allows the system to determine the current state of the components that are connected to the platform in real-time), multi-user conference (message sharing between a group of agents). These capacities provide new communication capabilities between agents, which make agents more versatile. As commented before, the SPADE platform can be applied in mobile devices. More specifically, SPADE was developed in Python. This allows the execution of the platform in several architectures and operating systems such as Windows, Linux, MacOS, Windows Mobile, PalmOS, SymbianOS for mobile phones, etc.

SPADE also enables organization design, based on the concept of Organizational Unit, which represents the minimum set of members' relationship inside an organization. There are three types of organizational units: simple hierarchy (formed by a supervisor who has control over all other members; and several subordinates that carry out the basic tasks and communicate with each other through the supervisor); a team (in which all members collaborate between them to reach a global and common goal, sharing all their information, and coordination is obtained using mutually accepted decisions and plans) and a flat structure (which represents an anarchy in which there is no fixed structure nor control of one member over another). More complex and elaborated organizational structures can be built in SPADE using those organizational units, such as bureaucracy, matrix, federations, congregations and so on. Moreover, SPADE offers a series of services related to an organizational unit for controlling agent interactions (allowing one to enable/disable communications, bilateral and multiple interactions), unit members (controlling agent identity, quantity of members, admission, expulsion and registration procedures), and organizational units (allowing to create, delete, configure or join an organization).

A real application of a multi-agent system architecture to offer services in the tourism industry has also been developed [48], following both organizational and ubiquitous concepts. Users can access the system using a Java-enabled mobile phone or PDA anytime, so they can obtain up-to-date information about the places they will visit and to plan a specific day. Currently, a hierarchical approach has been implemented, in which a broker agent is in charge of establishing and controlling communication between user and sight agents. But other more complex structures are faced, such as sight coalitions, in which places with similar activities offer services in common.

6. Mobility

In a wireless environment, most of the assumptions that guide the definition of the traditional client/server architecture are not valid: 1) fast, reliable and cheap communications; 2) robust and powerful devices; and 3) fixed locations of the participating devices. Thus, the client/server architecture is not adequate anymore for wireless environments, and several other agent-based software models have been proposed [67]:

- *Client/agent/server*. It is a three-tier architecture that introduces an agent on the server side (i.e., in the wired network). The agent becomes an intermediate for the interactions between the client (the mobile device) and the server. In this way, the server can communicate with the server agent even if the mobile device is unreachable at that moment, and the server agent will communicate appropriately with the client when the wireless connectivity is recovered.
- *Client/agent/agent/server* (also called *client/intercept/server*). Regarding the previous model, this one proposes the addition of a client-side agent. The purpose is to abstract the client from the intricacies of the wireless communications, as a server agent does for its server. The client and server agents interact to reduce the wireless communications and can divide the tasks among themselves according to the existing conditions. The client-side agent can also include optimizations such as *view materialization* [77] and an *asynchronous-disconnected mode* (requests that cannot be satisfied by the view are queued when connectivity is lost and resumed later when it is available again).
- *Mobile agents*. They are agents that have the ability to move autonomously from computer to computer to perform their tasks [51, 52, 47].

In the rest of this section we focus on the last model, as it is a general and flexible model which presents very interesting features for mobile environments.

6.1. Client/Server vs. Mobile Agents

In the traditional *client/server* architecture, a server at a certain computer offers a set of services to interested parties. Then, three steps take place: 1) a client located at another computer requests the execution of a service by interacting with the server, 2) the server performs the requested service, and 3) the server returns the result to the client.

Mobile agents arise as a promising alternative (and also as a complementary approach) to client/server for mobile environments. A mobile agent is a program that has the capability to move to other execution environments: it can decide itself when and where to move to perform its tasks. Mobile agents execute on context denominated *places* and can autonomously travel from *place* to *place* (usually, on different computers) resuming their execution there. Mobile agents are not bound to the computer where they are created; instead, they can move freely between *places* on different computers. Two types of mobility can be considered for mobile agents. If the whole agent's execution state is saved before a trip and restored at the target computer, we have *strong mobility*: on arrival at a new computer, the agent would resume by executing the statement that follows the movement statement. If the execution state is not saved, we have *weak mobility* [28]: on arrival at a new computer, the agent executes a certain *callback method* (predefined or specified by the programmer). While strong mobility is difficult to support, weak mobility has proven to be sufficient in most scenarios [6]. In the following, we analyze why mobile agents are beneficial to mobile environments.

6.2. Advantages of Mobile Agents

Due to their mobile nature, mobile agents offer many interesting benefits [47]. From the point of view of wireless networks, we would like to highlight the following:

1. *They simplify the maintenance of servers/devices.* As they can move to remote computers to achieve their goals, they avoid the need for installing specialized server processes on every machine to fulfill the requirements of all types of mobile devices and wireless applications. Instead, *only one server process* (the *mobile agent platform*, as explained in Section 6.3) *needs to be running* on a computer, and *many different agents* can travel from the mobile devices to that computer at any time carrying the required functionalities. Similarly, a mobile agent can travel with a the mobile device to provide a required service.

2. *They reduce the network load and latency.* A mobile agent can travel to the computer or mobile device that holds the necessary data, access them locally, and filter out the data that do not need to be sent over the wireless network. Moving the computation to the data, instead of the other way around, can save many wireless resources when large volumes of data must be analyzed. Besides, it improves the network latency, as the mobile agent obtains data quickly via local interactions.

3. *They are asynchronous and autonomous.* In traditional synchronous client/server architectures, the client must keep the connection active while its request is being processed by the server. If the connection fails (which may happen frequently with unreliable wireless connections), the client has to send the request to the server again, which will process it from the beginning. Alternatively, a mobile agent does not need to keep contact with its source computer while performing its tasks: a mobile device can send a mobile agent to a computer on the fixed network, and then go off-line or even be powered off. The agent becomes independent of its originating device, and thus it allows to dispatch a task into the network easily. When the device re-establishes the connection, it can collect the mobile agent and/or its results.

Furthermore, mobile agent technology also exhibits a *good performance* compared with the traditional client/server approach. For example, in [68] they evaluate the savings introduced by mobile agents when interacting with a remote database in a wireless environment, and in [50] they evaluate several strategies to download files from a wired network and show how mobile agents exhibit similar performance to client/server approaches. Due to all these benefits, mobile agents have been claimed to be very interesting for mobile and pervasive computing environments [68, 10, 72].

6.3. Mobile Agent Platforms

A mobile agent platform is an environment that allows agents to execute and provides them with different services, such as communication and mobility facilities. There are *many* available mobile agent platforms [49, 66, 18, 43], some developed by research groups and others by private companies. Aglets, Voyager, Grasshopper, and Tryllian are among the most popular alternatives. Most of the existing platforms have been developed in standard Java because it provides benefits such as platform independence (a key condition to allow agents to travel among heterogeneous mobile devices), secure execution, dynamic class loading, multithreading, and object serialization. Due to the impossibility of saving and restoring the execution stack in a standard Java system, they usually implement weak mobility.

The communication and mobility services that a platform must provide are interrelated. Particularly, mobile agents must be able to communicate among themselves, via remote method invocation or message passing, even if they move across computers. *Location transparency*, defined as the ability to communicate with mobile agents independently of their current locations, is a desirable feature. This is specially so in mobile environments (enough challenging on their own!), where placing this responsibility on the programmer should be avoided.

Some platforms are based on a remote invocation model for communications (e.g., Voyager, Grasshopper, and SPRINGS), through the idea of *proxy*, which is an abstraction used to communicate with an agent (similar to the idea of *stub* in *RMI*). On the contrary, others follow a message passing paradigm (e.g., Aglets, Tryllian and JADE[2]). Regarding message passing, there is an interest in the community to follow the FIPA standard (http://www.fipa.org/) to ensure agent interoperability. There is also a proposal specifically designed for mobile agents (*MASIF*, the *Mobile Agent System Interoperability Facility* [51]), adopted by OMG in 1998 to enable interoperability among different mobile agent platforms. However, the future of this specification is uncertain, since only a few platforms (Aglets and Grasshopper) implement it and it has not been modified since 2000.

6.4. The Future of Mobile Agents

Mobile agents have stirred up a lot of interest and research efforts during the last few years. However, despite their benefits, they have not been adopted outside the research area. In fact, the initial hype during the late nineties was followed by a more moderate period; while mobile agents continue to be an important focus of attention [82, 61], some doubts arise about their applicability and performance [74, 44, 42]. Thus, several issues have yet to be solved to increase the confidence of developers when pondering mobile agents as a practical approach to their problems.

A key problem is how to provide an efficient *location transparency* (i.e., supporting calls to target agents independently of their locations, as explained before)

---

[2]http://jade.tilab.com/

in environments with a high number of mobile agents. Location transparency requires a mechanism to keep track of the *places* where the agents are executing at every moment. This is important and challenging in distributed environments in general; even more in wireless environments, where other difficulties appear (e.g., loss of connectivity or unreliable/slow communications). Some platforms (such as Voyager, Grasshopper, and SPRINGS) provide location transparency through the use of *dynamic proxies* (proxies which continue being valid independently of agents' migrations). With dynamic proxies, building applications based on mobile agents is easier: the need of searching an agent every time a remote call is performed is avoided, as the same proxy is always used to route the communications as needed. Voyager implements dynamic proxies through *forwarding chains of proxies* (as agents move, they leave a trail of *footprints*). In Grasshopper, *region servers* are in charge of routing the calls on the proxies to their target agents. Other platforms (e.g., Tryllian and Aglets) do not offer location transparency. Some platforms, such as Tryllian or JADE, do not support proxies[3]. Not only keeping track of the current locations of the agents is challenging, but also how to ensure a reliable communication with agents that move very frequently [53] (especially in wireless environments, where connectivity can be lost at any time). This is also the concern of the platform *SPRINGS*[4] [43]. Some experimental results show that this platform achieves a good scalability, which is key for wireless environments where there may be many mobile users; thus, in a wired network SPRINGS supports several thousands of agents continually moving and calling among themselves [43].

While some issues need to be resolved to enable a massive adoption of mobile agent technology, we believe that it is a very useful paradigm for building applications for mobile environments. Thus, as we have explained in this section, mobile agents present very interesting advantages over the traditional client/server approach in a wireless context. However, mobile agent platforms have been designed mainly with fixed distributed environments in mind, and there is not enough experience with the use of mobile agents in real wireless networks. For example, some mechanisms used to keep dynamic proxies up-to-date may need to be adapted to the peculiarities of wireless contexts. We expect that promising developments will occur in the future.

7. Conclusions

In this chapter we have shown the appropriateness of multi-agent systems to the development of Ambient Intelligence applications. The importance of Ambient Intelligence environments, characterized by capacities such as transparency, ubiquity and intelligence, has notably grown in recent years and has become deeply-rooted

---

[3]In JADE, a message is sent to a certain agent by specifying its identifier. In Tryllian, the target address is also needed.
[4]*Scalable Platform foR movING Software*, it allows software agents to *spring* among computers, see http://sid.cps.unizar.es/SPRINGS.

in the information society. New solutions are required and the multi-agent systems are an excellent alternative for developing Ambient Intelligence applications.

In this sense, the main characteristics of Ambient Intelligence have been studied, illustrating the operation of different technologies. Particulary, this chapter focuses on agent technology. In this way, a brief summary of real developments in ambient intelligence using agent technology has been presented. Moreover, the advances on practical and theoretical applications of multi-agent systems in the fields of ubiquitous computing and mobile environments are presented.

One of the most important tasks that has to be accomplished for an agent to live in an intelligent environment is obtaining a context definition. In this chapter the importance of obtaining a good context definition has been emphasized, and different context aware applications have been presented. Moreover, different strategies for representing context information have been studied, focusing on ontologies. The importance of managing context information has also been noted, and tasks such as context delivery and context reasoning and aggregation have been illustrated.

Given the importance of the communication in multi-agent systems in Ambient Intelligence applications, defining ontologies helps to solve problems of interoperability, re-use and communication and differences about concepts, models and structures. The main concepts of an ontology have been presented and a proposal of a meta-ontology that focuses mainly on the definition of all the concepts in order to be valid for any environment or domain has been detailed. Furthermore, the ontology definition for agent communication and agent interaction have been shown, illustrating both processes with examples.

Ambient Intelligence environments require ubiquitous communication and ubiquitous computation. That implies the need of methodologies, frameworks and software that take care of situatedness, openness, locality in control and locality in interactions. An agent organization is a social entity composed of a specific number of members that accomplish several distinct tasks or functions. Dynamic agent organizations that self-adjust for making the most of their current environment are more and more important. In this chapter, the organizational models that have been recently used in agent theory for modeling coordination in open systems are presented. Moreover, an organization oriented multi-agent platform called SPADE is presented. The SPADE platform can be applied in mobile devices.

Mobile devices supporting wireless communication have become increasingly relevant in the development of multi-agent systems. They provide a framework for obtaining ubiquitous communication and building applications for mobile environments. Mobile agents present very interesting advantages over the traditional client/server approach in a wireless context. In this chapter, the advantages of mobile agents have been presented and mobile agent platforms have been studied. Finally, a discussion about the future of mobile agents is established.

Some issues need to be resolved to enable adoption multi-agent systems to develop Ambient Intelligence applications. The main tendencies and current issues have been presented within this chapter, but there is still a lot of work to do.

References

[1] E. Argente, V. Julian, and V. Botti. From Human to Agent Organizations. In *First International Workshop on Coordination and Organization (CoOrg'05)*, G. Boella and L.Van der Torre eds., pages 1–11, 2005.

[2] E. Argente, A. Giret, S. Valero, V. Julian, and V. Botti. Survey of MAS methods and platforms focusing on organizational concepts. *Frontiers in Artificial Intelligence and Applications*, 113:309–316, 2004.

[3] A. Baciu, and A. Nagy. Coordination and Reorganization in Multi-Agents Systems. In *Informatica*, vol. XLVIII, number 2, Studia Univ. Babes-Bolayi, pages 53–60, 2003.

[4] J. Bajo ,Y. de Paz , J.F. de Paz , Q. Martin, and J.M. Corchado. SMas: A Shopping Mall Multiagent Systems. In *Proccedings of IDEAL'06*, LNAI, vol 4224 pp. 1166-1173, Springer Verlag, 2006.

[5] J. Bajo, J.M. Corchado, and L.F. Castillo. Running Agents in Mobile Devices. In *Proccedings of IBERAMIA'06*, LNAI, vol 4140 pp. 58-67, Springer Verlag, 2006.

[6] L. Bettini and R. De Nicola. Translating strong mobility into weak mobility. In *5th International Conference on Mobile Agents (MA'01), Atlanta, Georgia, USA*, pages 182–197. Springer, 2001.

[7] Bohnenberger T., Jameson A., A. Krger, and A. Butz. Location-aware shopping assistance: Evaluation of a decision-theoretic approach. In *Proceedings of the Fourth International Symposium on Human-Computer Interaction with Mobile Devices*, Pisa, 155.169, 2002.

[8] G. Caire. JADE Tutorial. *Application-Defined Content Languages and Ontologies*, 2002

[9] M. Calisti, and D. Greenwood. Adaptive Service Access Management for Ubiquitous Connectivity In *4th International Workshop on Management of Ubiquitous Communication and Services, MUCS, May 21-25, 2007, Munich*

[10] R.S. Cardoso. Mobile agents: A key for effective pervasive computing. In *Second Pervasive Computing Workshop of ACM Conference on Object-Oriented Programming, Systems, Languages, and Applications (OOPSLA'02), Vancouver, British Columbia, Canada*, 2002.

[11] C. Carrascosa , J. Bajo, V. Julin, J.M. Corchado, and V. Botti. Hybrid multi-agent architecture as a real-time problem-solving model. *Expert Systems with Applications*. Pergamon-Elsevier Science LTD. doi:10.1016/j.eswa.2006.08.031, 2006.

[12] A. Chavez, D. Dreilinger, R. Guttman, and P. Maes. A Real-Life Experiment in Creating an Agent Marketplace. In *Proceedings of the Second International Conference on the Practical Application of Intelligent Agents and Multi-Agent Technology (PAAM'97)*, London, UK, 1997.

[13] H. Chen, T. Finin, and A. Joshi. An ontology for contextaware pervasive computing environments. *Knowledge Engineering Review. Special Issue on Ontologies for Distributed Systems*, 2003.

[14] H. Chen, F. Perich, T. Finin, and A. Joshi. Soupa: Standard ontology for ubiquitous and pervasive applications. In *International Conference on Mobile and Ubiquitous Systems: Networking and Services*, August 2004.

[15] J.M. Corchado, J. Pavn, E.S. Corchado, and L.F. Castillo. Development of CBR-BDI Agents: A Tourist Guide Application. In *Proceedings of the European Conference on Case-based Reasoning 2004 (ECCBR'04)*. LNAI vol. 3155 pp. 547-559, Springer Verlag, 2005.

[16] J.M. Corchado, J. Bajo, Y. de Paz, and D. I. Tapia. Intelligent Environment for Monitoring Alzheimer Patients, Agent Technology for Health Care. *Decision Support Systems*. Eslevier Science. doi: 10.1016/j.dss.2007.04.008, 2007.

[17] V. Dignum, J. Meyer, H. Wiegand, and F. Dignum. An organization-oriented model for agent societies. In *Proc. of International Workshop on Regulated Agent-Based Social Systems (RASTA'02)*, 2002.

[18] M. Dikaiakos and G. Samaras. A performance analysis framework for mobile-agent systems. In *Revised Papers from the International Workshop on Infrastructure for Agents, Multi-Agent Systems, and Scalable Multi-Agent Systems*, volume 1887, pages 180–187. Springer, 2001.

[19] Ducatel, K., Bogdanowicz, M., Scapolo, F., Leijten, J., Burgelman, J.C.. That's what friends are for. Ambient Intelligence (AmI) and the IS in 2010. In *Innovations for an e-Society. Congress Pre-prints, Innovations for an e-Society. Challenges for Technology Assessment*. Berlin, Germany, 2001.

[20] M. Escrivà, J. Palanca, G. Aranda, A. García-Fornes, V. Julian, and V. Botti. A Jabber-based Multi-Agent System Platform In *Proc. AAMAS06*, pages 1282–1284, 2006.

[21] M. Esteva, B. Rosell, J. A. Rodriguez, and J. L. Arcos. AMELI: An agent-based middleware for electronic institutions. In *Proc. of AAMAS04*, pages 236–243, 2004.

[22] M. Esteva, J.A. Rodriguez, C. Sierra, P. Garcia, and J.L. Arcos. On the formal specification of electronic institutions. *Agent Mediated Electronic Commerce*, 1991:126–147, 2001.

[23] A. Farquhar. *Ontolingua tutorial*.
http://ksl-web.stanford.edu/people/axf/tutorial.pdf, 1997.

[24] J. Ferber, O. Gutkenecht, and F. Michel. From agents to organizations: an organizational view of multi-agent systems. In *Proc. AAMAS03 - Workshop 4*, 2003.

[25] V. Fuentes, J. Carbo, and J.M. Molina. Heterogeneous domain ontology for location based information system in a multiagent framework. In *7th International Conference on Intelligent Data Engineering and Automated Learning*, Burgos, Spain, 2006

[26] V. Fuentes, N.Sanchez, J. Carbo, and J.M. Molina. Reputation in User Profiling for a Context-Aware Multi-Agent System. In *Fourth European Workshop on Multi-Agent Systems*, Lisbon, Portugal, 2006.

[27] V. Fuentes, N.Sanchez, J. Carbo, and J.M. Molina. Generic Context-Aware BDI Multi-Agent Framework with GAIA methodology. In *International Workshop on Agent-Based Ubiquitous Computing ABUC2007 in AAMAS 2007 Conference*, Honolulu. Hawaii, 2007.

[28] A. Fuggetta, G. P. Picco, and G. Vigna. Understanding code mobility. *IEEE Transactions and Software Engineering*, 24(5):342–361, 1998.

[29] L. Gasser. An Overview of DAI In *Distributed Artifical Intelligence: Theory and Praxis*, L. Gasser and N.M. Avouris eds., Kluwer Academic Publishers, pages 9–30, 1992.

[30] P. Giorgini, M. Kolp, and J. Mylopoulos. Multi-Agent Architectures as Organizational Structures. In *Journal of Autonomous Agents and Multi-Agent Systems*, Kluwer Academic Publishers, 2003.

[31] A. Gomez-Perez. Knowledge sharing and reuse. *Handbook of Applied Expert Systems*. Liebowitz, editor, CRC Press, 1998.

[32] J. J. Gomez Sanz. Modelado de Sistemas Multi-Agente. PhD dissertation. Universidad Complutense de Madrid, 2002.

[33] Tao Gu, Hung Keng Pung, and Da Qing Zhang. Toward an osgi-based infrastructure for context-aware applications. *IEEE PERVASIVE Computing*, pages 66–74, October-December 2004.

[34] T.R. Gruber. A Translation Approach to Portable Ontology Specification. *Knowledge Acquisition* 5:88 (1993), 199-220.

[35] M. Gruninger, and M.S. Fox. Methodology for the Design and Evaluation of Ontologies. In *Proceedings of the Workshop on Basic Ontological Issues in Knowledge Sharing, IJCAI-95*, Montreal, 1995.

[36] Hewlett-Packard: Understanding Wi-Fi. http://www.hp.com/rnd/library/pdf/, 2002.

[37] B. Horling, and V. Lesser. A Survey of multiagent Organizational Paradigms. In *The Knowledge Engineering Review*, Cambridge University Press, vol.19, pages 281–316, 2004.

[38] M. Hospers, E. Kroezen, A. Nijholt, R. op den Akker, and D. Heylen. Developing a generic agent-based intelligent tutoring system and applying it to nurse education. In *Proceedings IEEE International Conference on Advanced Language Technologies (ICALT '03)*, Athens, Greece, 2003.

[39] N. Howden, R. Ronnquist, A. Hodgson, and A. Lucas. JACK Intelligent Agents-Summary of an Agent Infrastructure. In *Proc. 5th International Conference on Autonomous Agents*, 2001.

[40] J.F. Hubner, J. S. Sichman, and O. Boissier. S-Moise+: A Middleware for developing Organised Multi-Agent Systems. In *Proc. Int. Workshop on Organizations in Multiagent Systems, from Organizations to Organization Oriented Programming in MAS*, pages 64–78, 2005.

[41] R.Ghizzioli, and D.Greenwood. The RASCAL System for Managing Autonomic Communication in Disruptive Environments In *1st IEEE Workshop on Autonomic Communication and Network Management (ACNM)*, Munich, May 21-25, 2007.

[42] R. S. Gray. Mobile agents: Overcoming early hype and a bad name. In *Fifth International Conference on Mobile Data Management (MDM'04)*, Berkeley, California, USA, pages 302–303. IEEE Computer Society, 2004.

[43] S. Ilarri, R. Trillo, and E. Mena. SPRINGS: A scalable platform for highly mobile agents in distributed computing environments. In *4th International WoWMoM 2006 workshop on Mobile Distributed Computing (MDC'06), Buffalo, New York (USA)*, pages 633–637. IEEE Computer Society, ISBN 0-7695-2593-8, June 2006.

[44] D. Johansen. Mobile agents: Right concept, wrong approach. In *Fifth International Conference on Mobile Data Management (MDM'04)*, Berkeley, California, USA, pages 300–301. IEEE Computer Society, 2004.

[45] T. Karygiannis, and L. Owens. Wireless Network Security 802.11, Bluetooth and Handheld Devices. National Institute of Standards and Applications. U.S. Department of Commerce. Special Publication 800-48, 2002.

[46] M. Klusch and A. Gerber Dynamic Coalition Formation among Rational Agents In *IEEE Intelligent Systems*, vol. 1094, pp. 42 - 47, 2002.

[47] D. Lange and M. Oshima. Seven good reasons for mobile agents. *Communications of the ACM*, 42:88–89, 1999.

[48] J.S. Lopez, F.A. Bustos, and V.J. Inglada Tourism Services Using Agent Technology: A MultiAgent Approach In *Proc. 1st Workshop on Industrial Applications of Distributed Intelligent Systems (INADIS)*, vol. CD-ROM, 2006.

[49] K. Ludwig, A. Josef, W. E. Edgar, S. Wolfgang, and G. Franz. Using mobile agents in real world: A survey and evaluation of agent platforms. In *Second Workshop on Infrastructure for Agents, MAS, and Scalable MAS at Autonomous Agents, Montreal, Canada*. AAAI, 2001.

[50] E. Mena, J.A. Royo, A. Illarramendi, and A. Goñi. Adaptable software retrieval service for wireless environments based on mobile agents. In *International Conference on Wireless Networks (ICWN'02), Las Vegas, Nevada, USA*, pages 116–124. CSREA Press, 2002.

[51] D. Milojicic, M. Breugst, I. Busse, J. Campbell, S. Covaci, B. Friedman, K. Kosaka, D. Lange, K. Ono, M. Oshima, C. Tham, S. Virdhagriswaran, and J. White. MASIF, the OMG mobile agent system interoperability facility. In *Mobile Agents (MA'98), Stuttgart, Germany*, volume 1477. Springer, 1998.

[52] D. Milojicic, F. Douglis, and R. Wheeler. *Mobility: processes, computers, and agents.* Addison-Wesley Professional, April 1999.

[53] A. L. Murphy and G. P. Picco. Reliable communication for highly mobile agents. *Autonomous Agents and Multi-Agent Systems*, 5(1):81–100, 2002.

[54] I. Nieto, J. Botia, and A. Gomez-Skarmeta. Information and hybrid architecture model of the ocp contextual information management system. *Journal of Universal Computer Science*, 12(3):357–366, 2006.

[55] N.F. Noy and D.L. McGuinness. Ontology Development 101: A Guide to Creating Your First Ontology. em Stanford Knowledge Systems Laboratory Technical Report KSL-01-05 and Stanford Medical Informatics Technical Report SMI-2001-0880, March 2001.

[56] A. Omicini. SODA: Societies and Infrastructures in the Analysis and Design of Agent-based Systems. In *Agent-Oriented Software Engineering*, vol.1957, pages 185–193, 2001.

[57] J. Pascoe N. S. Ryan and D. R. Morse. Human-computer-giraffe interaction - hci in the field. *Workshop on Human Computer Interaction with Mobile Devices*, 1998.

[58] Protege. *The Protege Project.* http://protege.stanford.edu 2000.

[59] D. Rios, P. Dockhorn Costa, G. Guizzardi, L. Ferreira Pires, J.G. Pereira Filho, and M. van Sinderen. Using Ontologies for Modelling Context-Aware Services Platforms. In *Workshop on Ontologies to Complement Software Architectures*, Anaheim, CA, USA, 2003.

[60] U. Rutishauser, J. Joller, and R. Douglas. Control and learning of ambience by an intelligent building, *IEEE Transactions on Systems, Man and Cybernetics Part*

A: Systems and Humans, Special Issue on Ambient Intelligence, Vol. 35, No. 1, pp 121-132, 2005.

[61] G. Samaras. Mobile agents: What about them? did they deliver what they promised? are they here to stay? In Fifth International Conference on Mobile Data Management (MDM'04), Berkeley, California, USA, pages 294–295. IEEE Computer Society, 2004.

[62] B.N. Schilit, N. Adams, and R. Want. Context-aware computing applications. In Proceedings of the Workshop on Mobile Computing Systems and Applications. IEEE, December 1994.

[63] W. Scott. Organizations: rational, natural, and open systems. Prentice Hall, 2002.

[64] M.K. Smith, C. Welty, and D.L. McGuinness. Owl web ontology language guide. w3c recommendation. Technical report, W3C, February 2004.

[65] J. Shao, W. A. Gray, N.J. Fiddina, T.J. Norma, A. Preece, P. Gray, S. Chalmers, N. Oren, N. Jennings, M. Luck, et al. Supporting Formation and Operation of Virtual Organisations in a Grid Environment In BT Technology Journal, vol. 24 no 1, 2006.

[66] A. R. Silva, A. Romäo, D. Deugo, and M. M. Silva. Towards a reference model for surveying mobile agent systems. Autonomous Agents and Multi-Agent Systems, 4(3):187–231, September 2001.

[67] C. Spyrou, G. Samaras, P. Evripidou, and E. Pitoura. Wireless computational models: Mobile agents to the rescue. In Second International DEXA Workshop on Mobility in Databases and Distributed Systems (MDDS'99), Florence, Italy, pages 127–133. IEEE Computer Society, 1999.

[68] C. Spyrou, G. Samaras, E. Pitoura, and P. Evripidou. Mobile agents for wireless computing: the convergence of wireless computational models with mobile-agent technologies. Mobile Networks and Applications, 9(5):517–528, 2004.

[69] The Foundation for Intelligent Physical Agents. Available : http://www.fipa.org, 2002.

[70] M. Uschold, and M. Gruninger. Ontologies: Principles, Methods and Applications. Knowledge Engineering Review 11(2), 1996.

[71] U.S. Department of Commerce. Radio Frequency Identification: Opportunities and Challenges in Implementation. Technical Report, 2005.

[72] L. Vasiu and Q.H. Mahmoud. Mobile agents in wireless devices. IEEE Computer, 37(2):104–105, 2004.

[73] J. Vazquez-Salceda, V. Dignum, and F.Dignum. Organizing Multiagent Systems. Institute of Information and Computing Sciences. Tech. Report. Utrecht University, 2004.

[74] G. Vigna. Mobile agents: Ten reasons for failure. In Fifth International Conference on Mobile Data Management (MDM'04), Berkeley, California, USA, pages 298–299. IEEE Computer Society, 2004.

[75] X. Wang. Ontology-based context modeling and reasoning using owl. In Context Modeling and Reasoning Workshop at PerCom 2004., 2004.

[76] R. Want, B.N. Schilit, N. Adams, R. Gold, K. Petersen, D. Greenberg, J. Ellis, and M. Weiser. An overview of the parctab ubiquitous computing environment. IEEE Personal Communications, 2(6), pages 28–43, 1995.

[77] O. Wolfson, P. Sistla, S. Dao, K. Narayanan, and R. Raj. View maintenance in mobile computing. *SIGMOD Record*, 24(4):22–27, 1995.

[78] M. Wooldridge, and N.R. Jennings. Agent Theories, Architectures, and Languages: a Survey. In *Wooldridge and Jennings, editors, Intelligent Agents, Springer-Verlag*, pp. 1-22, 1995.

[79] M. Wooldridge. *An Introduction to MultiAgent Systems*. Wiley & Sons, 2001.

[80] T. Yamashita, K. Izumi , and K. Kurumatani. Car Navigation with Route Information Sharing for Improvement of Traffic Efficiency. In *Proceedings of 7th Annual IEEE Conference on Intelligent Transportation Systems*, pp. 465-470, Washington, D.C., U.S.A, 2004.

[81] F. Zambonelli, and H.V.D. Parunak. From Design to Intention: Signs of a Revolution. In *Proc. AAMAS02*, pages 455–456, 2002.

[82] A. B. Zaslavsky. Mobile agents: Can they assist with context awareness? In *Fifth International Conference on Mobile Data Management (MDM'04), Berkeley, California, USA*, pages 304–. IEEE Computer Society, 2004.

José M. Molina
University Carlos III of Madrid,
Avenida de la Universidad Carlos III 22,
28270 Colmenarejo (Madrid),
Spain
e-mail: molina@ia.uc3m.es

Juan M. Corchado
University of Salamanca,
Plaza de la Merced s/n,
37008 Salamanca,
Spain
e-mail: corchado@usal.es

Javier Bajo
Pontifical University of Salamanca,
Calle Compania 5,
37002 Salmanca,
Spain
e-mail: jbajope@upsa.es

Whitestein Series in Software Agent Technologies, 59–85
© 2007 Birkhäuser Verlag Basel/Switzerland

Cognitive Abilities in Agents

Beatriz López and Susana Fernández

Abstract. The aim of this chapter is to describe the cognitive abilities deployed on agents and multi-agent systems by using examples from applications carried out by the authors. Particularly, the following agent abilities are reviewed: problem solving, memory, decision making and learning capabilities. These abilities, which involve most of the research done in Artificial Intelligence during decades of dealing with isolated agents, are revised in order to incorporate the interaction of agents in a multi-agent environment. The results of incorporating such capabilities to agents are the enhancement of the generality and flexibility of the systems.

1. Introduction

An agent is an artifact that can be viewed as perceiving its environment through sensors and acting upon that environment through actuators. The agent's choice depends on the observed sequence of inputs. Thus, **intelligent** agents are those that make the best possible selection according to its computational resources (*bounded optimality*). For this purpose, a variety of different agent designs are possible. According to [46], these range from pure reflex agents to pure deliberative agents: simple reflex agents, model-state reflex agents, goal-based agents, and utility-based agents. First, simple reflex agents select actions on the basis of the current input. Second, model-based reflex agents keep an internal state that captures the history of the inputs. Such a state is compared against an internal model of the world, so the agent can identify the results of its actions. Third, goal-based agents have some sort of goal that describes the situations that are desirable. In order to achieve those goals, agents use search and planning techniques. Finally, utility-based agents use utility functions to make decisions between conflicting goals, asses their importance, and determine if there is some uncertainty in the goal attainment.

Co-authors of this chapter: Javier Bajo, Juan M. Corchado, Raquel Fuentetaja, Manuel Gonzalez, David Isern, Sergio Jiménez, Aïda Valls.

Agents not only gather information from the environment in order to act, but also to learn from it. They can measure the effect of their actions and modify their behaviour from experience, adapting to the changing circumstances, updating incomplete knowledge, extending prior knowledge, etc.

Thus, intelligent agents are computational artifacts that should combine many cognitive abilities in an integrated system [35]: knowledge representation and memory (agent's beliefs, goals, knowledge representation of internal and world states), planning, decision making, and learning. Cognitive abilities can be achieved both at the agent and at the multi-agent levels, since intelligent systems do not function in isolation. The environment provides the opportunity to interact with and learn from other agents. They should interact to coordinate their goals, to rely on other agents, so they do not have to individually learn everything [28].

In this chapter, we review some cognitive abilities that characterise intelligent agents on the basis of practical examples of existing systems. The organisation of the chapter follows a set of well-known cognitive abilities, namely planning, memory, decision making and learning, trying to capture the different abilities of agents. An agent rarely exhibits a single cognitive ability; moreover, in a multi-agent system several agents try to provide a complementary ability to the system. Thus, in the conclusion section we discuss the different ways in which cognitive abilities have been integrated, and what are the open issues regarding further development of them.

2. Planning as problem solving

A problem is a situation experienced by an agent as different from the situation which the agent ideally would like to be in. There are many approaches to problem solving, depending on the nature of the problem. Most often, the way of solving a problem is executing a sequence of actions (plan) that reduce the difference between the initial and the desired situation. Planning then enables some agent to achieve its goals (solve their problems) given the current state of the world.

This section focuses on automated planning techniques and their use in intelligent agents. First, some basic issues about planning are provided. Then, several approaches that have been used to combine automated planning and multi-agent systems are introduced. The next subsection provides an illustrative example of a cognitive architecture SAMAP [12] that contains a planner agent. Finally, the difficulties of building agents with problem solving capacities are discussed.

2.1. General concepts about planning

Any form of general problem solving has these three components:

- A *conceptual model*, i.e., the description of the problems to solve. Problem solving is concerned with the selection and organization of actions to change the state of a dynamic system so it uses a *conceptual model* able to describe dynamic systems. Most of the planning approaches take as their *conceptual model* the model of state-transition systems but making several assumptions to make it more operational:

1. *Finite state space.* The dynamic system has a finite set of states.
2. *Deterministic world.* When an action is applicable to a state, its execution brings the dynamic system to a single other state.
3. *Static world.* The dynamic system stays in the same state until a new action is executed.
4. *Full observable world.* There is complete knowledge about the current state of the dynamic system.
5. *Restrictive goals.* The planner objective is to find a sequence of state transitions that ends at one of the states satisfying the goals.
6. *Implicit time.* Actions have no duration. The state transitions are instantaneous.

- *A representation language,* i.e., the elements used to describe the problems to solve. In automated planning these languages are notations for representing syntactic and semantically planning problem models. Most of them declaratively describe the objects, actions, states and goals through variants of the first order logic.
- *An algorithm,* i.e., the technique used to solve the problems. The algorithms used to solve planning problems are search algorithms. These algorithms explore graphs systematically, trying to find a path to arrive at some goal node n_g starting from a given initial node n_0.

When an agent does not have a complete knowledge of the environment it needs some mechanisms to revise and adapt its plans. Regarding this, the planning model is extended in two different dimensions:

1. *Actions' effects.* In many environments the agent can not assume their actions have deterministic effects. Actions may produce different outcomes so the planning algorithms should not look just for a sequence of actions that solve a problem but does so with high probability.
2. *World observability.* In many environments the agent can not always have a complete description of the current state of the world where it is acting.

As follows, there is a classification of the different planning paradigms according to how these two dimensions are extended:

- *Deterministic planning* is the task of generating a plan to arrive at a state where a set of conditions, the goals, are true starting from a given state, the initial state, in a completely known environment. In these cases the agents can do the planning offline, as they need no feedback from the execution of their actions in the world. Most of the research work in automated planning has focused on deterministic planning. Thanks to that choice, deterministic planning is now a well formalized and well characterized problem with algorithms and techniques that scale-up reasonably well.
- *Probabilistic planning* is the task of finding a robust sequence of actions to satisfy the goals in a completely observable environment where actions can

produce possible different states determined by a probability distribution. Sometimes there is no plan guaranteeing always the goals satisfaction. So it is important to maximize the probability of reaching them, and hence it is important to use information on the probabilities of different effects of agent actions. There are three main approaches to tackle planning problems in these environments: combining deterministic planning and replanning [33], extending classical planning [36] and Solving Markov Decision Processes (MDPs) [44].

- *Contingent planning* is the task of solving a planning problem in environments where the current state is not completely known but it is possible to observe some aspects of the current state during the actions execution. Contingent planning needs to represent planning problems with two extra functionalities. First, the agent handles a probability distribution over states rather than exactly the current state. These probability distribution over states are called belief states. And the agent has to describe the acquisition of information about the current state in execution time. This can be achieved by enriching the action model with sensing actions [6].

- *Conformant planning* is the problem of finding a safe plan in a non-deterministic and non-observable environment. In this kind of environments the agent has to find a sequence of actions able to achieve a goal state for all possible contingencies without any sensing during the plan execution. There are three main approaches to tackle planning problems in these environments: via Model Checking Planning [13], extending deterministic planning paradigms [8], and compiling conformant planning problems into deterministic planning problems [45].

2.2. Planning systems and multi-agent systems

Multi-agent approaches and planning systems have been combined in two different senses:

1. To develop intelligent systems able to address the "whole" planning problem (deliberation, execution and control). Thus, the goal of the multi-agent system is to solve a planning problem, and each individual agent has one or more abilities to carry out one or more processes involved in the achievement of this goal.
2. In environments where individual agents generate their own plans but they should coordinate with other agents to solve dependencies and conflicts between their plans.

Both approaches are motivated by the fact that usually a unique agent is not enough to deal with real-world problems.

Regarding (1), an isolated planner can not address realistic planning problems. To carry out plans in the real world, the planning task has to be complemented with some other processes. First, there have to be processes that interface

with the sensors and actuators of the system to put the planned actions into prac-
tise. Second, as real environments usually are non-deterministic, there have to be
processes that allow monitoring of the actions executions [18]. And finally, there
have to be processes that modify the plans when the actions executions have unexpected outcomes [24]. All these functionalities can be easily implemented in a
multi-agent architecture where each of these processes is fulfilled by an individual
agent. An example of this approach is O-plan [22], where a planning agent deals
with plan generation while other agents are concerned with aspects such as task
elicitation, plan analysis, reactive execution, plan repair, monitoring, etc. Another
example is SAMAP [12], whose architecture is described in the next subsection.

With respect to (2), when in real-life problems we have multiple agents having
their own goals, it is often impractical or undesirable to create the plan for all
agents centrally. These agents may be people or companies simply demanding
to plan their actions themselves, or refusing to make all information necessary for
planning available to someone else. Consequently, agents are able to make their own
plans independently of what the other agents are planning to do. However, in many
cases dependencies between the tasks of the agents make independent planning
impossible. That is, if the agents do not take into account the dependencies between
their plans, then they might come into conflict when they try to execute them. To
solve their dependencies, agents must coordinate their efforts. From this point of
view, a *multi-agent planning problem* [19] is a problem where given an initial state,
a set of global goals, a set of agents and for each agent a set of its capabilities and
private goals, each agent should find a plan that achieves its private goals, such
that these plans together are coordinated and the global goals are meet.

According to [19], the process of solving a multi-agent planning problem has
the following phases:

- Refine the global goals or tasks until subtasks remain that can be assigned
  to individual agents.
- Allocate this set of subtasks to the agents.
- Define rules or constraints for the individual agents to prevent them from
  producing conflicting plans (coordination before planning).
- For each agent: find a plan to reach its goals (individual planning).
- Coordinate the individual plans of the agents (coordination after planning).
- Execute plans and synthesise the results of the subtasks.

There are several plan coordination methods such as: *coordination throughout
filtering*, to filter out those options that are incompatible with the agent's goals;
Generalized Partial Global Planning (PGP), where agents cooperate because no
agent has complete information; and *plan merging*, which is used for agents that
are able to create a valid plan on their own. A more detailed description of these
methods can be found in [19] and [20].

An example of the application of coordination techniques to planning in a
multi-agent system is [50]. The goal of this system is to produce an applicable
action sequence under complex constraints for spacecraft missions. In that system,

each spacecraft subsystem is represented by a planning agent, and they cooperate with each other in order to build plans of actions needed to achieve the given goals. The knowledge space is partitioned into sub-spaces and each agent is in charge of managing and operating upon a given subset of the domain, called the agent domain. The multi-agent planning system can lead to several improvements in terms of efficiency and reliability of planning activity over distributed environment.

2.3. SAMAP

SAMAP is an example of a cognitive agent architecture that combines several cognitive abilities in an integrated system. The goal of SAMAP is to build a software tool to help different people visit different cities. It dynamically captures and updates a user model of different city visits, analyses past planning behaviour of the tourist and similar tourists in the same type of visit, and selects, through a case-based reasoning (CBR) approach, a list of places that have a high probability to be interesting for the tourist. Then, taking into account distances, places timetables, etc., it computes a plan, and also shows how to go from one place to the next in the plan. This system is intended to work in portable devices (mobile phones, PDAs, etc,) with Internet connection.

SAMAP has been built as a multi-agent system, consisting of three main agents: user modelling and interface agent, case-based agent, and planning agent. It also integrates an ontology to facilitate the information exchange among these agents. The ontology stores information about the tourists and their preferences, the activities that can be performed in a city and the city itself.

The first step consists of building the user model. This requires the tourist to enter personal information, that is, personal data, interests and preferences about, i.e., art, monuments, meals, etc. Also, the tourist should specify which city is going to be visited, on what schedule, etc. This information can be gathered by using any device with Internet connection. In order to obtain more interesting data about the tourist, the system (by means of machine learning techniques) can use past information about the same tourist (provided the tourist has used the application before). This information is stored in the ontology.

The second step consists of the generation of a list of activities that the tourist might like to perform in the current visit according to the preferences. The activities might come directly from the tourist, or be automatically generated by CBR from similar tourists' plans in the city or similar cities. Each activity will also be described with the expected utility that this activity might have for the tourist. This utility can be directly specified by the tourist, or computed by SAMAP from knowledge about similar tourists.

The last step is the computation of the tourist plan by taking into account the previously computed list of activities.

At the multi-agent level, the ontology shared by all agents constitutes the first cognitive ability of the system (memory). At the agent level, the user modelling agent is provided with the learning abilities, and the planning agent with the problem-solving abilities.

2.3.1. Planning agent. One of the inputs of the planning agent is the list of activities selected by the CBR agent. This list is not directly the goal of the planning problem. If the CBR has ranked activities and made a selection, it can still contain more places than the tourist would be able to visit because of schedule or movement constraints among places. Therefore, the planner must select which of them should be included in the plan. Moreover, the planner must schedule each visit according to the place timetable, deal with the city map, etc. This planning task has several features that make it hard for current planners:

- **Time management:** each visit should be scheduled according to the opening hours of each place and the expected duration of the visit according to the user model. Also, it should consider the time to go from a place to another.
- **Preferences:** the ontology contains knowledge about user preferences or constraints such as time-to-eat, utilities of visiting, places, types of food...
- **Management of numerical values:** the prices of the visits, meals and transports must not exceed the available budget.
- **Locations:** the planner should indicate how to go from one place to another, that is, which transport the tourist should take. In case it is preferable to walk, the planner should specify which route the tourist should follow.
- **Goals:** three types of goals have been specified. They are the following:
  - totally instantiated goals, i.e., visit a specific museum,
  - partially instantiated goals, i,e., generic goals like visiting any museum,
  - a metric indicating that the plan must maximize its utility.

  Moreover, not all the available places must be visited, that is, not all goals would be achievable, because of scheduling constraints related to timetables (one cannot enter the Prado's museum at night) or to the available time of the tourist (one cannot visit five places if there is time to visit only two). This problem is related to the over-subscription problem in planning [48] and scheduling [34].

As it is difficult to use any of the current planners for solving the whole planning problem, a hybrid system was proposed based on the ideas in [25]. Thus, besides the planner module, the planner agent in SAMAP is composed of four more modules: the Translator module that transforms the original list of activities into the predicates required by the planner; the Control module that coordinates the rest of the modules providing the input that they need; the Selector of activities module that selects the most appropriate actions to be solved by the planner each time, and the Transport module that receives an origin and a destination point and returns the transport subplan for moving a person from the origin to the destination.

As said above, the input of the system is a ranked list of activities that represents the places of interest of the tourist (including eating and leisure places) together with a number indicating their utility, i.e, the *satisfaction degree* of the tourist when visiting such site (computed by the CBR agent). Each activity can be totally or partially instantiated, as in "visit museum of Modern Art" or "visit any museum". The output is one or more tourist plans which contain a list of scheduled visits along with the indications about how to move from one place to another. The system also computes the cost of the plans trying to maximize its quality according to the established metric. By default, the quality metric is to maximize the total utility, but it could be to diminish the cost, a combination of both or any one else.

The final step of the planning system is to store the generated plans into the ontology.

2.4. Discussion

The straightest way to endow an agent with a problem solving capacity is to integrate an existing planner in the agent architecture. However, the planning task resulting from real world problems can be computationally too hard even for state-of-art planners. So, it is necessary to help the planner somehow.

In the SAMAP particular case, the planner agent assists tourists in their visit to a city, using a PDA or a third generation mobile phone. Visits are adapted according to the tourist preferences. So the system only proposes a list of activities that could be really interesting and achievable for the tourist. The input of the planning agent is an original list of activities, selected by a CBR agent, that represents the places of interest to the tourist (including eating and leisure places) together with their utility. The output is one or more tourist plans that maximize the utility, including as many visits as possible, along with the indications about the transports needed to move between the different places (the transport subplans). This planning task resulting from the analysis of this tourist problem was a difficult task even for the state-of-art planners. Therefore, SAMAP uses an hybrid planner agent composed by a planner and other modules that reduce the task of planning itself. This way, the planning agent can solve complex problems that otherwise the planner alone could not solve.

Another solution might have been to use a CBR mechanism throughout the system. The use of a planning approach with "classical" operators was chosen because (a) there is not a CBR planning tool that allows one to develop applications quickly and (b) in big cities where there are a number of different goals and ways to go from one place to another and scheduling the visits, a very rich adaptation agent could be needed. Therefore, it seems reasonable to adopt the following solution: the planner takes this information as input together with information about the city (streets and intersections, situation of each place, etc.) to compute the plan for the user.

3. Memory and BDI

The BDI model [9] has traditionally been used to describe the agents' mental process as intentional entities. However the BDI model presents certain limitations. One of these limitations is its memory management. The method proposed in

[16, 26] facilitates the incorporation of Case-based Reasoning (CBR) and Case-based Planning (CBP) systems as a deliberative mechanism within BDI agents. CBR is a type of human thinking based on reasoning about past experiences. CBP is a type of CBR system specially designed for planning construction. The CBR and CBP systems allow the BDI agents to learn and adapt themselves, lending them a greater level of autonomy than pure BDI architecture [9].

In this section a deliberative agent architecture based on the integration of deliberative Beliefs-Desires-Intentions (BDI) agents within Case-based Reasoning and Case-based Planning systems is presented. First, some generalities are provided, and then a practical case illustrates the approach. Finally, some conclusions and the future research line are presented.

3.1. CBR-BDI and CBP-BDI agent architectures

The relationship between CBR or CBP systems and BDI agents can be established by implementing cases as beliefs, intentions and desires which lead to the resolution of the problem. In the CBR-BDI agent [16, 26], each state or problem description is considered as a belief; the objective to be reached or problem description, once the objective has been reached, may also be a belief. The intentions are plans of actions that the agent has to carry out in order to achieve its objectives, so an intention is an ordered set of actions [4, 15, 14]. Each change from state to state is made after carrying out an action (the agent remembers the action carried out in the past, when it was in a specified state of similar characteristics, and takes a decision depending on the subsequent result). A desire is any of the final states reached in the past (if the agent has to deal with a situation, which is similar to one in the past, it will try to achieve a similar result to the one previously obtained). Moreover, in order to obtain a complete integration, the agent has to execute a CBR reasoning cycle. A CBR-BDI agent implements a CBR cycle by means of behaviours executed sequentially. All the behaviours concerning one of the stages of the CBR cycle are defined into an agent capability. CBR-BDI agents possess three (if the revision stage is external to the system) or four capabilities in charge of the implementation of the CBR cycle [16, 14]. Each of the capabilities contains the behaviours (one or more) required to complete its corresponding task: case retrieval task (case memory indexing, similarity algorithms), solutions reuse task (adaptation algorithms to reuse past solutions or to search new solutions, planning algorithms in the case of CBP), proposed solution revision task (algorithms to evaluate the solution proposed in the reuse stage) and learning task (algorithms to update both case memory and knowledge memory). The CBP-BDI agent architecture incorporates a model based on variational calculus, providing the option of planning and replanning in execution time [11]. Every time the environmental changes interrupt the intentions or plans carried out by the agent in order to achieve its objectives, the agent is able to react without "undoing" the previous executed actions, and constructs a new plan [4, 11, 15].

3.2. A practical point of view

From a practical point of view, some of the architectures successfully implemented in the last years look at CBR-BDI agent architectures as frameworks. CBR-BDI agent architecture, as well as CBP-BDI agent architecture have been applied to different real problems in order to obtain a preliminary evaluation and conclusions about their behaviour working in real environments. In particular, this agent architecture has been applied to resolve a wide range of problems, such as the monitoring and evaluation of the carbon dioxide exchange rate between the ocean water surface and the atmosphere [3, 2, 14], the development of a guiding system to be applied not only in tourism recommendation problems [17] but also in a guiding system for the users of a shopping mall that helps them to identify bargains, offers, leisure activities, etc. [5, 4], the automation of the management of internal mail in a department using mail robots responsible for mail delivery [11] or the incorporation of ambient intelligence techniques for health care in geriatric residences [15]. The results obtained have been very promising and demonstrate the versatility of the architecture.

3.2.1. Carbon dioxide exchange monitoring.

One of the factors of greatest concern in climactic behaviour is the quantity of carbon dioxide (CO_2) present in the atmosphere. Traditionally, it has been considered that the main system regulating CO_2 in the atmosphere is the photosynthesis and respiration of plants. However, in the last decades it has been shown that the ocean plays a highly important role in the regulation of carbon quantities, the full significance of which still needs to be determined. The implementation of an open multi-agent system which incorporates a CBR-BDI agent, facilitates to automatically monitor the interaction between the ocean surface and the atmosphere. Initially, the system is being used in order to evaluate and predict the amount of CO_2 absorbed or expelled by the ocean in the North Atlantic. The initial results have been very successful from the technical and scientific point of view [3, 2, 14].

3.2.2. Route planning.

A multi-agent system that includes deliberative and pure reactive processes has been implemented using the SIMBA platform [29]. The approach allows the integration of unbounded deliberative processes with critical real-time tasks. In the case study proposed for the evaluation of the hypothesis, the SIMBA architecture was integrated with both ARTIS agents [7], (which are capable of guiding mobile robots in real time), and CBP-BDI deliberative agents (which generate and distribute plans in the execution time of the ARTIS agents). Therefore, the deliberative agents were responsible for planning the routes that should be followed by the mobile robots, and the ARTIS agents put these plans into action until insurmountable obstacles were encountered, in which case an alternative plan is requested from the deliberative agent [11].

3.2.3. Intelligent guidance and suggestions.

The CBR-BDI and CBP-BDI architectures have also been used to construct a model for recommending plans in dynamic environments [5, 4, 17]. The proposal presented in [5, 4] has been used to develop a guiding system for the users of a shopping mall that helps them to identify bargains, offers, leisure activities, etc. CBP-BDI is a highly appreciated tool that optimizes the time spent in the shopping mall. Both users of the tourism [17] and mall [5, 4] applications have noticed the utility of the dynamic replanning, since it is quite usual for them to change opinions/objectives in the middle of a plan.

3.2.4. Alzheimer patient monitoring.

Finally, an autonomous intelligent agent has been developed for ambient intelligence health care in geriatric residences [15]. The agent operates in wireless devices and is integrated with complementary agents into a multi-agent system, named ALZ-MAS (ALZheimer Multi-Agent System), capable of interacting with the environment. Ambient Intelligence (AmI) provides an effective way to create systems with the ability to adapt themselves to the context and users necessities. The vision of AmI assumes seamless, unobtrusive, and often invisible but also controllable interactions between humans and technology. The AGALZ (Autonomous aGent for monitoring ALZheimer patients) is designed to plan the nurses' working time dynamically, to maintain the standard working reports about the nurses' activities, and to guarantee that the patients assigned to the nurses are given the right care.

3.3. Discussion

In this section we have described the particular model of a BDI agent in which memory is managed though a case-based approach. The proposed method facilitates the automation of agents' construction. Implementing agents in the form of CBR or CBP systems also facilitates learning and adaptation, and therefore a greater degree of autonomy than with a pure BDI architecture. This software-engineering approach, however, should be analyzed in the context of future agent designs. It is a general feeling that, in coming years, new proposals to design agents will emerge in order to build up a type of architecture for agents from biological and situated cognitive abilities. The combination of both approaches would allow the deployment of complex behaviors that would make intelligent agents capable of tackling dynamic environments. Regarding cognitive abilities, it would be important to be able to develop architectures in which building up representations and using them to plan ahead will emerge from agent-environment interaction.

Thus, future explorations in the agent field should include implementations of sufficient environmental complexity to allow for the possibility of causal correlations between ordered states of evolving organisms and ordered states of their environments. Such inclusions are likely to provide a base from which minimally cognitive artifacts can survive and constitute artificial individuals capable of the acquisition of novel information in their individual lifetimes.

4. Decision making

While problem solving techniques, such as planning or searching, deal with goal achievement, decision making aims at choosing a goal among a set of conflicting goals, establishing the importance among them, or dealing with uncertainty in the goal attainment. This cognitive capability is then particularly important when intelligent agents support the users in the complex task of taking decisions (where to go, which place to visit, etc.).

Intelligent agents can have the cognitive ability of knowing the preferences of its owner and use this information to make recommendations in order to allow the user to take a better decision. Particularly, in this section the case of agents that give decision support when the user is faced with a set of alternatives described by means of multiple criteria is presented. First, an introduction to multiple criteria decision making (MCDM) models as a cognitive ability for agents is provided. Then, an example is described of the use of such methods in a multi-agent system called HeCaSe2 [30], which provides patient-oriented services in the healthcare domain.

4.1. Multiple criteria decision making

When a person has to analyse a set of alternatives with respect to a set of criteria in order to take a decision, we say that this is a multiple criteria decision making problem. In the 19th century economists and mathematicians started to study the laws and behaviour of this type of problems (Pareto, VonNeumann, Morgenstern). In the end of the 20th century it became again a widely studied area, and many methods have been developed for helping in this common human task. An MCDM problem is one that, having a set of alternatives A, with respect to a set of criteria C, either aims to find a subset of alternatives that contain the best ones (selection problem), an assignment of the alternatives into predefined categories (sorting into ordered categories or classification into unordered ones) or a ranking of the alternatives from the best to the worst (ranking problem) [23]. The main difficulty lies in the fact that it is an ill-defined mathematical problem because there is no objective or optimal solution for all the criteria. Thus, some trade-off must be done among the different criteria to determine an acceptable solution for the decision problem.

There exist two main approaches to the solution of a MCDM problem, which are based on multi-attribute utility theory and outranking methods. The first one, named MAUT, is based on the idea that any decision-maker attempts unconsciously to maximise some function U that aggregates the utility of each different criterion. The key issue in utility-based approaches is the determination of the marginal utility functions, U_j. These functions transform the scale of the corresponding criterion into utility values. The second approach, called outranking relations, is based on the fact that the decision-maker provides pairwise comparisons of the alternatives to determine the preference of each alternative over the other ones for each particular criterion. Each criterion usually leads to different evaluation of the alternatives, so the problem is to find a consensus in the ranking. The outranking methods are based on the definition of a concordance relation and a discordance relation. They are used to find the dominance relation over the alternatives, which is the basis for solving the decision problem.

Focusing on the MAUT-based solutions, the methods consider two stages. In the first stage, called aggregation stage, a global utility rating for each alternative is computed $U(a)$; then, the second stage proceeds to sort out the decision problem, selecting the best alternatives according to its rating, ranking them, or sorting or classifying them into some predefined categories.

The problem of aggregating information has been widely studied and there exist several methods to aggregate numerical values as well as linguistic terms. A description of the operators and the properties required for decision making can be found in [10]. Although a wide range of operators is available, in most cases, the aggregation is done using some form of weighted arithmetic mean. This operator reflects a compromise behaviour among the various criteria. However, sometimes this is not a good approach because a compensative behaviour is not desired. In [38], a study of this type of operators and its generalisation is done.

4.2. The HeCaSe2 system

HeCaSe2 is a multi-agent system that provides healthcare services to patients and medical professionals [30]. Several agents that play different roles coordinate their activities to provide a user-centred assistance. In Figure 1 the architecture of HeCaSe2 is shown, which includes different medical structures organised hierarchically (doctors, nurses, medical devices, departments and the medical centre at the top level). Inside this scheme, several organisational and medical rules guide the behaviour of the agents. HeCaSe2 is designed as an open-architecture of agents. Any healthcare institution can be modelled with different topologies and organisation rules and patterns. In any case, agents that represent doctors and patients (*i.e.*, users) are always required.

In order to provide patient-centred services, the system maintains a user's profile that stores his/her preferences with respect to some aspects of patient care. In addition, the User Agent stores the agenda of its owner (which is private and is only used by this agent).

The case of arranging an appointment between a patient and a medical unit can illustrate the possibility of assigning decision support abilities to the agents. This is one of the problems that requires more communication and negotiation between the entities involved in patient care.

In HeCaSe2 the decision-making process is performed by a Doctor Agent, using a set of possible alternatives (*e.g.*, proposals of appointments in different units that can perform the activity required by the doctor, such as a blood analysis). To obtain those alternatives, the system must start a communication with other agents at different levels of the hierarchy shown in Figure 1. The Doctor Agent collects all the possible appointments proposed by the different units (through the

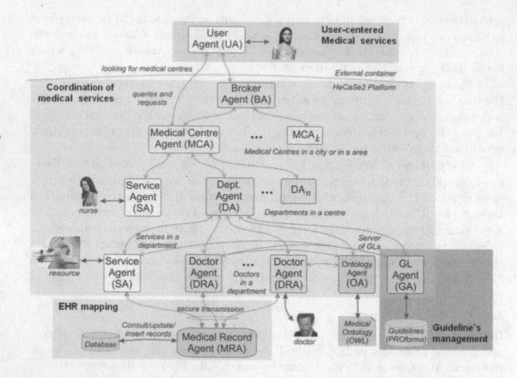

FIGURE 1. HeCaSe2 multi-agent system.

Service Agents) and then uses the patient profile to rank and filter them, in order to recommend to the patient only the best N options.

A set of five criteria to make that recommendation were selected. As has been said, the personal preferences for these criteria are stored in the user's profile. In particular the most relevant information of any appointment proposal considered is: the day of the week, the period of the day (morning, afternoon, night), the medical centre where the test should be performed, the distance between the centre where the doctor performs the medical visit and the centre where the test should be performed and the number of days to wait for the test. Some of that information is stored using numbers and others using a fixed set of linguistic terms. In the following section, the transformation of that data into utility values is explained.

4.3. Decision support in HeCaSe2

HeCaSe2 agents use a multi-attribute utility approach to give decision support to the patient when he/she needs an appointment for a medical test or visit. That is, each alternative is described using a set of utility values (one for each criterion). Then those marginal utilities are aggregated to obtain a global rating value. Using those ratings the system selects the best N options, which are presented to the user.

To obtain the utility value of each criterion of an alternative, the user's preferences are taken into account, given by different types of transformation functions, depending on the type of value ([32]). For the case of numerical values (distance and waiting time), the case of linear, polynomial, exponential and logarithmic transformation functions were studied. The conclusions showed that the exponential function is the most adequate because it allows one to distinguish better the close samples. The result is a numerical value in the interval [0,1]. For the case of linguistic variables (day, period and medical centre), the user associates to each possible term in the domain of the variable, a linguistic preference value in a fixed scale S. For example, $U_{period}(morning)=low$, $U_{period}(afternoon)=high$, and $U_{period}(night)=none$. The selection of the vocabulary S is very important because it determines the degree of expressiveness of the criterion and its semantics. In addition, it definitely influences the rest of the decision making process. In [32], this aspect was analysed in detail. Finally, the linguistic term set used was formed by nine symmetrically ordered terms, $S=\{none, very low, low, almost medium, medium, almost high, high, very high, perfect\}$.

As has been said, to determine the rating of the alternatives, an aggregation operator must be used. In this case, the Linguistic OWA operator [27] was selected. It belongs to the family of OWA operators (Ordered Weighted Averaging operators [51]), whose main characteristic is the possibility to establish different decision making polices with respect to the aggregation of the values. The OWA operators are in the class of mean operators; they are idempotent, monotonic and commutative. The LOWA aggregation operator works with linguistic values instead of numbers. In [21], the numerical-linguistic and linguistic-numerical transformation processes are defined. Those processes are used in the HeCaSe2 system.

In Figure 2, a representation of the decision making process is presented. At first, each of the possible appointments is described using the corresponding partial utilities according to the patient's preferences. Secondly, the system puts all the utilities into the common linguistic domain S. Then, it performs the aggregation-based rating of alternatives received using LOWA and find the best options and, finally, the learning stage allows us to adapt the user's preferences. This last stage is explained in the next section.

4.4. User's profile adaptation

As explained above, when the user receives a set of alternatives to consider for an appointment, the list of proposals is rated and ranked according to the preferences stored in the user's profile. The following action done by the patient, through his User Agent, is the selection of the most appropriate alternative for him. This action gives to the system a very important feedback. If he selects the first option, it means that the decision support process works fine, but if he selects another alternative, it means that for some reason the algorithm has rated too low the most appropriate alternative to the user. The main goal now is to adapt the user's

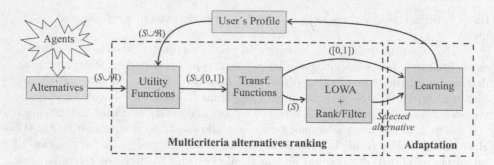

FIGURE 2. Decision making procedure implemented.

profile with this information, in order that if the same situation is repeated in the future, the alternative selected by the user becomes the first one.

In [31] the adaptation algorithm designed and used in HeCaSe2 is explained. It basically consists in comparing the appointment selected by the user (proposal a_i) with the ones that were ranked in higher positions (proposals from a_0 to $a_i - 1$). However, the comparison of a_i to all of them are not directly performed, instead, all are automatically gathered into two clusters, and a_i is compared with the two prototypes with the purpose of identifying the closest prototype, which is selected as the target to reach. With this approach the algorithm tries to adapt the patient's profile smoothly along a time line. Similarly, the user's profile is not changed completely at each decision. Only the most relevant utility values are modified (those that differ more from the target with respect to the selection made).

4.5. Discussion

This section explains how a MCDM-based method is applied to a distributed problem that requires adaptation of some results to the user's preferences. All required data is scattered among different partners and the user's preferences are used both to rate and filter the results.

Adding this kind of cognitive abilities to the agents allows the system to improve the quality of its responses to the user. Moreover, it provides personalised services that make specific recommendations to each user depending on his/her profile. The key point of this approach is that the user provides some kind of information about his/her preferences, which sometimes is not possible to obtain.

In the case study presented, a method for implicitly adapting the user's profile with some feedback information obtained from the use of the system have been mentioned briefly. This is also another key point to take into account in the design of agents based on profiles. The preferences of the user may change through time, and the profile must be adapted accordingly. However, an automatic user's profile adaptation must be done carefully because different parameters must be defined, which can lead to a bad updating.

Finally, it is important to mention that in MCDA there are some basic elements of the problem that influence the goodness of the final result: the set of criteria considered, the set of linguistic terms to express preferences or the aggregation operator and its parameters. First of all, the criteria must be representative enough of the information considered by the user to make the decisions. As the number of criteria increases, the performance of the aggregation and profile updating increases. The second issue is the selection of the set of linguistic terms and its semantics. At least five different terms should be included in the vocabulary and no more than eleven. With respect to their semantics, there are different approaches, but the most common one is the use of fuzzy membership functions, which should be tuned appropriately to the problem characteristics. Finally, the selection of the aggregation operator (which is the most important cognitive element of the process) must be according to the properties required in each particular decision problem (*i.e.*, neutrality, monotonicity, compensativeness).

5. Learning

According to Minsky [39], agents can learn by useful changes in their workings. From observation, agents can combine several descriptions into one. Agents can also accumulate descriptions and form new concepts, or modify descriptions, as well as functions or actions. From observation, agents can be aware of the effects of their actions, giving them the opportunity to learn about their decision making process. From an operational point of view, machine learning researchers have been dedicated to the study of how to construct computer programs that automatically improve with experience [40]. The incorporation of machine learning methods to agents opens the opportunity to automatically incorporate new capabilities to agents, adapt their behavior, and improve their performance.

Learning in a multi-agent system can be achieved at different levels: individual (isolated learning) or collective (interactive learning) [47]. In the former, agents learn to improve their individual performance. While in the latter, agents learn about other agents in order to obtain the maximum revenues from a collectivity. In this section two practical experiences of both situations are reviewed. First, a diagnosis system is explained in which an agent improves its diagnosis capabilities by both its individual experience and with the cases provided by other agents in the neighborhood. And second, a recommender system that forgets according to its individual experience and learns about the other agents' behavior is described.

5.1. Diagnosing from experience

In [37] a case-based agent was proposed to diagnose acute strokes. Medical treatment of such illnesses have changed quickly in the last years. Drugs are quite specific depending on the kind of stroke, and physicians require supporting tools that help them to identify the clinical category of strokes.

In order to facilitate exchange of experiences, the case-based agent was integrated in a multi-agent system. The multi-agent system is organized according

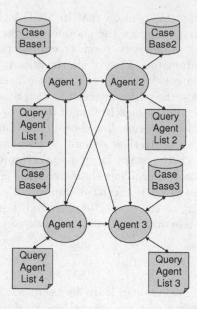

FIGURE 3. The multi-agent system in which agents cooperate when solving a problem.

to the different hospitals in a given zone (see Figure 3). Currently, four hospitals are represented by a different case-based agent (CB-agent) in the architecture. Then, each CB-agent assesses the diagnosis process according to the criteria of the physicians in a given hospital, and cooperates with other CB-agents when the assessment provided within a hospital is not significant.

At the agent level, each agent relies on a Case-Based Reasoning (CBR) approach. CBR is applied with two different goals: when trying to find a diagnosis, and when trying to provide cases to another agent. In the first case, the four steps of the CBR cycle according to [1] have been extended to include using cases provided by other agents (see Figure 4). In the second case, a single retrieval step is enough. Learning, in any of the situations, is performed by accumulating new cases, because accumulating experiences is a key issue in medical practice.

One particularity of the approach is the case structure, since cases are trees. A case was formally defined as follows:

$$C_i = <D_i, S_i>$$
(5.1)

where D_i is the problem description, and S_i the problem solution.

The notation used to represent the attributes is a set of nested attribute-value pairs. That is, D_i is defined as follows:

$$D_i = \{(x_j, v_j)\}$$
(5.2)

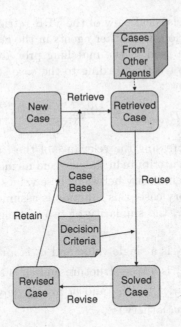

FIGURE 4. The different phases of the CBR cycle.

where $x_j \in X$, X is the set of attributes used to describe the problem, and v_j is the value of x_j which can be a list $\{(x_k, v_k)\}$ or a single value.

The problem solution of the case consists in the clinical category. Formally,

$$S_i = (clinicalCategory, v_j) \tag{5.3}$$

where v_j is one of the five possible values of clinicalCategory (*atherothrombothic, cardioembolic, small vessel disease , other, undefined*).

Regarding the CBR cycle (see Figure 4), different methods have been defined for retrieval, reuse, revise and retain.

First, in the retrieve phase, given a current (new) case to be diagnosed, the most similar cases are retrieved from the case-base. This phase of the cycle consists of the following steps:

1. Matching the current case against all cases in the memory.
2. If the most similar cases have a similarity degree less than a given threshold θ, then:
    (a) Let be $\theta' = \theta$.
    (b) While there are agents to ask and $\theta' \geq \theta$,
        (i) Ask the next agent for relevant cases.
        (ii) θ = highest similarity degree of the provided cases.
3. Selecting the k most similar cases

Note, then, that the classical view of the CBR retrieve has been extended in order to include collaboration with other agents in the environment.

The similarity metric used in the matching procedures is defined based on the similarity between two trees, according to the case structure. It is defined as a weighted average as follows:

$$sim(D_{new}, D_{mem}) = \frac{\sum_{i \in D_{new}} \omega_i sim_i(v_i^{new}, v_i^{mem})}{\sum_{i \in D_{new}} \omega_i} \qquad (5.4)$$

where ω_i is the weight expressing the relevance of the i attribute, and v_i^{new} and v_i^{mem} are the values of the i attribute in the new and memory case correspondingly, and $sim_i(v_i^{new}, v_i^{mem})$ the similarity between these values. Note that if attribute i is not present in the memory case, this function is assumed to be 0.

Given an attribute x_i, the similarity of two of their values is computed as follows:

$$sim_i(v_j, v_k) = \begin{cases} 0 & \text{if } v_j \text{ is a single value and } v_k \text{ is a tree structure,} \\ 0 & \text{if } v_j \text{ is a tree structure and } v_k \text{ is a single value,} \\ 1 - \delta(v_j, v_k) & \text{if } v_j \text{ and } v_k \text{ are single values,} \\ sim(v_j, v_k) & \text{otherwise,} \end{cases} \qquad (5.5)$$

where δ is the Hamming distance of two values, and $sim(v_j, v_k)$ is the similarity between two trees. On one hand, δ is computed as follows:

$$\delta(v_j, v_k) = \begin{cases} 1, & \text{if } v_j \neq v_k, \\ 0, & \text{otherwise.} \end{cases} \qquad (5.6)$$

On the other hand, note that using $sim(v_j, v_k)$ inside the definition of $sim_i(v_j, v_k)$ makes the similarity measure recursive.

Once all the similarities of the current case with the memory cases have been computed, the selection step consists of choosing the most similar cases. In the CB-agents, a k-neighbor approach was followed (so the k-most similar cases were retrieved). Particularly, with k=5 the results were good enough.

Note that always some cases are gathered either from the memory or from other agents. In the best case, the retrieved cases are over the θ threshold .

In the reuse phase the k-most similar cases are used to elaborate the solution of the current case. In the revision phase, the case-based agent requires some feedback from the user in order to know when it has been successful and when not. Finally, all cases are retained in the memory because accumulating experiences is a key issue in medical practice.

5.2. Recommending from experience

GenialChef [42] is a recommender system based on case-based learning and trust. From the former, the agent is able to improve its recommendations to a user. From the latter, the agent also improves its recommendations and gives innovative proposals to the user thanks to the information provided by other agents' interactions.

5.2.1. Case-base learning. The case-base system consists of a set of previous items explicitly and/or implicitly assessed by the user. The initial case base is empty, and the CBR agent uses a training set to learn an initial profile of the user preferences from a set of training cases. The profile is improved by accumulating experiences.

One of the most relevant issues of the approach in GenialChef is the incorporation of a drift attribute in order to adapt the case-base to the user interest over time. The drift attribute belongs to the case description and its function is to age the cases in the case base. For this purpose, a reinforcement mechanism was used to update the drift values.

As described in [42], the drift attribute works as follows:

- The drift attribute value is confined to the [0-1] interval.
- New items are inserted in the case base with the maximum drift value when the user shows some interest about them.
- The value of the drift attribute δ_q of a case q is decreased by multiplying the last drift value by a factor β of between 0 and 1,

$$\delta_q = \delta_q * \beta. \tag{5.7}$$

The system decreases drift attributes each time a new item is incorporated into the case base, emulating the gradual process of people losing interest in something. When a case reaches a drift value under a certain threshold (ξ), it is discarded.

- The value of the drift attribute is increased (rewarded) if the retrieved case results in a successful recommendation. The drift attribute δ_q of a case q is increased by dividing the last drift value by a factor λ of between 0 and 1,

$$\delta_q = \delta_q / \lambda. \tag{5.8}$$

Both, the decreasing and increasing operations define a reinforcement mechanism.

5.2.2. Trust learning. The incorporation of trust in GenialChef enables the definition of what has been call the opinion-based filtering method of recommended systems [43]. Each agent has a list of friendly agents in the neighborhood in which it relies: $C_i = \{(a_{i_1}, t_{i,i_1}), (a_{i_2}, t_{i,i_2}), \ldots, (a_{i_n}, t_{i,i_k})\}$, where a_{i_j} is an agent identifier and t_{i,i_j} is a number between [0,1] that represents the truth value the agent a_i has on agent a_{i_j}. The opinion-based filtering method consists of querying these agents in a lack of information situation (see more details on [43]).

Initially the contact list is empty. Thus, agents contact other agents in the world and learn the initial trust using a *playing agents* procedure following [49].

Trust values are updated according to a reinforcement mechanism, so the recommender agent learns about the benefits of the interaction performed with other agents in the neighborhood. Thus, for every agent a_{e_i} in the contact list of the agent a_q, its trust value $t_{q,i}$ is updated as follows:

$$t_{q,i} = \varphi * t_{q,i} + (1 - \varphi) * r_{real} \tag{5.9}$$

where r_{real} is the real interest of the user in the product (see details in its computation on [41]) and φ is a parameter of the system that manages the evolution dynamics of trust.

Other approaches to trust are described in chapter 4.

5.3. Discussion

Practical applications have shown that a case-based approach facilitates learning from experience. On one hand, isolate learning allows improvement of the agents decisions (how to improve diagnosis, how to improve recommendations) . On the other hand, learning by interaction with other agents allows us to improve agents collaboration (when to rely on other agent's outcomes, trust).

One of the major issues regarding leaning, however, is the cold-start problem, that is, the set up of the learning mechanism employed by agents. In the GenialChef system described, this problem is bypassed by the use of a training set which is used for both, training the internal problem solving capability of agents, and for training the interaction model of the neighbour agents (trust).

Other problems such as the tradeoff between diversity and coverage should also be taken into account. That is, not all agents experiences should be accumulated, and only the ones that provide some diversity should be retained. The system studied in this section proposes a drift attribute; but some other maintenance mechanism should be explored. Finally, the different parameters that configure a learning mechanism, such as learning threshold, learning rates, which numbers increase in a multi-agent environment when learning other agents' behavior, are also a matter of discussion in the design of learning capabilities.

6. Conclusions

This chapter has described several cognitive abilities in multi-agent systems. These have been illustrated by means of several practical applications. First, planning as a kind of problem solving, has been analysed in the context of recommending tours to citizens. Second, complex memory structures have been described in the deployment of Belief-Desire-Intention agent architectures that have been proved useful for dealing with carbon dioxide exchange monitoring, recommender systems, and Alzheimer patients monitoring. Third, decision making methodologies have been used to asses the adaptation of user preferences, as shown by practical applications in the healthcare domain. And fourth, case based learning and reinforcement learning have been explained as part of the agent learning abilities in a medical diagnosis problem and a restaurant recommendation query.

Some of the analysed intelligent agents combine different cognitive capabilities, while other approaches integrate different abilities at the multi-agent level. Whether to integrate several abilities at the agent level or to combine them in a multi-agent architecture is a difficult design decision. At the agent level, for example, there are different agents in the HeCase system able to make decisions, as well as learn from the environment and build a user model. Another interesting example is the CBP-DBI agents analysed in Section 3 which uses case-based reasoning to deal with memory management, and combines planning and adaptation techniques to achieve agents' goals. In general, case-based reasoning seems to be a promising approach to deal with a valid practical integration of problem solving, memory, and learning

On the other hand, at the multi-agent level, some multi-agent systems that integrate cognitive abilities have been described. For example, the SAMP system is composed by a set of agents, each of them exhibiting a particular cognitive ability, mainly case-base reasoning and planning. A particular case is the multi-agent system described in Section 5.1 in which all the agents have the same cognitive capabilities, but they differ in their past experiences. Note, however, that agent interaction is being used from a complementary point of view, assuming that all the agents are collaborating to achieve a common goal. In the future, it is important to consider other scenarios, especially competitive scenarios, in which cognitive abilities would play an important role. Such capabilities, combined with the new paradigms coming from the research on agents and multi-agents systems, namely, negotiation, argumentation, etc., are the right way to create artifacts that enhance generality and flexibility of intelligent systems.

Thus, agents and multi-agents systems have found the way of integrating different subfields of intelligence, planning with learning, decision-making with learning, and others. However, throughout the chapter, several problems have been highlighted in the design of cognitive capabilities, mainly the parameters required by the cognitive mechanisms that influence the goodness of the final results. For example, in the decision making methods, the set of linguistic terms, the set of criteria, or the aggregation operators have been identified as critical elements in the definition of a MCDA method. Other examples are the learning rates and thresholds of case-base reasoning. The definition of this kind of parameters depends, to some extent, on the skill of the intelligent agent designer and it is a difficult issue to automate.

References

[1] A.Aamodt and E. Plaza. Case-based reasoning: Foundational issues, methodological variations, and system approaches. *Artificial Intelligence Communications*, 7(1):39–59, 1994.

[2] J. Bajo and J. Corchado. Multiagent architecture for monitoring the North-Atlantic carbon dioxide exchange rate. In *XI edition of the International Conference of the Spanish Association for Artificial Intelligence (CAEPIA'05), Santiago de Compostela (Spain)*, volume LNAI 4177, pages 321–330. Springer Verlag, November 2005.

[3] J. Bajo and J. Corchado. Evaluation and monitoring of the air-sea interaction using a cbr-agents approach. In *6th International Conference on Case Based Reasoning (ICCBR'05), Chicago, Illinois (USA)*, volume LNAI, 3620, pages 50–62. Springer Verlag, August 2006.

[4] J. Bajo, J. Corchado, and L. Castillo. Running agents in mobile devices. In *X Ibero-American Conference on Artificial Intelligence (IBERAMIA'06), Burgos (Spain)*, volume LNAI 4140, pages 58–67. Springer Verlag, October 2006.

[5] J. Bajo, Y. de Paz, J. de Paz, Q. Martín, and J. Corchado. A shopping mall multiagent systems. In *7th International Conference on Intelligent Data Engineering and Automated Learning (IDEAL'06), Burgos (Spain)*, volume LNAI 4224, pages 1166–1173. Springer Verlag, November 2006.

[6] S. Biundo, K. Myers, and K. Rajan, editors. *Contingent Planning via Heuristic Forward Search with Implicit Belief States*, 2005.

[7] V. Botti, C. Carrascosa, V. Julian, and J. Soler. *The ARTIS Agent Architecture: Modelling Agents in Hard Real-Time Environments*, volume 1, pages 63–76. Springer Verlag, 1999.

[8] R. Brafman and J. Hoffmann. Conformant planning via heuristic forward search: A new approach. In S. Koenig, S. Zilberstein, and J. Koehler, editors, *Proceedings of the 14th International Conference on Automated Planning and Scheduling (ICAPS-04)*, 2004.

[9] M. Bratman, D. Israel, and M. Pollack. Plans and resource-bounded practical reasoning. *Computational Intelligence*, 4:349– 355, 1988.

[10] T. Calvo, G. Mayor, and R. e. Mesiar. *Aggregation Operators: New Trends and Applications*, volume 97 of *Studies in Fuzziness and Soft Computing*. Physica-Verlag, 2002.

[11] C. Carrascosa, J. Bajo, V. Julian, J. Corchado, and V. Botti. Hybrid multi-agent architecture as a real-time problem-solving model. *Expert Systems with Applications*, 34(1):2–17, 2008.

[12] L. Castillo, E. Armengol, E. Onaindía, L. Sebastiá, J. González-Boticario, A. Rodríguez, S. Fernández, J. D. Arias, and D. Borrajo. Samap. An user-oriented adaptive system for planning tourist visits. *Expert Systems With Applications*, 2008.

[13] A. Cimatti and M. Roveri. Conformant planning via model checking. In *5th European Conference on Planning: Recent Advances in AI Planning*, volume 1809 of *LNCS*, pages 21–34, 1999.

[14] J. Corchado, J. Aiken, and J. Bajo. A CBR agent for monitoring the co_2 exchange rate. In *Petra Perner (ed), Case-Based Reasoning on Signals and Images*, pages 213–246. Springer Verlag (Studies in Computacional Science, 73), 2007.

[15] J. Corchado, J. Bajo, Y. de Paz, and D. Tapia. Intelligent environment for monitoring Alzheimer patients, agent technology for health care. *Decision Support Systems*, pages In Press, Corrected Proof, Available online 8 May 2007.

[16] J. Corchado and R. Laza. Constructing deliberative agents with case-based reasoning technology. *International Journal of Intelligent Systems*, 18(12):1227– 1241, 2003.

[17] J. Corchado, J. Pavón, E. Corchado, and L. Castillo. Development of CBR-BDI agents: A tourist guide application. In *Advances in Case Based Reasoning (EC-CBR'04), Madrid (Spain)*, volume LNAI 3155, pages 547–559. Springer Verlag, August-September 2004.

[18] M. de la Asunción, L. Castillo, J. Fdez.-Olivares, O. García-Pérez, A. González, and F. Palao. Knowledge and plan execution management in planning fire fighting

operations. *Workshop on Planning and Scheduling: Bridging Theory to Practice. European Conference on Artificial Intelligence*, 2004.

[19] M. de Weerdt, A. ter Mors, and C. Witteveen. Multi-agent planning – an introduction to planning and coordination. Technical report, Delft University of Technology, 2005.

[20] M. M. de Weerdt. Plan coordination. In *Proceedings of the Doctorial Consortium of the International Conferenence on AI Planning and Scheduling*, pages 142–145, 2003.

[21] M. Delgado, F. Herrera, E. Herrera-Viedma, and L. Martínez. Combining Numerical and Linguistic Information in Group Decision Making. *Information Sciences*, 107:177–194, 1998.

[22] B. Drabble and A. Tate. O-plan: A situated planning agent. In M. Ghallab and A. Milani, editors, *New Directions in AI Planning*, pages 247–260. IOS Press (Amsterdam), 1996.

[23] J. Figueira, S. Greco, and M. e. Ehrgott. *Multiple Criteria Decision Analysis:State of the Art Surveys*, volume 78 of *International Series in Operations Research and Management Science*. Springer, 2005.

[24] M. Fox, A. Gerevini, D. Long, and I. Serina. Plan stability: Replanning versus plan repair. *Proceedings of the 16th International Conference on Automated Planning and Scheduling (ICAPS'06)*, pages 193–202, 2006.

[25] M. Fox and D. Long. Hybrid STAN: Identifying and managing combinatorial optimization sub- problems in planning. In *IJCAI*, pages 445–452, 2001.

[26] M. Glez-Bedia, J. Corchado, E. Corchado, and C. Fyfe. Analytical model for constructing deliberative agents. *Engineering Intelligent Systems*, 3:173–185, 2002.

[27] F. Herrera and E. Herrera-Viedma. Linguistic decision analysis: Steps for solving decision problems under linguistic information. *Fuzzy Sets and Systems*, 115:67–82, 2000.

[28] M. Huhns and L. Stephens. Miultiagent systems and society of agents. In *Multiagent Systems- A Modern Approach to Distributed Artificial Inteligence*. G. Weiss (eds), 1999.

[29] V. J. J. Inglada, C. C. Casamayor, M. R. Pedruelo, J. V. S. Bayona, and V. B. Navarro. *SIMBA: An Approach for Real-Time Multi-agent Systems*, volume 2504, pages 282–293. Springer Verlag, 2002.

[30] D. Isern and A. Moreno. Distributed guideline-based health care system. In *4th International Conference on Intelligent Systems Design and Applications (ISDA-2004)*, pages 145–150, Budapest, Hungary, 2004. IEEE Press.

[31] D. Isern, A. Valls, and A. Moreno. Learning the user's preferences for multiple criteria ranking. In *XIII Congreso Español sobre Tecnologías y Lógica Fuzzy (ESTYLF'06)*, pages 325–330, Ciudad Real, Spain, 2006.

[32] D. Isern, A. Valls, and A. Moreno. Using aggregation operators to personalize agent-based medical services. In B. Gabrys, R. J. Howlett, and L. C. Jain, editors, *Knowledge-Based Intelligent Information and Engineering Systems (KES06)*, volume 4252 of *LNAI*, pages 1256–1263, Bournemouth, UK, 2006. Springer Verlag.

[33] S. Jiménez, A. Coles, and A. Smith. Planning in probabilistic domains using a deterministic numeric planner. In R. Qu, editor, *Proceedings PLANSIG-06 Nottingham, UK*, 2006.

[34] L. Kramer and S. Smith. Maximizing availability: a commitment heuristic for over-subscribed scheduling problems. In J. K. S. Z. . S. K. (Eds), editor, *Proceeding of ICAPS'05*, pages 272–280, Monterey, CA, USA, 2005. AAAI Press.

[35] P. Langley. Cognitive architectures and general intelligent systems. *AI Magazine*, pages 33–44, Summer 2006.

[36] I. Little and S. Thiébaux. Concurrent probabilistic planner in the GraphPlan framework. In *Proceedings of the Sixteenth International Conference on Automated Planning and Scheduling (ICAPS '06), The English Lake District, Cumbria, UK*, 2006.

[37] B. López, C. Pous, J. Serena, and J. Piula. Cooperative case-based agents for acute stroke diagnosis. In *ECAI Workshop on Agents Applied in Health Care*. Riva di Garda, Italia, 2006.

[38] X. Luo and N. R. Jennings. A spectrum of compromise aggregation operators for multi-attribute decision making. *Artificial Intelligence*, 171:161–184, 2007. doi:10.1016/j.artint.2006.11.004.

[39] M. Minsky. *The Society of Mind*. Simon & Schuster, 1985.

[40] T. Mitchell. *Machine Learning*. McGraw-Hill, 1997.

[41] M. Montaner, B. López, and J. L. de la Rosa. Developing trust in recommender agents. In *First International Joint Conference on Autonomous Agents and Multiagent Systems (AAMAS'02)*, pages 304–305. Bologna, Italia, 2002.

[42] M. Montaner, B. López, and J. L. de la Rosa. Improving case representation and case-based maintenance in recommender agents. In *Lecture Notes in Computer Science (Artificial Intelligence) 2416*, pages 234–148, 2002.

[43] M. Montaner, B. López, and J. L. de la Rosa. Opinion-based filtering through trust. In *Lecture Notes in Computer Science (Artificial Intelligence) 2446*, pages 164–178, 2002.

[44] O. B. O. and D. Aberdeen. The factored policy gradient planner (ipc-06 version). In *Proceedings of the Fifth International Planning Competition*, June 2006.

[45] H. Palacios and H. Geffner. Compiling uncertainty away: Solving conformant planning problems using a classical planner (sometimes). In *Proc. 21st Nat. Conf. on Artificial Intelligence (AAAI-06)*, 2006.

[46] S. Russell and P. Norvig. *Artificial Intelligence. A Modern Approach (second edition)*. Prentice-Hall, 2003.

[47] S. Sen and G. Weiss. Learning in multiagent systems. In *Multiagent Systems- A Modern Approach to Distributed Artificial Inteligence*. G. Weiss (eds), 1999.

[48] D. Smith. Choosing objectives in over-subscription planning. In *Proceeding of ICAPS-04*, pages 393–401, Whistle, Canada, 2004.

[49] L. Steels and P. Vogt. Grounding adaptive language games in robotic agents. In *Proceedings of ECAL'97*, pages 476–484, 1997.

[50] R. Xu, P. Yuan-Cui, and X.-F. X. H.-T. Cui. Multi-agent planning system for spacecraft. In *Proceeding of the International Conference on Machine Learning and Cybernetics (ICMLC'03*, volume 4, pages 1995–1999, Xi-an, China, 2003.

[51] R. R. Yager. On Ordered Weighted Averaging Aggregation. Operators in Multicriteria Decisionmaking. *IEEE Transactions on Systems, Man and Cybernetics*, 18:183–190, 1988.

Acknowledgment

Many thanks to the AgentCities.ES for supporting the collaboration of the authors. This work has been partially funded by the Spanish MCyT under project TIC2002-04146-C05-05, MCYT TIC2003-07369-C02-02, JCYL-2002-05 project SA104A05, the Spanish MEC under project TIN2004-063540-C02-02, and DURSI AGAUR under grant SGR 00296 (AEDS).

Beatriz López
University of Girona,
Campus Montilivi, edifice P4,
17071 Girona,
Spain
e-mail: `blopez@eia.udg.es`

Susana Fernández
University Carlos III of Madrid,
Avd. Universidad 30, edificio Sabatini,
28021 Leganés, Madrid,
Spain
e-mail: `sfarregu@inf.uc3m.es`

Whitestein Series in Software Agent Technologies, 87–115
© 2007 Birkhäuser Verlag Basel/Switzerland

Trust and Security

Sergi Robles

Abstract. This chapter gathers a global view of trust and security in multi-agent systems. Sharing a common rationale, each section tackles a different aspect of this area, ranging from the cryptographic protection of agents to the formalization and modeling of trust and reputation. Practical issues such as applications and the designing of testbeds are also included in the chapter.

1. Introduction

Trust and security have been two major research areas for the agent concerned scientific community. In recent years important results in these two related areas have been achieved. This chapter describes the main contributions in trust and security, devoting its sections to specific aspects of these areas.

Security is critical in any distributed system, and especially in multi-agent systems (MAS). There are scenarios though in which traditional straightforward security mechanisms cannot be directly applied. This can be either due to the social nature of MAS, or due to some special security requirements such as the protection of agent mobility. For the first case, common cryptography is hard to use in MAS with large numbers of independent autonomous social agents interacting with each other. It is difficult to establish trusted third parties in open environments, and thus building trust models for agents has become the standard mechanism to face the problem. Different models can coexist in the same MAS as they are only for the internal use of the agents themselves. By using trust models, every agent has its own metrics for ultimately deciding whom to trust and why. In the social and continuous context of a MAS, this award/punishment system self regulation leads to a fair and secure execution environment, avoiding misconduct or dishonest behaviour.

Co-authors of this chapter: Aurora Vizcaíno, Juan Pablo Soto, Javier Portillo-Rodríguez, Jordi Sabater-Mir, Javier Carbó, Esteve del Acebo, Ramon Hermoso, Enrique de la Hoz, Bernardo Alarcos.

For the second case, in which there exist special security requirements such as agent mobility, traditional cryptographic mechanisms cannot be used either. However, there have been several breakthroughs in this field allowing the protection of agents along with their data, state, and itinerary. These mechanisms, unlike trust models, are applied to prevent fraud and dishonest behaviour in a shorter term.

Like the two sides of the same coin, trust and direct security are part of a larger concept for which it is difficult to find a name other than global security. This chapter gives a general state of the art of trust and security in MAS, and describes some of the last breakthroughs in this area contributed by the groups of the AgentCities.ES Spanish network.

The rest of the chapter is structured as follows. Section 2 describes the main models for trust and reputation in the literature, focusing on those devised by the IIIA-CSIC group of the network. The next three sections show specific contributions to trust in MAS, namely using organisational structures, managing reputation and trust in knowledge management, and applying fuzzy contextual corrective filtering (FCCF). Section 6 presents the ART testbed for trust models, with an example of how FCCF can be applied there. Sections 7 and 8 are devoted to cryptographic agent security, first describing the problems and advances in securing mobile agent applications, and then a practical example of protecting intelligent agents in smart offices. Conclusions are outlined in Section 9.

2. Modeling reputation in MAS

Since many costly services and products can be provided through electronic means, remote interactions soon played a central role in open distributed systems such as agent systems. The availability of these interactions among agents is increasing the interest in how to achieve/acquire the acceptance of electronic services. However this acceptance faces several challenges [1]. One of these issues is how to select providers and partners that are geographically and culturally distant.

Most current electronic services assume that secure and reliable communication (including contracts and signatures) is enough to assure trust. But with the growing impact of agent systems a broader concept of trust becomes more and more important. Often, there are some possible objective criteria to evaluate the quality of services, and in a more general way the behaviour of partners. Then, trust comes from reliable authorities (often called Trusted Third Parties) that certify a positive satisfaction of these properties.

Unfortunately, when there is no set of universal/shared objective evaluation criteria, this kind of trust will not be easily asserted. In real life, such local and subjective trust plays a very important role in social organizations as a mechanism of social control. There are several application domains where interpersonal communications are the main source of trust due to the subjective nature of the evaluation criteria. Therefore, modelling subjective trust in agent systems becomes a critical issue, since their offline and large-scale nature weaken the social control of direct interactions. This broad concept of trust has been present in human societies from the beginning of written history. But there is no universally accepted definition. Several disciplines have studied and used it: psychology, sociology, and economy. Although there are several ways to define trust, numerous studies have shown that in real life one of the most effective channels to avoid deception is through reputation-based mechanisms.

Reputation consists of the opinion others have of us, or in other words, how we are considered in the eyes of others. It affects us indirectly, through other peoples' behaviour toward us. Sometimes reputation is defined as equivalent to the notion of past history, previous knowledge or familiarity among partners of interaction. On the other hand, game theorists put strong emphasis on reputation as information that players receive about the behaviour of their partners from third parties, and that they use to decide how to behave themselves

Many computational and theoretical models and approaches to reputation have been developed in the last few years. We can classify them in two main trends:

- Computational models of reputation-based trust that involve a numerical approach, made up of utility functions, probabilities and evaluations of past interactions.
- Computational models of reputation that involve a cognitive approach [2]: a symbolic model of opponents. Therefore reputation is then made up of underlying beliefs, and trust is inferred from the truth value of these beliefs. Trust is then the result of a mental process about reputation in a cognitive sense.

The combination of both approaches aspires to reproduce the reasoning mechanisms behind human decision-making as agents have been observed to do (the so-called social metaphor).

2.1. Computational trust and reputation models from IIIA-CSIC

During recent years, a group of researchers at the IIIA-CSIC in collaboration with several international groups[1], has been working in the area of computational trust and reputation models. Their contribution to the area has focused in two main directions:

- Developing different computational trust and reputation models, each one confronting the problem from a different perspective and exploring also different technical solutions.
- Founding and contributing actively, together with a set of international partners, to the ART testbed initiative, a testbed for trust and reputation models.

The work has been centered around four models: ReGreT[6], RepAge[35, 36], CREDIT[34] and the Sierra–Debenham model[37]. Each model puts special emphasis on a different aspect. *ReGreT*'s main characteristic is the use of the social

---

[1]Research partially supported by the European Union project OpenKnowledge, IST-4-027253-STP

environment of the agent as a relevant source of information to establish the trust of a partner. *RepAge* is a cognitive model based on a well-founded cognitive theory about reputation from Conte and Paolucci[33]. In this case, the model is designed with special attention to the internal representation of the elements used to build images and reputations as well as the inter-relations of these elements. The main idea behind this approach is that the internal process followed to arrive at a final trust and reputation value is as important as the final result itself, opening the possibility of a new area of research like the management of its own reputation or the argumentation of a reputation value. *CREDIT* models a normative environment that helps in simplifying the dialogues of the agents, as some issues do not need to be fully specified when the norms guarantee certain behaviour and uses fuzzy sets to model the qualitative thinking that most humans use in contract execution evaluation. Finally, the Sierra–Debenham model has a solid probabilistic foundation to model its basic tenet: all communication in negotiation is, in fact, about information. When offers are made or rejected, when arguments are interchanged, agents pass information to each other. Modelling this information is the basic activity that an agent in this model is dealing with. Acceptance of proposals is made after enough information about the contract and the satisfaction of the agent's needs is gathered in the agent's world model. Trust is nothing else than a measure of the uncertainty of the opponents behaviour.

2.1.1. ReGreT. ReGreT[6] is a modular trust and reputation system oriented to complex societies where the social component of the agents behaviour has a special relevance. The system uses knowledge about the social structure of the society as a method to overcome the lack of direct experiences and to evaluate the credibility of witnesses. By combining direct experiences, third party information and social knowledge, the system can improve the computation of trust and reputation values. It also provides a degree of reliability for these values and can adapt to situations of partial information, improving gradually its accuracy when new information becomes available.

The ReGreT model takes into account three types of computation of indirect reputation depending on the information source: system, neighborhood and witness reputations. Note that witness reputation is the one that corresponds to the concept of reputation that we (and most of the authors) are considering. ReGreT includes a measure of the social credibility of the agent and a measure of the credibility of the information in the computation of witness reputation. The first of them is computed from the social relations shared between both agents. It is computed in a similar way to neighborhood reputation, using third party references about the recommender directly in the computation of how its recommendations are taken into account. In addition, the second measure of credibility (information credibility) is computed from the difference between the recommendation and what the agent experienced by itself. The similarity is computed matching this difference with a triangle fuzzy set centered at 0 (the value 0 stands for no difference at all). The information credibility is considered as relevant and taken into account in the experiments of this present comparison. Both decisions are also, in some way, supported by the authors of ReGreT, who also assume that the accuracy of previous pieces of information (witness) are much more reliable than the credibility based on social relations (neighborhood), and they reduce the use of neighborhood reputation to those situations were there is not enough information on witness reputation. The complete mathematical expression of both measures can be found in [6].

2.1.2. RepAge. Repage[35, 36] is a reputation model, that is being developed together with the ISTC-CNR institute in Rome under the eRep European project[2], based on the cognitive theory of Conte and Paolucci [33]. The main point behind this theory is the distinction between *Image* and *Reputation*. Although both are social evaluations, image and reputation are distinct objects. Image is an evaluative belief; it says that the target is "good" or "bad" with respect to a norm, a standard, or a skill. Reputation is a belief about the existence of a communicated evaluation. Consequently, to assume that a target t is assigned a given reputation implies only to assume that t is reputed to be "good" or "bad", i.e., that this evaluation circulates, but it does not imply sharing the evaluation. Repage provides evaluations on potential partners and is fed with information from others and outcomes from direct experience.

The main element of the Repage architecture is the memory that is composed of a set of *predicates*. Predicates are objects containing a social evaluation, belonging to one of the main types accepted by Repage (image, reputation, shared voice, shared evaluation), or to one of the types used for their calculation (valued information, evaluation related from informers, and outcomes). These predicates have a tuple of five numbers to represent the evaluation, plus a strength value that indicates the confidence the agent has in this evaluation. Predicates are conceptually organized in different levels and interconnected to reflect their dependencies.

Predicates are connected by a network of dependencies, that specifies which predicates contribute to the value of other predicates. Each predicate in the *Repage* memory has a set of antecedents and a set of consequents. If an antecedent is created, removed, or changes its value, the predicate is notified, recalculates its value and notifies the change to its consequents.

2.1.3. CREDIT. CREDIT [34] is a computational trust model (**C**onfidence and **RE**putation **D**efining **I**nteraction-based **T**rust) that is similar to ReGreT. It combines *confidence* in an agent built from direct interactions and *reputation* that is gathered from the experiences of other agents in the community, gossip or by analyzing signals sent by the agent. The difference here is the method based on fuzzy sets used to compute these measures. [3]

---

[2]European Union-CIT5-028575-STP

[3]Fuzzy sets are here used to characterise the inherent imprecision in the perception of the performance of an opponent and to provide agents with a high-level means of assessing the extent to which an opponent satisfies the issues of a contract. Thus an opponent may be characterised as having a high degree of membership to the fuzzy set 'delivery-on-time' and a low degree of

The use of norms to model the expectations of environment evolution is a differentiating factor in evaluating the trust of opponents. In so doing, it prevents agents from trusting those opponents that are only performing well because of the prevailing norms. Further CREDIT allows interacting agents, with different norms, to negotiate those issues for which they have different expected values (guided by the norms) and avoid negotiating over those issues for which they have coherent expectations. This, in turn, minimises losses and saves negotiation time. Finally trust can be used to adjust the stance that an agent takes during negotiation so as to minimize the utility loss incurred when it believes its opponent is likely to defect by different degrees from a signed contract. To summarize, CREDIT not only consists of the basic constructs needed to build meaningful measures of trust, it contains the hooks that allow an agent's reasoning mechanism to use measures of trust in trust-based negotiation (TBN).

2.1.4. Sierra–Debenham model. This model of trust [37, 38] is based on information theory. It is developed from the observation that any illocutionary exchange between agents give away information, which can be used to build information models of them. Argumentative dialogues change this information model with respect to the ongoing relationship between them. This temporal model builds up trust measures which in turn can be used to select partners for collaboration or to select strategies for argumentation with the chosen partner.

A trust model based on information theory is particularly suited for open scenarios as it assumes almost nothing about the agents, nor about the environment, but builds up a model dynamically based on argumentation. It is further based on commitments, thus assumes nothing about the internal architecture of the agents (e.g., beliefs, intentions). Another feature is its honour model, a measure of the integrity of the information exchanged (in appeals) and conditional promises made (in threats and rewards) which supports sustainable partnerships over long periods.

The essence of "information-based agency" is described in the following. An agent observes events in its environment, including what other agents actually do. It chooses to represent some of those observations in its world model as beliefs. As time passes, an agent may not be prepared to accept such beliefs as being "true", and qualifies those representations with epistemic probabilities. Those qualified representations of prior observations are the agent's *information*. This information is primitive — it is the agent's representation of its beliefs about the environment, and about other agents' prior actions. It is independent of what the agent is trying to achieve, or what the agent believes the other agents are trying to achieve. Given this information, an agent may then choose to adopt goals and strategies, to evaluate situations and to act. To enable the agent's strategies to make good use of its information, tools from information theory are applied to summarise and

---

membership in the fuzzy set 'sells-high-quality' to denote that it is expected to deliver on time and sell goods of relatively poor quality.

process it: Maximum Entropy Inference, and Minimum Relative Entropy Inference. Such an agent is called *information-based*.

2.2. Other reputation models

Two of the most cited reputation models are SPORAS and HISTOS [3]. SPORAS is inspired in the foundations of the chess players evaluation system called ELOS. The main point of this model is that trusted agents with very high reputation experience much smaller changes in reputation than agents with low reputation. SPORAS computes the reliability of agents' reputation using the standard deviation of such measure.

HISTOS is designed to complement SPORAS by including a way to deal with witness information (personal recommendations). HISTOS includes witness information as a source of reputation through a recursive computation of weighted means of ratings. It computes reputation of agent i for agent j from the knowledge of all the chain of reputation beliefs corresponding to each possible path that connects two agents. It also permits limiting of the length of paths that are taken into account. To make fair comparison with other proposals, that limit should be valued as 1, since most of the other views consider that agents communicate only its own beliefs, but not the beliefs of other sources that contributed to its own belief of reputation.

Another well-known reputation model is from Singh and Yu. This trust model [5] uses Dempster–Shafer theory of evidence to aggregate recommendations from different witnesses. The main characteristic of this model is the relative importance of failures over success. It assumes that deceptions cause stronger impressions than satisfactions. It then applies different gradients to the curves of gaining/losing reputation in order to make reputation easy to lose and hard to acquire. The authors of this trust model assign different equations to the sign (positive/negative) of the received direct experience (satisfaction/deception) and the sign of the previous reputation corresponding to the given agent.

Instead of Dempster–Shafer theory, Sen's reputation model [8] uses learning to cope with recommendations from different witnesses. Unfortunately learning requires a high number of interactions and a relatively high number of witnesses to avoid colluding agents benefiting from reciprocative agents.

Another recent successful model is FIRE [7] that integrates four types of information sources: interaction trust, role-based trust, witness reputation and certified reputation. Interaction trust is built from the direct experience of an agent, in particular, the direct trust component of ReGreT is exploited in this model. Role-based trust is based on relationships between the agents, which is mostly domain-specific. Witness information is built from reports of witnesses about an agent's behavior. Certified reputation is a novel type of reputation introduced by the authors which is built from third-party references provided by the agent itself. Certified reputation plays a similar role to what we call advertisements, since in both cases an agent i that has just joined the environment can make some assessment of the trustworthiness of another agent j based on the certified reputation or advertisements provided by the agent j itself. The main limitation of the FIRE model in [7] is that all agents are assumed to be honest in exchanging information.

Another approach when agents are acting in uncertain environments, is to apply adaptive filters such as Alpha Beta, Kalman and IMM [9, 10]. They have been recognized as a reasoning paradigm for time-variable facts. Making time-dependent predictions in a noisy environment is not an easy task. They apply a temporal statistical model to the noisy observations perceived through a linear recursive algorithm that estimates future state variables. Particularly, when they are applied as a reputation model, the state variable would be the reputation, while observations would be the results from direct experiences.

Other researchers have proposed a socio-cognitive view of trust. Castelfranchi and Falcone [11] claim that some other beliefs rather than reputation are essential to compute the amount of trust in a particular agent: its competence (ability to act as we wish), willingness (intention to cooperate), persistence (consistency along time) and motivation (our contribution to its goals). For the authors, these beliefs should be taken into consideration in determining how much trust is placed in this agent. Brainov and Sandholm [12] highlight the relevance of modeling an opponent's trust, since if this outside trust was not taken into account, this would lead to an inefficient trade between agents involved. So both agents would be interested in showing the trustworthiness of the counterpart to efficiently allocate resources.

Another example of a socio-cognitive approach is AFRAS from Carbo et al. [13]. It supports the fuzzy nature of the reputation concept itself. It uses fuzzy logic to represent reputation since this concept is built up with: vague evaluations (they depend on personal and subjective criteria), uncertain recommendations (malicious agents, different points of view) and incomplete information (untraceability of every agent in open systems). Furthermore, reliability of fuzzy reputation is implicit in the shape of the corresponding fuzzy set. Additionally, it includes other beliefs in the AFRAS trust model that aims to represent an emotive characterization of agents: shyness, egoism, susceptibility. It also includes a global belief of the agent noted as *remembrance*. This attribute determines the relevance given to the last direct interaction in the updating of trustworthiness. It represents the general confidence of the agent in its own beliefs. The more success is achieved in predicting the behaviour of a particular agent, the more relevance is applied to our already asserted beliefs over future experiences with any agent (not only that particular agent).

3. Organisational structures to improve trust and reputation

Organisational abstractions can be used to impose some structure on a society of agents and can endow MAS with certain behaviours. Agents joining an organisation play specific *roles* in different *interactions* and they are supposed to act conforming to the prescriptions of these concepts. Furthermore, these prescriptions may be complemented by a more general set of *norms* and some kind of mechanisms that make it difficult for agents to transgress norms. Multi-agent systems with such organisational structures will be called *Virtual Organisations* (VOs) [20] [21].

VOs can be considered as limiting the freedom of choice of agents because they regulate the interactions within a MAS. However, especially within low regulated organisations, agents will still have to tackle the problem of choosing appropriate counterparts for their interactions according to their own beliefs and goals. Within this scenario, trust and reputation mechanisms can be integrated into VOs providing support to agents' decision-making processes.

The structure provided by a VO can be used to construct more effective trust mechanisms. In particular, the structural elements defined in a VO (e.g., roles and interactions) provide a certain notion of similarity which allows agents to infer the expected behaviour of acquaintances within totally new situations by analysing their past behaviour within *similar* situations. This property is especially useful in situations where agents can not count on their own past experiences, e.g., when they have just joined an organisation, or within very volatile or dynamic environments.

3.1. Basic Local-Based Trust Model for Virtual Organisations

Similarly to other approaches [22][23], the trust model presented in this section is based on the idea of *confidence* and *reputation*. Both are ratings agents use in order to evaluate the trustworthiness of other agents in a particular issue (e.g., playing a particular role in a particular interaction). *Confidence* is a local measure that is only based on an agent's own past experiences, while *reputation* is an aggregated value an agent gathers by asking its acquaintances about their opinion regarding the trustworthiness of another agent. Thus, reputation can be considered as an external or *social* measure. *Trust* is defined as a rating resulting from combining *confidence* and *reputation* values.

A typical scenario for the use of a trust model is the following: an agent A wants to evaluate the trustworthiness of some other agent B – playing the role R – in the interaction I. This trustworthiness is denoted as $t_{A \to \langle B,R,I \rangle}$, with $t_{A \to \langle B,R,I \rangle} \in [0..1]$, and it measures the trust of A in B (playing role R) being a "good" counterpart in the interaction I. When evaluating the trustworthiness of a potential counterpart[4], an agent can combine its local information (confidence) with the information obtained from other agents regarding the same counterpart (reputation).

Confidence, $c_{A \to \langle B,R,I \rangle}$, is collected from A's past interactions with agent B playing role R and performing interactions of type I. We construct a LIT – *Local Interaction Table* –, an agent's data structure dedicated to storing confidence values for past interactions with any counterpart the agent has interacted with.

---

[4]Potential counterpart will be an agent which is a candidate to interact with.

TABLE 1. An agent's local interaction table (LIT_A).

$\langle X, Y, Z \rangle$	$c_{A \to \langle X,Y,Z \rangle}$	$r_{A \to \langle X,Y,Z \rangle}$
$\langle a_9, r_2, i_3 \rangle$	0.2	0.75
$\langle a_2, r_7, i_1 \rangle$	0.7	0.3
$\vdots$	$\vdots$	$\vdots$
$\langle a_9, r_2, i_5 \rangle$	0.3	0.5

Each entry corresponds to an *issue*: an *agent* playing a specific *role* in a particular *interaction*. LIT_A denotes agent A's LIT. An example is shown in Table 1.

Each entry in a LIT consists of: i) the Agent/Role/Interaction identifier $\langle X, Y, Z \rangle$, ii) the confidence value for the issue ($c_{A \to \langle X,Y,Z \rangle}$), and iii) a reliability value ($r_{A \to \langle X,Y,Z \rangle}$). The confidence value is obtained from some function that evaluates past experiences on the same issue. It is supposed that $c_{A \to \langle X,Y,Z \rangle} \in [0..1]$ and higher values to represent higher confidence.

Each direct experience of an agent regarding an issue $\langle X, Y, Z \rangle$ changes its confidence value $c_{A \to \langle X,Y,Z \rangle}$. In this sense, it is supposed that the agents have some kind of mechanism to evaluate the behaviour of other agents they interact with. Let $g_{\langle X,Y,Z \rangle} \in [0..1]$ denote the evaluation value an agent A calculates for a particular experience with the agent X playing role Y in the interaction of type Z. The following equation will be used to update confidence:

$$c_{A \to \langle X,Y,Z \rangle} = \lambda \cdot c'_{A \to \langle X,Y,Z \rangle} + (1 - \lambda) \cdot g_{\langle X,Y,Z \rangle}, \qquad (3.1)$$

where $c'_{A \to \langle X,Y,Z \rangle}$ is the confidence value in A's LIT before the interaction is performed and $\lambda \in [0..1]$ is a parameter specifying the importance given to A's past confidence value. In general, the aggregated confidence value from past experiences will be more relevant than the evaluations of the most recent interactions.

Reliability ($r_{A \to \langle X,Y,Z \rangle}$) measures how certain an agent is about its own confidence in an issue. It is supposed that $r_{A \to \langle X,Y,Z \rangle} \in [0..1]$. Furthermore, it is assumed that $r_{A \to \langle X,Y,Z \rangle} = 0$ for any tuple $\langle X, Y, Z \rangle$ not belonging to LIT_A. Reliability is calculated by taking into account the number of interactions a confidence value is based on and the variability of the individual values across past experiences, similarly as it is done in other approaches [4] [22].

An agent may build trust directly from its confidence value or it may combine confidence with reputation. Reputation will be particularly useful when an agent has no experience on an issue or if the reliability value for the confidence is not high enough. Social reputation may be obtained by asking other agents about their opinion on an issue, but this will not be taken into account for this chapter. Agents that have been asked for their opinion will return the corresponding confidence and reliability ratings from their LIT. The requester might then be able to build trust by calculating a weighted mean over its own confidence value and the confidence values received from others, as it is represented in equation (3.2):

$$t_{A \to \langle B,R,I \rangle} = \begin{cases} c_{A \to \langle B,R,I \rangle}, & if \ \ r_{A \to \langle B,R,I \rangle} > \theta \\ \dfrac{\sum\limits_{X \in AA \cup \{A\}} c_{X \to \langle B,R,I \rangle} \cdot w_{X \to \langle B,R,I \rangle}}{\sum\limits_{X \in AA \cup \{A\}} w_{X \to \langle B,R,I \rangle}} & otherwise. \end{cases} \qquad (3.2)$$

$\theta \in [0..1]$ is a threshold on the reliability of confidence. If the reliability is above θ, then an agent's own confidence in an issue is used as the trust value. Otherwise trust is built by combining confidence and reputation. AA is a set of acquaintances an agent asks about their opinion regarding the issue $\langle B,R,I \rangle$. Within a VO, the structural abstractions may provide hints for the proper selection of such a set of acquaintances. For instance, in some scenarios it may be useful to ask other agents that play the same role as A, since they may have similar interests and goals.

The weights $w_{X \to \langle B,R,I \rangle}$ given to the gathered confidence values are composed of the corresponding reliability value and a constant factor α that specifies the importance given to A's own confidence in the issue, as it is shown in the following equation:

$$w_{X \to \langle B,R,I \rangle} = \begin{cases} r_{X \to \langle B,R,I \rangle} \cdot \alpha, & if \ \ X = A, \\ r_{X \to \langle B,R,I \rangle} \cdot (1 - \alpha), & otherwise. \end{cases} \qquad (3.3)$$

3.2. Confidence Inference using Organisational Structure Similarities

In this section a local way is proposed for building trust on an issue when no past interactions have been performed and without relying upon social reputation. This section proposes to use the agent/role confidence $c_{A \to \langle B,R,\_ \rangle}$ (or the agent confidence $c_{A \to \langle B,\_,\_ \rangle}$) as an estimation for $c_{A \to \langle B,R,I \rangle}$ if agent A has no reliable experience about issue $\langle B,R,I \rangle$. This approach relies on the hypothesis that, in general, agents behave in a similar way in all interactions related to the same role. It argues that, exploiting this idea, the more similar I' and I are, the more similar the values $c_{A \to \langle B,R,I' \rangle}$ and $c_{A \to \langle B,R,I \rangle}$ will be. The same applies to roles. Using this assumption, confidence ratings accumulated for similar agent/role/interaction tuples may provide evidence for the trustworthiness of the issue $\langle B,R,I \rangle$. Based on this idea, it is proposed to build trust by taking into account all the past experiences an agent has, focusing on their degree of similarity with the issue $\langle B,R,I \rangle$. In particular, trust will be calculated as a weighted mean over all the confidence values an agent has accumulated in its LIT. This is shown in the following equation:

$$t_{A \to \langle B,R,I \rangle} = \frac{\sum\limits_{\langle X,Y,Z \rangle \in LIT_A} c_{A \to \langle X,Y,Z \rangle} \cdot w_{A \to \langle X,Y,Z \rangle}}{\sum\limits_{\langle X,Y,Z \rangle \in LIT_A} w_{A \to \langle X,Y,Z \rangle}}, \qquad (3.4)$$

$w_{A \to \langle X,Y,Z \rangle}$ is the weight given to agent A's confidence on issue $\langle X,Y,Z \rangle$. The weights combine the confidence reliability with the similarity of the issue $\langle X,Y,Z \rangle$ to the target issue $\langle B,R,I \rangle$ in the following way:

$$w_{A \to \langle X,Y,Z \rangle} = r_{A \to \langle X,Y,Z \rangle} \cdot sim(\langle X,Y,Z \rangle, \langle B,R,I \rangle). \qquad (3.5)$$

The similarity function $sim(\langle X, Y, Z \rangle, \langle B, R, I \rangle)$ is computed as the weighted sum of the similarities of the individual elements (agent, role and interaction) as it is shown in the following equation:

$$sim(\langle X, Y, Z \rangle, \langle B, R, I \rangle) = \left\{ \begin{array}{cc} \beta \cdot sim_R(R, Y) + \gamma \cdot sim_I(I, Z), & if \quad B = X, \\ 0, & otherwise, \end{array} \right.$$

(3.6)

where $sim_R(R, Y)$, $sim_I(I, Z) \in [0..1]$ measure the similarity between roles and interactions, respectively, and β and γ, with $\beta + \gamma = 1$, are parameters specifying the sensibility regarding the individual similarities.

It is supposed that organisational models include taxonomies of roles and/or interactions from which role and interaction similarity measures can be derived. In this case, $sim_R(R, R')$ and $sim_I(I, I')$ can be implemented by *closeness functions* that estimate the similarity between two concepts on the basis of their closeness in the concept hierarchy. Some useful functions to determine similarity between concepts in a taxonomy can be found in [24] and [25].

Equation (3.4) can be used as an alternative way to build trust. Especially if an agent has no reliable experience about a particular agent/role/interaction issue, this model can be used to estimate trust without the necessity to rely on the opinions of other agents. Thus, the proposed model makes agents less dependent on others, which is an important issue, in particular in VOs that do not provide mechanisms to keep its members from cheating.

4. Using Reputation and Trust in Knowledge Management

The concepts of trust and reputation can be also very useful in the knowledge management domain since to store many data is not equal to acquiring valuable information. On the other hand, employees sometimes introduce not very useful information in a knowledge base. This fact decreases the trust that employees have in their organizational knowledge and reduces the probability that people will use it. In order to avoid this situation we have developed a multi-agent architecture in charge of monitoring and evaluating the trustworthiness of the knowledge that is stored in a knowledge base. To design this architecture it has been considered how people obtain information when they are working in communities of practice since they are a hub for sharing knowledge within an organization. Bearing in mind the advantages of working with groups of similar interests, the agents have been organized into communities where there are two types of agents: the User Agent and the Manager Agent. The former is used to represent each person that may consult or introduce knowledge in a knowledge base. The User Agent can assume three types of behaviour or roles similar to the tasks that a person can carry out in a knowledge base. Therefore, the User Agent plays one role or another depending upon whether the person that it represents carries out one of the following actions:

- The person contributes new knowledge to the communities in which s/he is registered. In this case the User Agent plays the role of Provider.

- The person uses knowledge previously stored in the community. Then, the User Agent will be considered as a Consumer.
- The person helps other users to achieve their goals, for instance by giving an evaluation of certain knowledge. In this case the role is that of a Partner. So, in a Community there could be two User Agents playing the role of Partner (Pa), one User Agent playing the role of Consumer (Co) and another being a Provider (Pr).

4.1. Concept of reputation

Part of the conceptual model of a User Agent, whose goals are to detect trustworthy agents and sources, is based on two closely related concepts: trust and reputation. The definitions that are used in this approach are the following: trust is considered as the confidence in the ability and intention of an information source to deliver correct information [27] and reputation as the amount of trust an agent has in an information source, created through interactions with information sources. This definition is the most appropriate for our research, since the level of confidence in a source is based on previous experience with the source. It is for this reason that the remainder of this document deals solely with reputation. However, if we attempt to imitate the behaviour of the employees in a company when they are exchanging and obtaining information, it is observed that apart from the concept of reputation other factors also exert influence. For this reason, we argue that reputation is not a single notion but one of multiple parts. These parts are:

- Position: employees often consider information that comes from a boss as being more reliable than that which comes from another employee in the same (or a lower) position as him/her [31]. However, this is not a universal truth and depends on the situation. For instance in a collaborative learning setting, collaboration is more likely to occur between people of a similar status than between a boss and his/her employee or between a teacher and pupils [29]. Because of this, as will be explained later, in our research this factor will be calculated by taking into account a weight that can strengthen the factor to a greater or to a lesser degree.
- Expertise: this term can be briefly defined as the skill or knowledge of a person who knows a great deal about a specific thing. This is an important factor since people often trust in experts more than in novice employees. Moreover, tools such as expertise location [28] are being developed with the goal of promoting the sharing of expert knowledge.
- Previous experience: People have greater trust in those sources from which they have previously obtained more "valuable information". Therefore, a factor that influences the increasing or decreasing reputation of a source is "previous experience" and this factor can help us to detect trustworthy sources of knowledge.
- Intuition: When people do not have any previous experience they often use their "intuition" to decide whether or not they are going to trust something. Other authors have called this issue "indirect reputation or prior-derived

reputation" [30]. In human societies, each of us probably has different prior beliefs about the trustworthiness of strangers we meet. Sexual or racial discrimination might be a consequence of such prior belief [30]. We have tried to model intuition according to the similarity between the user profiles: the greater the similarity between one agent and another, the greater the intuition level.

Taking all these factors into account, we have defined our own "concept of reputation". The reputation of $agent_j$ in the eyes of $agent_s$ is a collective measure defined by the previously described reputation factors and is computed as follows:

$$R_{sj} = w_e * E_j + w_p * P_j + w_i * I_j + (\sum_{j=1}^{n} QC_j)/n \qquad (4.1)$$

where R_{sj} denotes the reputation value that $agent_s$ has in $agent_j$ (each agent in the community has an opinion about each of the other agent members of the community which it has interacted with). E_j is the value of expertise which is calculated according to the degree of experience that a person has in a domain. P_j is the value assigned to the position of a person. This position is defined by the organizational diagram of the enterprise. Therefore, a value that determines the hierarchic level within the organization can be assigned to each level of the diagram. I_j is the value assigned to intuition which is calculated by comparing each of the users profiles. In addition, previous experience should also be calculated. We suppose that when an agent A consults information from another agent J, the agent A should evaluate how useful this information was. This value is called QC_j (Quality of j's Contribution). To attain the average value of an agent's contribution, we calculate the sum of all the values assigned to their contributions and we divide it between their total. In the expression, n represents the total number of evaluated contributions.

Finally, w_e, w_p and w_i are weights with which the Reputation value can be adjusted to the needs of the organizations. For instance, if an enterprise considers that all their employees have the same category, then $w_p = 0$. The same could occur when the organization does not take its employees intuitions or expertise into account.

In this way, an agent can obtain a value related to the reputation of another agent and decide to what degree it is going to consider the information obtained from this agent. Moreover, when a user wants to join a community in which no member knows anything about him/her, the reputation value assigned to the user in the new community is calculated on the basis of the reputation assigned from other communities where the user is or was a member. For instance, a User Agent called j will ask each community manager where he/she was previously a member to consult each agent that knows him/her with the goal of calculating the average value of his/her reputation (Rj). This is calculated as:

$$R_j = (\sum_{j=1}^{n} R_{ij})/n \qquad\qquad (4.2)$$

where n is the number of agents who know j and R_{ij} is the value of j's reputation in the eyes of i. In the case of being known in several communities the average of the values R_j will be calculated. Then, the User Agent j presents this reputation value (similar to when a person presents his/her curriculum vitae when s/he wishes to join a company) to the Manager Agent of the community to which it is "applying". This mechanism is similar to the "word-of-mouth" propagation of information for a human [26]. We do realize that reputation is clearly a context-dependent quantity. For instance, one's reputation as a computer scientist should have no influence upon one's reputation as a cook [30]. However, if we are trying to emulate the behavior of people working in communities of practice, then we should observe how some people's opinions influence others. In the case of the user being new in the community, then this user is assigned a "new" label in order for the situation to be identified. Once the Community Manager has obtained a Reputation value for j, it is added to the community member list. Besides these agents there is also another in charge of initiating new agents and creating new communities. This agent has two main roles: the "creator" role is assumed when there is a petition (made by a User Agent) to create a new Community and the "initiator" role is assumed when the system is initially launched. This agent, which is not included in any of the communities, is called the Creator Agent.

5. Application of Fuzzy Contextual Corrective Filtering

A point seems to have been so far overlooked by the formalisms for trust modeling that have been developed over the last years: *It is not necessary to trust an agent (in the sense of believing it is saying the truth) in order to get some utility from the information provided by it.* The information can be useful even if it is false, provided we had some method to correct it.

The key concept in order to be able to correct information coming from other agents is reliability (in the sense of "giving the same result in successive trials". [19]). If an agent tends to communicate similar information under similar circumstances, a moment will arrive when we will be able to extrapolate the circumstances, more or less correctly, from the received messages. On the contrary, if an agent emits just random messages it will be very difficult, if not impossible, to obtain from them any utility at all.

The corrective mechanisms or filters can have very different structures. The ARLab research group(Agent Research Laboratory) of the University of Girona, has defined Fuzzy Contextual Corrective Filters (FCCF) [14, 15] as reliability modeling methods loosely based on system identification and signal processing

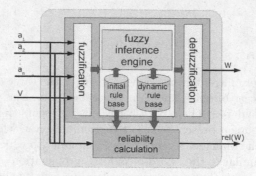

FIGURE 1. Structure of a fuzzy contextual corrective filter

techniques. They have also proved their usefulness by applying them to the appraisal variance estimation problem in the Agent Reputation and Trust (ART) testbed.

5.1. Fuzzy Contextual Corrective Filters

Think about the following problem: An agent A interacts with several other agents in a multi-agent environment requesting from them some kind of information, which they supply. Suppose also that the correct answers to A's requests are made available to A by the environment in a posterior time instant, in such a way that A is able to know which agents told the truth and which agents lied, and how much. Our point is: for A to be able to perform well in this kind of environment it has to maintain a set of filters (one of them for each agent it interacts with) which allows it to correct the information received from the other agents, as well as to assess the possible utility of the corrected information. These filters must be dynamic, in the sense that they must evolve and adapt to changes in the environment and in the behavior of the other agents. So filters act as a translative layer that eases the process of interpretation of the messages sent by other agents.

It is also very important for the agent that owns the filter to have some kind of measure of the correctness of the filtered information, that is, the degree to which it can be expected to reflect the reality. We will call this value *reliability* and the filter will compute it from the observed regularities in the behavior of the filtered agent in past interactions.

Figure 1 shows the suggested structure for the construction of these filters, called fuzzy corrective contextual filters (FCCF) [14, 15]. A FCCF F has two parts, the *corrective module* and the *reliability calculation module*. The corrective module is a special case of a Mamdani fuzzy inference system [18] where the fuzzy rules have the form:

If A_1 is S_1 and ... and A_n is S_n and V is L_1, then W is L_2.

We call $A_1, A_2, \ldots, A_n$ the *context variables*, V the *main variable* and W the *filtered variable*. The corrective module of a FCCF filters the values (fuzzy sets) of the main variable to obtain new values (fuzzy sets over the same universe or another one) which are expected to be more suitable for some purpose.

The rule base of the corrective module has two components, the static and dynamic rule bases. The static rule base is fixed (and possibly the same) for every agent. It expresses the *a priori* assumptions about the behavior of the other agents in the environment and serves as a departing point in the interpretation of other agents's assertions. The dynamic rule base is built upon the information extracted (in the form of fuzzy rules) from the interactions between the agent which owns the filter and the filtered agents. The reliability calculation module, is in charge of the computation of the reliability of the filtered value obtained by the corrective module. Reliability is, then, a function of the input and context variables and depends upon the number of prior similar interactions between filtering and filtered agents, as well as upon the regularities observed during those interactions.

In the next section we will see how FCCF is applied to the ART testbed.

6. From models to testbeds: the ART testbed initiative

As shown in Section 2, a diverse collection of trust modeling algorithms for multi-agent systems has been developed in recent years, resulting in significant breadth-wise growth without unified direction or benchmarks. The ART (Agent Reputation and Trust) Testbed Initiative[32, 17] was born as a collaboration among several international research groups in the area of computational trust and reputation models, with the objective of establishing a testbed for agent trust- and reputation-related technologies. This testbed serves in two roles: (1) as a competition forum in which researchers can compare their technologies against objective metrics, and (2) as a suite of tools with flexible parameters, allowing researchers to perform customizable, easily-repeatable experiments.

As a versatile, universal experimentation site, the ART Testbed fosters a cohesive exploration of trust research problems; researchers are united toward a common challenge, out of which can come solutions to these problems via unified experimentation methods. Through objective, well-defined metrics, the testbed provides researchers with tools for comparing and validating their approaches. The testbed also serves as an objective means of presenting technology features—both advantages and disadvantages—to the research community. In addition, the ART Testbed places trust research in the public spotlight, improving confidence in the technology and highlighting relevant applications.

6.1. Operation

The ART testbed is based on the art appraisal domain, for experimentation and comparison of trust-modeling techniques. Agents function as painting appraisers with varying levels of expertise in different artistic eras. Clients request appraisals for paintings from different eras; if an appraising agent does not have the expertise to complete the appraisal, it can request opinions from other appraiser agents.

Appraisers receive more clients, and thus more profit, for producing more accurate appraisals.

When an agent A does not have enough confidence in its own expertise to guarantee a good appraisal for a given painting, it can buy the opinion of other, more expert, agents. The process is the following: first, agent A asks all or some of the other agents to provide a value stating their confidence in the accuracy of their appraisal of the painting. Then, A decides, upon the received confidence values, which agents to trust, that is, which opinions to purchase.

This is the main point at which the communication of false or misleading information can appear in the ART testbed. An agent can declare a greater confidence in its appraisal than it actually has, and then produce a very bad appraisal. This can result in a big error in the requesting agent's appraisal and, consequently, a big loss for the client. On the other hand, the requesting agent has no way of knowing what the confidence value provided by an agent means. It is a value over an arbitrary range that has to be interpreted. It is perfectly possible for a given confidence value to mean completely different confidence levels for different agents.

6.2. Application of Fuzzy Contextual Corrective Filtering to the ART testbed

The main issue faced in the construction of the ART agent was the following: given two appraisals, it is known how to compare them in order to obtain the appraisal with the minimal expected relative error. A way is needed, however, to determine each appraisals' variances from the supplied confidence values.

The problem was solved by providing the agent with a set of FCCF (see Section 5.1), one for each participating agent other than itself. Their structure is very simple. They have, as input variable, the confidence value stated by the seller agent, and, as context variable, the era to which the painting belongs. The filtered variable is the square of the relative error of the appraisal.

Rules in the initial rule base are predefined by design and serve the purpose of providing a sensible starting point to the interpretation process. Rules in the dynamic rule base, on the other hand, are continuously obtained from interactions between the agent and the filtered agents. Each of the rules in the rule bases, then, has the same form:

$$R_i : \text{If } era = E_i \text{ and } conf = C_i, \text{ then } qError = Q_i$$

where E_i and Q_i are singleton fuzzy sets over the sets of the eras and the positive reals, respectively and C_i is a fuzzy real number. So, for instance, if an appraisal for a cubist painting is purchased for which the seller agent declares to have a confidence 0.5, and the provided appraised value is 20000 but the real price of the painting turns out to be 25000 (giving a relative error of 0.2), we will add to the dynamic rule base the following rule: If $era = cubism$ and $conf = 0.5$ then $qError = 0.04$.

Now consider the possibility of purchasing an appraisal for a painting of a given era e from an agent which states that it has a confidence c in its appraisal. How do we estimate the variance of the appraised value? The variance is defined as the expectation of the quadratic error, so, in principle it would be enough to gather all the interactions in which the agent has stated the very same confidence in its appraisal of a painting of the same era and estimate the variance from these data as the mean of the quadratic errors made. Unfortunately, confidence values will be, in general, scattered along a big range of values, so it can hardly be expected to have enough of them to make the estimation accurate. It is possible, nevertheless, to estimate the variance by computing the output of the fuzzy system in the following way:

$$\sigma_{e,c}^2 = \frac{\sum_i \pi_i(e) \cdot \mu_i(c) \cdot Q_i}{\sum_i \pi_i(e)\mu_i(c)}, \tag{6.1}$$

where $\pi_i(e)$ will take the values 1 or 0 depending on whether the era of the painting corresponding to fuzzy rule R_i was e or not, Q_i is the quadratic error corresponding to fuzzy rule R_i and $\mu_i(c)$ is the degree to which the value c belongs to the fuzzy number C_i. The implementation of the reliability calculation module for the problem is based in previous work by the authors [16]. It mainly takes into account the completeness of the rule bases (roughly speaking, the number of rules that are activated in the calculation of the variance).

Results look very promising. A first version of the agent finished second in the 2007 Spanish ART contest and a evolved version of it, called Spartan, finished fourth (from sixteen teams all over the world) in the 2007 International ART Competition, which took place within the AAMAS 2007 conference.

7. Securing agents in practice

So far, it has been shown how trust can play an important role in multi-agent systems, as well as the details on how to use it in practice. Trust is very useful when dealing with complex systems involving the interaction of many independent agents. There are some actions though that need certain mechanisms running reliably, such as the admission of agents in the system, electronic payments, or authorizations. There are special security requirements which regard the protection of agents. Even though this could seem a trivial thing to achieve, the tangled nature of agents makes of this problem a tough one. In this section we will analyze how to bring into practice the straightforward concepts of confidentiality, authentication, integrity and authorization when dealing with all types of agents, including mobile agents. In fact, the rest of the section will be focused on mobile agents, for mobility is a feature that can be present in any agent and all results apply to stationary agents as well. Moreover, other related issues will be introduced, such as the development of secure agent-based applications and the secure migration of agents between platforms.

7.1. Self-protection of agents

As a starting point for designing agent security, the worst case scenario is taken, in which agents must move around carrying their own data and state from one execution environment to the next, and resuming their execution upon arrival at their destination. Mobile agent systems raise a well-known set of security issues [39, 40] that have to be addressed by any platform providing free-roaming mobile software agents. These security concerns can be classified in two broad categories, according to whether the agent's or the platform's security is at stake.

On the one hand, host platforms receiving and executing mobile agents must be protected against malicious code. Common mechanisms addressing this issue include cryptographic authentication and integrity checks, code signing and encryption, etc. On the other hand, mobile agents must protect themselves against hosts trying to tamper maliciously with either the code or the data carried by incoming agents. This issue, known as the *malicious host problem* [41, 40], is usually addressed by the introduction of application-level cryptographic protocols [42, 43, 44] whose aim is providing two basic guarantees: confidentiality and integrity.

Confidentiality issues arise specially in the context of mobile agents carrying data that must be accessible only to specific, authorized hosts in their itinerary. Besides barring access to reserved information, the roaming agent must also ensure the integrity of the data it carries, i.e., any tampering with pre-existing data must be detected by the agent's owner and, if possible, other hosts in the agent's itinerary.

Previous schemes have addressed the confidentiality and integrity problems with different degrees of success, but, as shown in [42], never in a completely satisfactory way. In any case, all of them are based on standard cryptographic schemes, often relying on public key infrastructures, via platform-driven protection mechanisms. Unfortunately, these security solutions often rely on a static prospect, implying the modification of all the involved platforms.

The UAB group's research team has presented a general software architecture for the protection of mobile agents, with the aim of minimizing or even getting rid of some of the main difficulties of existing solutions. The scheme merges the agent and platform driven approaches into a flexible method for the protection of agent's code and data. Existing cryptographic protocols can be easily embedded in this solution, avoiding in the process some of their shortcomings. The key idea of this approach lies in enhancing agents with an independent, fully encapsulated protection mechanism carried by the agents themselves. This security layer interacts with platforms in very definite circumstances via clear-cut interfaces, minimizing the impact (in terms of new developments and legacy code reuse) of adopting the new mechanism or even modifying the underlying security policies and techniques. This is a telling argument of the approach, for the infrastructure of platforms becomes tenable. Users need not provide security since the mobile agents carry their own self-protection mechanisms, obscuring the application layer. Last but not least, domain-specific or home-brewed security mechanisms can easily coexist with the new architecture.

It is worth stressing that existing agent-based applications can benefit from this solution. Making mobile agents secure involves only minor changes to both the platform and the agent's code.

Finally, the ideas behind this approach are not limited to a theoretical speculation on the benefits of the solution. A fully functional proof-of-concept implementation of the work described in this section (using the well-known JADE agent platform), has been developed and put into practice in a real-world application [45].

7.2. Simplifying the development of secure applications

In order to definitively unblock this technology, it is not enough to provide security breakthroughs. Development of secure mobile agent applications should be encouraged as well. There is still a barrier to overcome for achieving this: the difficulties that programmers have for implementing and using this type of applications. The security systems that protect mobile agents may be theoretically and technically valid, but this does not suffice. It is also necessary to provide a handy and convenient way of developing these systems, without requiring a deep knowledge and expertise in cryptography. A new methodology for the design and development stages has to be created, simplifying to the greatest extent possible the tasks carried out by the designer of new cryptographic protocols and by the developer of new applications. It will be also necessary to provide this methodology with the basic tools that enable its practical application and facilitate development and deployment.

There is very little literature about these specific aspects, mainly because the main work done on this area has been focused on agent protection mechanisms. More basic usability issues concerning the developer (humans) are left aside. The UAB research group has already worked on the basic ideas behind this new approach to assist in the development of secure applications, and has developed a proof-of-concept of a cryptographic architecture compiler [46].

This research group has proposed a methodology for the design of applications based on mobile agents protected with cryptographic architectures. This kind of protection mechanism has represented an inflection point for the security of mobile agents, because it is the first scheme that introduces an agent-driven approach [47], instead of the traditional platform-driven one. The main tool in the scheme is the agent builder, which is the key element for the generation of secure mobile agents. It takes an XML representation of the itinerary, and a specification of the cryptographic architecture represented in the IPL language, and creates the protected mobile agent. This set of tools brings new possibilities to both the application developer and the cryptographic architecture designer.

7.3. Agent migration and security

Mobility is a feature from which information agents can get a lot of benefits. For instance, information retrieval applications [45] show that agent mobility enables a uniform, distributed, autonomous and efficient way to process vast and heterogeneous amounts of information at Internet scale.

In the development of mobile agent-based applications two main problems are faced: security and interoperability. Security is mandatory in any reliable application based on mobile agents. No commercial application will be built until security in mobile agents can be assured. Solutions such as those presented in previous sections facilitate the deployment of secure mobile agent applications.

Interoperability is also an important problem for agents. Since the initial proposals of mobile agent systems, a wide number of platforms have been implemented. The platforms, typically developed by research groups, focus their implementation on several areas of mobile agents research. While some of the platforms focus their implementation on bringing security, others try to build high-performance mobile agents, methods to attain resource access control, communication among agents, and so on. These differences in the platform designing goals cause differences in programming languages, architectures or patterns chosen to design the frameworks and, also, the use of different communication protocols to transport agents or messages among platforms. This set of heterogeneous platforms is one of the main obstacles to agent interoperability and movement through different platform implementations. This fact is critical in some mobile agent applications, especially involving information retrieval, where a great number of reachable platforms are supposed to be present, each one with several resources for agents.

Although several proposals have been presented to provide interoperability among mobile agent systems, this is not an area with as much maturity as in security. Most of these works are focused on software engineering techniques to provide portability of agents between platforms. However, these works often suppose a common programming language and a common communications infrastructure. Others like IEEE FIPA or MASIF, try to standardize some aspects of communication between mobile agent platforms to provide a minimum degree of interoperability to those systems implementing this standard.

The UAB group has presented a global approach to the interoperability problem based on the use of FIPA standards. The main reason for such an approach is that important interoperability problems solved by FIPA specifications are isomorphic to mobile agents interoperability problems, which justifies the use of FIPA solutions to make mobile agent systems inter-operable. This research group is now working on the next FIPA standard for interoperability, defining a flexible scheme of different protocols to perform the required operations for agent migration.

8. Secure intelligent agents in smart offices

In this section it is shown how security can be applied to protect agents in the specific case of smart offices.

One of the first challenges that has to be faced while shifting from smart homes to smart offices is the design of the security architecture. In smart home environments the main goals are user comfort and easy deployment of new devices, so security is usually left apart or focuses mainly on transparency and privacy enhancement. Smart office security, however, has more rigorous security requirements, especially if we are dealing with large organisations, where there may be hundreds of employees with different access needs and security clearances. In this section, an extension to the iEAP (Intelligent Environment Agent Platform)[48] agent-based architecture in order to provide security services to the smart office is proposed.

8.1. The iEAP agent architecture

The iEAP architecture relies on the concept of *smart spaces*, which are specific, self-contained locations within the environment, which may be hierarchically arranged if required by the specific characteristics of the environment. In our application to the smart office, we have a Building Smart Space, which contains several Floor Smart Spaces, each one containing several smart spaces related to offices, corridors, elevators... . This hierarchical approach allows us to provide different layers of services, context information, and security.

To meet its goals, the architecture relies on a set of devices distributed throughout the environment. According to the degree of autonomy and intelligence provided by the devices, mainly determined by its computational capacity to include agents, the devices that we can find in a given iEAP smart space can be divided in four groups: *Smart Space Agent Platform (SSAP)* that contains the agent platform which supports the existence of all other agents in the smart space, *Devices with Agents*, *Devices without Agents* (sensors and effectors without autonomy or intelligence, controlled from the SSAP), *Identification Devices* carried by users and *Personal Devices*, which not only provides the functionality of the identification devices above, but also hosts the necessary agents to learn, maintain and try to satisfy user preferences, and to display adequate interfaces to the available services when needed.

There are different kinds of software agents in a typical iEAP smart space:

- *Smart Space Coordination Agent (SSCA):* Provides device and service discovery to all other users or agents in the smart space, and to SSCAs of other smart spaces. It resides in the SSAPs.
- *Device agents.*
- *System Agents:* They reside in the SSAP, and add an additional layer of intelligence between sensors and effectors in the environment. Security agents, presented in the next section, and context agents are System Agents.
- *Service Agents:* These agents are intended to provide services directly to the user, and usually upon user's request. In the iEAP architecture, two different classes of service agents can be found:
    - Persistent Service Agents: These agents provide services directly related to each specific smart space.

– Non-persistent Service Agents. These agents provide services more related to the user, such as content access or unified messaging. These
agents are able to move from the SSAP to the personal device, and
move again to another SSAP when the user enters another space.

• *Personal Agents (PA):* Personal agents are directly associated to users.

8.2. Security Proposal

The security architecture proposal is focused on setting up a trust relationship
among the agents that exchange information, by using mechanisms of authentication, authorization of users and agents. This requires protecting the information
exchanged by the agents using authentication, integrity and confidentiality. The
principal security assumptions in this scenario are the use of a building certification authorization (BCA) associated to each Smart Space Agent Platform (SSAP)
and the use of Identification Devices by the users to access smart services.

• Connectivity to a centralized building certificate authority (BCA) is available
to the Smart Space Agent Platform (SSAP) associated to each space in the
building.

• Each user in the system can be required to carry a personal identification
device (PDA, smartphone, badge,...) to access the smart services provided in
the building.

8.2.1. Message authentication, confidentiality and integrity.
In pervasive environ-
ments, the nature of the communication being secured and the devices taking part
in the communication must be leveraged to get a trade-off between security and
performance due to limitations of resources. In our proposal, we assume the use of
asymmetric cryptography is acceptable at the SSAPs and at the personal devices
(PDAs or smart phones). However, since personal devices are battery powered, the
use of this kind of cryptography should be minimized. Taking this into account the
security architecture uses asymmetric cryptography to agree on a shared secret between the communicating parties, using a simple handshake protocol. The shared
secret is used to derive symmetric keys which are used to provide the different
security services (confidentiality and integrity of the messages). The use of mobile
agents raises numerous security considerations [39]. At the moment, the architecture only allows mobility to non-persistent service agents The SSAP generates
temporary symmetric shared keys whenever a mobile agent needs to communicate with another principal. Those keys are revoked if the mobile agent leaves the
SSAP.

8.2.2. Key Distribution and User Personal Devices.
As stated above, each SSAP
has its own asymmetric key pair, furthermore the public key is stored at the BCA.
Whenever a new user is added to the system, key pairs are generated for use within
the building. If the user has a personal certificate issued by a trusted root certificate
authority, a mechanism is provided so that the user can securely generate its own
key pair and have its public key stored and published at the BCA. If no electronic
proof of the user identity is available, human intervention is required. The nature

of the physical device holding user cryptographic material may vary depending on the manner the user will interact with the system. For users with access to service personalisation, a Personal Agent (PA) is created and launched on their Personal Device agent platform. An additional asymmetric key pair is generated for the PA, so that it can act on behalf of the user to adapt the environment to his preferences. Having two different key pairs for the user and the PA allows the system to distinguish between automated requests and direct requests from the user, and also allows the system to ask for user confirmation when dealing with sensitive tasks.

8.2.3. User, Device and Agent Authentication. User authentication is performed by means of certificates. Every user can not be supposed to have a personal certificate. Therefore, the building must have its own Building-level Certificate Authority Agent (BCAA) to issue Building-level Certificates (BCs) for any user entering the building. A BC associates the user identity to a public key and to roles (i.e., employee, visitor). Building-level Certificates are used to authenticate users to the Smart Space Coordinator Agents (SSCA) whenever they enter a new space. Each individual space within the building has its own BC, which is used to authenticate system agents and persistent service agents running in the Smart Space Agent Platform. Each SSAP has its own asymmetric key pair and its own associated BC. All system agents and persistent service agents running in the SSAP share this key pair and can use it to authenticate users, personal agents and other SSAPs and to exchange session keys with them as described. Similar assumptions cannot be made regarding the security of other devices in the smart space. As the physical security of light bulbs for example, can not be guaranteed, it is inappropriate to share the SSAP key with these devices and the agents controlling them, so the communication with them is secured using secret key cryptography. Each SSCA shares a secret key with each device in the space which is imprinted on the devices[49]. By means of these keys, it is possible to share symmetric session keys between devices, user and agents. Non-persistent service agents, having mobility features, are not considered secure enough to share the SSAP asymmetric key pair. Taking this into account, the same secure communication schema that this one used for devices is used here too.

8.2.4. Authorization and delegation. Once users, devices and agents are authenticated and can establish secure communications among themselves, a credential-based approach[50] to provide authorization services is used. The basic idea is that users and agents are allowed to perform an action if they can show a valid credential signed by a Smart Space Authorization Agent (SSAA). There is one SSAA for each SSAP, and there can be a SSAA associated to groups of SSAPs to provide a hierarchical tree of authorization agents.

Building-level credentials are usually associated to user roles, defining, for example, which spaces can be accessed by visitors implementing a particular form of RBAC [51]. For users not carrying a personal device with enough resources, or for those users not having a Personal Agent acting on their behalf, the system provides an alternative mechanism where the service agents themselves ask the authorization agents for user credentials. This will be the typical scenario for unknown visitors provided with a smart card to access certain spaces of the building.

Delegation is handled as a particular case of authorization, where the authorisation authority which issues a credential to allow a principal A to perform action X is not an SSAA, but another principal B which is allowed to perform that action.

9. Conclusions

This chapter has provided an overview of trust and security in multi-agent systems. The approaches presented here have been contributed by the groups of the AgentCities.ES Spanish network, and have meant an important step forward in the state of the art of the area. The reputation models presented in this chapter, combined with some strategies like organisational structuring or the use of fuzzy contextual corrective filtering, provide new prospects for trust and reputation applications. In the later sections we have presented some breakthroughs in agent security and how they can be applied in the scenario of smart offices. It is possible now, with the currently existing technology in agent trust and security, to deploy secure agent-based applications that adapt to complex social interactions.

Far from being an already solved problem, security and trust in MAS still have a number of open issues such as agent replay attacks, the protection of open agent itineraries, or improving reputation models for the dynamic adaptation to ever-changing environments. This is a continuously evolving subject, and as time goes by new requirements arise due to other technologies coupling, new application domains, etc. We plan to go on with the research on these topics, especially in the validation of trust models and in the inter-operability of security.

References

[1] C. Sierra and F. Dignum, *Agent-Mediated Electronic Commerce: Scientific and Technological Roadmap* Lecture Notes in Artificial Intelligence **1991**, Springer Verlag (2001), 1–18.

[2] S. Marsh. *Trust in distributed artificial intelligence*, Lecture Notes in Artificial Intelligence **830**, Springer Verlag (1994), 94–112.

[3] G. Zacharia, P. Maes *Trust Management through Reputation Mechanisms* Applied Artificial Intelligence **14** (2000), 881–907.

[4] J. Sabater and C. Sierra *Regret: a reputation model for gregarious societies* Proc. 4th Workshop on Deception, Fraud and Trust in Agent Societies (2001), 61–69.

[5] B. Yu and M. P. Singh *A social mechanism for reputation management in electronic communities.* Lecture Notes in Computer Science **1860** (2000), 154–165.

[6] J. Sabater *Trust and Reputation for agent societies* PhD Thesis, Universitat Autònoma de Barcelona, 2003.

[7] T.D. Huynh, N.R. Jennings and N.R. Shadbolt *An integrated trust and reputation model for open multi-agent systems.* Autonomous Agents and Multi-Agent Systems **13(2)** (2006), 119–154.

[8] S. Sen, A. Biswas and S. Debnath *Believing others: pros and cons* Proc. 4th International Conference on MulitAgent Systems (2000), 279–285.

[9] J. Carbo, J. Garcia and J.M. Molina *Subjective Trust Inferred by Kalman Filtering vs. a Fuzzy Reputation.* Lecture Notes in Computer Science **3289**, Springer-Verlag (2004), 496–505.

[10] J. Carbo, J. Garcia and J. M. Molina *Convergence of agent reputation with Alpha-Beta filtering vs. a fuzzy system,* Intl. Conference on Intelligent Agents, Web Technologies and Internet Commerce (2005).

[11] C. Castellfranchi and R. Falcone *Principles of trust for multi-agent systems: Cognitive anatomy, social importance and quantification* Proc. 3rd Intl. Conference on Multi-Agent Systems (1998), 72–79.

[12] S. Braynov and T. Sandholm *Trust revelation in multi-agent interaction.* Proc. Workshop on The Philosophy and Design of Socially Adept Technologies (2002), 57–60.

[13] J. Carbo, J.M. Molina and J. Davila *Trust management through fuzzy reputation* Int. Journal of Cooperative Information Systems **12**(1) (2003), 135–155.

[14] E. del Acebo and J. L. de la Rosa. *A fuzzy system based approach to social modeling in multi-agent systems.* Proc. 1st International Joint Conference on Autonomous Agents & Multi-Agent Systems (2002), 463–464.

[15] E. del Acebo, N. Hormazábal, and J. L. de la Rosa. *Beyond trust. fuzzy contextual corrective filters for reliability assessment in MAS. application to the art testbed.* Proc. Trust in Agent Societies Workshop. The Seventh International Joint Conference on Autonomous Agents & Multi-agent Systems, (2007)

[16] E. del Acebo, A. Oller, J. L. de la Rosa, and A. Ligeza. *Statistic criteria for fuzzy systems quality evaluation.* IEA/AIE (vol. 2) Lecture Notes in Computer Science vol. **1416**, Springer (1998), 877–887.

[17] K. Fullam, T. Klos, G. Muller, J. Sabater, A. Schlosser, Z. Topol, K. S. Barber, J. Rosenschein, L. Vercouter, and M. Voss. *A Specification of the Agent Reputation and Trust (ART) Testbed: Experimentation and Competition for Trust in Agent Societies.* Proc 4th International Joint Conference on Autonomous Agents and Multi-Agent Systems, ACM Press (2005), 512–518.

[18] J.S.R. Jang, C.T. Sun, and E. Mizutani. *Neuro-Fuzzy and Soft Computing.* MATLAB Curriculum Series. Prentice-Hall, first edition, 1997.

[19] Merriam-Webster. Merriam-webster online dictionary, 2007. http://www.m-w.com/.

[20] R. Hermoso, H. Billhardt, and S. Ossowski. *Integrating trust in virtual organisations.* Proc. Workshop on Coordination, Organization, Institutions and Norms in agent systems (2006), 121–133.

[21] M. Schumacher and S. Ossowski. *The governing environment.* Environments for Multi-Agent Systems II, vol. **3830**, Springer-Verlag (2006), 88–104.

[22] T. Dong Huynh, N. R. Jennings, and N. R. Shadbolt. *FIRE: An integrated trust and reputation model for open multi-agent systems.* Proc. Proceedings of the 16th European Conference on Artificial Intelligence (2004).

[23] S. D. Ramchurn, C. Sierra, L. Godó, and N. R. Jennings. *A computational trust model for multi-agent interactions based on confidence and reputation.* Proc. 6th International Workshop of Deception, Fraud and Trust in Agent Societies (2003), 69–75.

[24] Y. Li, Z. A. Bandar, and D. McLean. *An approach for measuring semantic similarity between words using multiple information sources.* IEEE Transactions on Knowledge and Data Engineering **15(4)** (2003), 871–882

[25] P. Ganesan, H. Garcia-Molina, and J. Widom. *Exploiting hierarchical domain structure to compute similarity.* ACM Trans. Inf. Syst., **21(1)** (2003), 64–93.

[26] A. Abdul-Rahman and S. Hailes. *Supporting trust in virtual communities.* Proc. 33rd Hawaii International Conference on Systems Sciences (2000).

[27] K. Barber and J. Kim. *Belief revision process based on trust: Simulation experiments.* Proc. 4th Workshop on Deception, Fraud and Trust in Agent Societies (2004)

[28] R. Crowder, G. Hughes, and W. Hall. *Approaches to locating expertise using corporate knowledge.* International Journal of Intelligent Systems in Accounting Finance & Management (2002), 185–200.

[29] P. Dillenbourg. *Introduction: What Do You Mean By "Collaborative Learning"?* Collaborative Learning Cognitive and Computational Approaches. Dillenbourg (Ed.). Elsevier Science, 1999.

[30] L. Mui, A. Halberstadt, and M. Mohtashemi. *Notions of reputation in multi-agents systems: A review.* Proc. International Conference on Autonomous Agents and Multi-Agents Systems (2002), 280–287.

[31] S. Wasserman and J. Glaskiewics. *Advances in Social Networks Analysis.* Sage Publications, 1994.

[32] *ART testbed.* http://www.art-testbed.net.

[33] R. Conte and M. Paolucci. *Reputation in artificial societies: Social beliefs for social order.* Kluwer Academic Publishers, 2002.

[34] S. D. Ramchurn, C. Sierra, L. Godo, and N. R. Jennings. *Devising a trust model for multi-agent interactions using confidence and reputation.* Int. J. of Applied Artificial Intelligence, **18** (2004), 833—852.

[35] J. Sabater, M. Paolucci, and R. Conte. *Repage: Reputation and image among limited autonomous partners.* Journal of Artificial Societies and Social Simulation, **9(2)** (2006).

[36] J. Sabater-Mir and M. Paolucci. *On representation and aggregation of social evaluations in computational trust and reputation models.* International Journal of Approximate Reasoning, In press, (2007).

[37] C. Sierra and J. Debenham. *An information-based model for trust.* Proc. 4th Intl Conference on Autonomous Agents and Multi-Agent Systems, ACM Press (2005), 497–504.

[38] C. Sierra and J. Debenham. *Information-based agency.* Proc. 20th Intl Joint Conference on Artificial Intelligence (2007)

[39] W. Jansen and T. Karygiannis. *Mobile Agent Security*, National Institute of Standards and Technology. Special publication **800-19** (2000).

[40] S. M. Chess *Security issues in mobile code systems*. Lecture Notes in Computer Science, vol. **1419**, Springer-Verlag (1998), 1–14.

[41] V. Roth. *On the robustness of some cryptographic protocols for mobile agent protection*. Lecture Notes in Computer Science, vol. **2240** (2001), 1–14.

[42] V. Roth. *Empowering mobile software agents*. Proc. 6th IEEE Mobile Agents Conference, Lecture Notes in Computer Science, vol. **2535**, Spinger-Verlag (2002), 47–63.

[43] S. Robles, J. Mir, and J. Borrell. *Marism-a: An architecture for mobile agents with recursive itinerary and secure migration*. Proc. 2nd. IW on Security of Mobile Multi-Agent Systems (2002).

[44] J. Mir and J. Borrell. *Protecting mobile agent itineraries*. Proc. Mobile Agents for Telecommunication Applications. Lecture Notes in Computer Science, vol. **2881**, Springer-Verlag (2003), 275–285.

[45] P. M. Vieira-Marques, S. Robles, J. Cucurull, R. J. Cruz-Correia, G. Navarro, and R. Martí. *Secure Integration of Distributed Medical Data Using Mobile Agents*. IEEE Intelligent Systems **21(6)** (2006), 47–54.

[46] C. Garrigues, S. Robles, A. Moratalla, and J. Borrell, *Building Secure Mobile Agents using Cryptographic Architectures*. Proc. 2nd European Workshop on Multi-Agent Systems (2004), 243–254.

[47] J. Ametller, S. Robles, and J. A. Ortega, *Self-Protected Mobile Agents*. Proc. of the 3rd Intl Joint Conference on Autonomous Agents and Multi-Agent Systems. IEEE Computer Society (2004), 362–367.

[48] I. Marsá-Maestre. *A hierarchical, agent-based architecture for smart spaces*. Technical Report TR-2005-101, Grupo de Ingeniería de Servicios Telemáticos, http://ist.aut.uah.es (2005).

[49] F. Stajano, R. Anderson. *The resurrecting duckling: security issues for ubiquitous computing*. IEEE Computer **35** (2002), 22–26.

[50] C. Ellison, B. Frantz, B. Lampson, R. Rivest, B. Thomas and T. Ylonen. *SPKI certificate theory*. IETF RFC **2693** (1999).

[51] D. Ferraiolo and D. Kuhn. *Role based access control*. Proc. 15th National Computer Security Conference (1992).

Sergi Robles
Universitat Autònoma de Barcelona
08193 Bellaterra - Spain
e-mail: Sergi.Robles@uab.es

Whitestein Series in Software Agent Technologies, 117–143
© 2007 Birkhäuser Verlag Basel/Switzerland

Physical Agents

Vicente Julián and Carlos Carrascosa

Abstract. This chapter reviews different approaches for the development of new models, architectures and real applications of physical agents. The chapter starts by identifying this kind of agents and their main requirements. After that, it presents one approach to allow deliberation while the world changes, and some specific applications that have been implemented by different participants of the AgentCities.ES network: a multi-agent system architecture to control a single robot, a submarine robot, and a container terminal management system for the port of Valencia.

1. Introduction

Physical agents are agents situated in an environment of real-world, physical objects. This simple definition implies many of constraints and requirements imposed by the physical environment that need not be considered by agents dealing with concepts and ideas. For this reason, physical agents can be considered as an special type of agent with specific individual characteristics. This chapter analyzes physical agents showing some important issues to take into account when developers try to employ agent technology in physical environments. As an example, the development process of this kind of system should include a simulation development prior to the one interacting with the physical world. This simulation development is done to abstract or to forget the peculiarities of this kind of environment in a first step of the development process.

Once a new development is fully tested in simulation, there may exist problems to take it to the real world. It is due, in part, to the peculiarities belonging to the real world environment, that may not be simulated. So, when talking about agents, it may not be the same to work with a simulated robot, as to work with a real robot. Physical agents are developed with the intention to interact with a

---

Co-authors of this chapter: Juan Manuel Corchado, Javier Bajo, Esteve Acebo, Bianca Innocenti, Vicente Botti.

physical world, therefore, the obtained systems are always real applications. Moreover, it is only through working in a real physical environment that one of the main purposes of any research may be carried out, the transference of technology.

The chapter is structured as follows. Section 2 introduces a more specific definition of the term "physical agent", insisting on the particularities and concluding the necessity of appropriate architectures to obtain agency benefits in physical environments. According to the proposed definition, some of the main problems related to this needed physical interaction are detailed in Section 2.1. Section 3 analyzes one of the main issues to overcome, the efficient interaction of complex deliberation processes with physical restrictions. The section also explains a bounded deliberative technique as a solution for this problem. Section 4 presents some experiences in test examples or even transference of technology carried out by AgentCities.ES nodes. The presented experiences cover different application areas. There are two examples applied in mobile robots. The first one presents a generic architecture for an autonomous management of a mobile robot in a complex and dynamic environment. The former is applied in a more specific environment, designing a system to manage an autonomous underwater vehicle. Finally, the last presented system is an industrial application, where a multi-agent system is designed to solve the automatic allocation problem in a container terminal.

2. What are physical agents?

As it has been stated above, physical agents can be defined as agents situated in a physical real world. Some examples of this kind of agents are, for instance, robots as the *aibot* ones in the *Robocup* competition (http://www.robocup.org/), or autonomous unmanned vehicles as in the [45] and NASA missions [33].

From a very abstract perspective, the basic architecture of a physical agent should consist of three components: a set of sensors, a set of effectors, and a cognitive capability which can compute actions in a physical environment from sensor perceptions, probably in a bounded time. More specifically, there must be a module that estimates the current state of the environment (perception), a module of cognition which is in charge of computing the set of actions allowing the agent to reach its goals, and a module of action which acts on the environment. This basic architecture proposed for a physical agent is shown in Figure 1. However, it is necessary for all of these modules to have a bounded worst case execution time, in order to determine whether the system reacts according to its temporal restrictions.

The main problem in this architecture is with the cognition module. This module uses AI techniques as problem-solving methods to compute more *intelligent* actions. In this case, it is difficult to extract the time required by this module because it can either be unbounded or if bounded, its variability is very high. When using AI methods, it is necessary to provide techniques that allow their

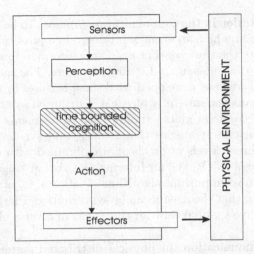

FIGURE 1. General structure for a Physical Intelligent Agent.

response times to be bounded. These techniques are based on RTAIS techniques [20].

With regard to the concept of agent, an agent may have a set of features associated to it. These features add specific differences not available in more classic software systems. When researchers talk about concepts like autonomy, sociability, reactivity, proactivity, etc. they want to provide an agent with its own identity. Some of the most important features of agency are the following capacities: to work autonomously, to adapt to the environment, to reason, to learn, to predict the future effect of the performed actions and to predict the future behavior of the environment. It is obvious that, if a specific software achieves any or all of these features, it is due to an extra effort in its development process. Therefore, even minimal fulfillment significantly complicates the implementation and functionality of an agent. If the agent must operate in a physical environment, the agent construction complexity is increased enormously. Evidently, different environments require different software structures. Therefore, in an agent context, it is necessary to define an appropriate structure in order to use agent features in physical environments.

2.1. Main Problems

The term *physical* applied in the agent or multi-agent area is still in a premature state of development which is why we don't have clear and consolidated definitions. Nevertheless, we can perform a characterization of some requirements of this kind of systems. The requirements that should be met are:

Access to continuous data. A physical agent must have access to a physical real environment where the information is produced in a continuous way, not in a discrete one.

Time representation in the communication process. To be able to reason over the temporal instant at which an event is produced in a physical environment, it is necessary to integrate the time concept inside the information transmitted among the different entities that make up a distributed system. The agent communication language FIPA ACL was not developed with these features in mind.

Global time management. In a physical distributed system it is absolutely necessary to have a common global time for all the elements that make up the system. There are several strategies that manage and synchronize the clocks of each computer. Different levels of precision are obtained with each of them. The Network Time Protocol (NTP) [32] for Internet, or Cristian's algorithm for intranet [15] are some of the most important algorithms. Platform Agents must provide this global time service, so that the agents can be synchronized. Platform agents should also be adapted to have a global time for the agents of diverse platforms that want to interact.

Real-time Communication. In physical distributed systems, it is necessary to be able to assure the communication. This supposes communication protocols with a low and restricted latency (interval between the sending of a message and its reception), as well as fault detection. One example is the CAN protocol [43]. The applications where it is feasible to use the MAS paradigm does not need such strict restrictions for communication. However, there is no doubt about the need for efficient protocols to assure a maximal delivery message time to the developed applications.

Hard resource management. The execution of tasks in this kind of systems is assured, by exercising a strict control on the available resources. There is a planning algorithm that assures the task execution and the coherent use of resources. The agent platforms must implement hard resource management. This is very important, for instance, when facilitating agent mobility among platforms.

Fault tolerant execution. This kind of systems are considered to be predictable. However, it is also indispensable for them to develop fault tolerant systems. This is fundamental since the systems that are controlled are usually critical and a system fall would be catastrophic. A relevant work in this area is [14]. The fault tolerance in MAS must be twofold. First, the execution of the agents must be assured after an internal failure, as well as after a failure in the communication process. Platform agents must be capable of assuring certain requirements in order to offer communication mechanisms and strategies that permit agent execution recovery.

2.2. Related Work

Over the last years, a number of researchers have used agent technology in attempts to resolve the above presented problems, whereas only a few testbeds and real applications have been developed and reported.

Some members of the AgentCities.ES have developed applications of this kind, as will be explained in the next sections. These applications may be classified into two big groups:

- Application of generic architectures to specific problems, as the classical subsumption architecture [8] which is the most widely known robot architecture, the ARCHON platform created for industrial multi-agent systems [24], or the applications of ARTIS agent architecture to mail robots [39, 12], or the application of CIRCA agent architecture to Unmanned Aerial Vehicles (UAVs) under development by the military and deep space probes being developed by NASA [13].
- Ad-hoc developments to solve problems regarding robotics, industrial processes or any related physical environment. In these cases the solutions must deal with concrete problems and their extrapolation to other problems or domains is very difficult. With respect to robotics we can find many works or proposals developed to control a robot, and more specifically a mobile robot. It is difficult to identify a small set of the best or most useful works. We can, howewer, cite in particular the work of Mackenzie [31] where an agent-based method for designing controllers is presented, or the work of Van Breemen [44] which describes a method for modeling complex control problems. On the other hand, for industrial applications, we can recommend the control of a line of production developed by the industrial consortium of Daimler-Chrysler [9] where a flexible and robust system was provided for the control of a production line in a factory. Or the electricity transport management developed by the Spanish company Iberdrola [25] where a process was realized for monitoring and controlling the generation, transport and distribution of electrical energy. Other works of particular note are the General Motors system for control of the air supply in painting vehicle cabins [17] or the air traffic control described in [28]. We can also cite the Spanish system for control of a port container terminal [35] where global management of a terminal is realized, including the control of physical devices such as cranes or transtainers. In following sections this latter work will be explained in more detail.

3. Deliberating while the physical world changes

One of the main problems that needs to be overcome when applying generic agent architectures to physical environments is the efficient integration of high-level, multi-agent planning processes within this kind of architectures. These complex deliberative processes, which allow the agent to adapt and learn, are unbounded and it is difficult to integrate them in physical and restricted systems. Typically, in the multi-agent area these processes are carried out by so-called deliberative agents, which decide what to do and how to do it according to their mental attitudes. In a deliberative agent, it is relatively simple to identify decision processes and choose how to perform them. However, the main drawback in such an agent lies in finding a mechanism that permits its efficient and bounded execution.

Therefore, it would be interesting to integrate complex deliberative processes for decision-making in physical systems in a simple and efficient way.

Intelligent agents may use a lot of reasoning mechanisms. One of them is based on planning techniques [2]. Planning-based agents decide the course of an action before it is realized. Thus, a plan represents the structure of such action. A planning-based agent will execute plans allowing it to reach its goals. To do this, the agent begins from an initial state and tries to get to a final state or set of states. The mechanism used to reach the goals is to apply a set of operators over the objects composing the agent's environment.

3.1. A bounded deliberative technique

In this section, the objective of integration of new bounded deliberative techniques into an agent architecture is pursued. More specifically, this technique is applied to the ARTIS agent architecture [7, 40]. This kind of agent will be able to incorporate a new planning proposal known as CBP-BDI (Case Base Planning-Beliefs Desires Intentions) in order to carry out deliberative planning tasks at the moments where the timing restrictions will not be considered critical. This proposal has been applied to the specific problem of a mail robot whose work is to collect and to deliver mail to people working at a company department. The action of the robot is developed in a restricted and well-known test environment. Moreover, the example has been tested in order to proof the proposal.

The case study consists in solving the automatization of the internal mail management of a department that is physically distributed in a single floor of a building plant. At the department, there is a mail robot in charge of attending sending requests, carried out by a user from a department office through a PDA to send a letter or packet to another office of the same department. In this way, the robot will be in charge of picking up and delivering the external mail received by the department or the mail that is going to be sent to the outside. The robot is going to be controlled by an ARTIS agent. Each ARTIS agent has a reflex server able to plan tasks in real-time and a second level deliberative server in charge of non-critical timing restrictions. The deliberative server will plan the execution of CBP-BDI techniques [29], and it will be in charge of generating optimal plans to pick up and deliver mail at slack time (the spare time once critical time restrictions are satisfied). A CBP-BDI agent uses a case-based reasoning mechanism, thus allowing it to learn from an existing knowledge base; i.e., to autonomously interact with the environment, the users and the rest of the system's agents; and to have a great capability of adapting to the environment's needs. So, case-based reasoning is a suitable technique to implement a planner for the mail robot problem. The CBP-BDI agent generates plans, where a plan is a sequence of pick-up and delivery points. In the same way, the CBP-BDI agent will be available to replan in situations where the robot is unable to fulfil the assigned plans, such as finding obstacles, closed doors, low battery level, or receiving new requests for picking up or sending mail while the robot is executing a plan.

The case study has been implemented in a simulated environment in order to evaluate the proposal. To do this, different experiments have been carried out investigating, basically, the performance of the system and the planning/replanning behaviour. The results have shown the benefits obtained with the integration of the CBP-BDI deliberative behaviour into the ARTIS agent while maintaining the fulfilment of the critical time restrictions. A detailed version of this proposal can be found in [10].

3.1.1. ARTIS Agent: A Hard, Real-Time, Intelligent Agent.
This subsection provides a short description of the ARTIS Agent (AA) architecture, for hard real-time environments (a more detailed description can be found in [7, 39]). The AA architecture could be labelled as a vertical-layered, hybrid architecture with added extensions to work in a hard real-time environment [7].

One of the main features of the AA architecture is its hard real-time behavior. It guarantees the execution of the entire system's specification by means of an off-line analysis of the specification. This analysis is based on well-known predictability analysis techniques in the RTS community, and it is defined in [19].

The off-line analysis only ensures the schedulability of real-time tasks. However, it does not force the task sequence execution. The AA decides the next task to be executed at run-time, allowing it to adapt itself to environment changes, and to take advantage of the tasks using less time than their *wcet* (*worst-case execution time*).

The AA reasoning process can be divided into two stages. The first one is a mandatory time-bounded phase. It obtains an initial result of satisfactory quality. After that, if there is available time left (also called *slack time* in the RTS literature), the AA may use this time for the second reasoning stage. This is an optional stage and it does not guarantee a response. It usually produces a higher quality result through intelligent, utility-based, problem-solving methods. This split reasoning process is described in detail in [7].

ARTIS Agent Architecture The architecture of an AA can be viewed from two different perspectives: the user model (high-level model) [11] and the system model (low-level model) [42]. The user model offers the developer's view of the architecture, while the system model is the execution framework used to construct the final version of the agent.

From the **user model** point of view, the AA architecture is an extension of the blackboard model which is adapted to work in hard real-time environments. It is formed from the following elements:

- A set of **sensors** and **effectors** that interact with the environment. Due to the environment features, the perception and action processes are time-bounded.
- A set of **beliefs** comprising a world model (with all the domain knowledge which is relevant to the agent) and the internal state, that is the mental states of the agent. This set is stored in a frame-based blackboard [5].
- A set of **behaviors** that models the answer of the AA to different situations. It can be said that a *state* (internal along with an environment representation)

defines a *situation* (represented by the current beliefs and goals) which activates a behavior or allows it to go on being active. This behavior determines the agent's current set of *goals and restrictions*, along with the *knowledge* needed to control the situation.

Each one of these behaviors is formed by a set of **in-agents**. The main reason to split the whole problem-solving method is to provide an abstraction which organizes the problem-solving knowledge in a modular and gradual way. (see Figure 2).

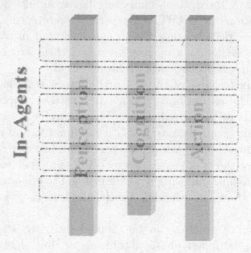

FIGURE 2. Modular division of an AA into in-agents.

Each in-agent periodically performs a specific task. An in-agent is also an agent according to Russell's agent definition [37]. Each in-agent has to solve a particular subproblem, but all the in-agents of a particular AA cooperate to control the entire problem, and an in-agent may use information provided by other in-agents.

In-agents can be classified into critics and acritics. The first ones are in charge of solving essential problems of the AA, so its execution is assured at least for calculating a low-quality answer. The last ones are in charge of solving non-essential problems of the AA to improve its performance quality. A **critic** in-agent is characterized by a period and a deadline. The available time for the in-agent to obtain a valid response is bounded. It must guarantee a basic response to the current environment situation. From a functional point of view, an in-agent consists of two layers: the reflex layer and the real-time deliberative layer. The reflex layer assures a minimal quality response (an offline schedulability analysis of the AA, considering all the in-agents in the AA, guarantees that this reflex layer will be fully executed). On the other hand, the real-time deliberative layer tries to improve this response (this level will be executed in slack time). The reflex layer of all the in-agents make up the AA mandatory phase. On the other hand, the real-time deliberative layers form the optional phase. An **acritic** in-agent only has the real-time deliberative layer.

- A **control module** that is responsible for the real-time execution of the in-agents that belong to the AA. The temporal requirements of the two in-agent layers (reflex and deliberative) are different. Thus, the control module must employ different execution criteria for each one.

  – **Reflex server (RS)** This module is in charge of controlling the execution of reactive components, that is, the components with critical temporal restrictions. Due to these restrictions, it is part of a Real-Time Operating System (RTOS)[1] [42]. It includes the First Level Scheduler (FLS) that must schedule the execution of all the reactive components, in order to guarantee their temporal restrictions. This scheduler is implemented according to a common RTS scheduling policy, a Fixed-Priority, Preemptive Scheduling Policy [4].

    Once the execution of the critical parts is assured, there are slack time intervals between the execution of these critical parts. These slack times (calculated using an algorithm based on the Dynamic Slack Stealing algorithm [16]) can be employed by the second submodule of the control module in order to do different functions, the goal of which is to refine the reactive response and to improve its quality.

    This module carries out the following functions to accomplish its purpose:

    * To schedule the execution of all in-agents with critical temporal restrictions. This process must guarantee the fulfillment of these restrictions.
    * To cede the agent control to the DS during the system idle time.
    * To inform the deliberative server of the execution state of the in-agent reflex part and the time it has available to use. This slack time is calculated just before informing the DS to take into account the tasks using less time than their wcet.

  – **Deliberative server (DS)** This module is in charge of controlling the execution of the deliberative components. Therefore, this server is the intelligent element of the control module, but with soft real-time restrictions.

The **system model** provides a software architecture for the AA that supports all the high level features expressed in the user model. The main features of this model are [19]:

- Off-line schedulability analysis.
- Task Model that guarantees the critical temporal restrictions of the environment.

---

[1]The current version of the AA architecture uses RT-Linux as its RTOS

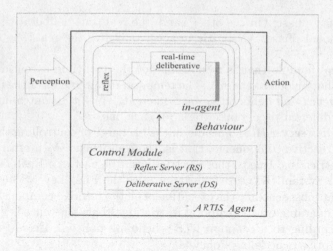

FIGURE 3. ARTIS Agent architecture.

- Slack extraction method to calculate on-line the available time for executing the real-time deliberative layer.
- Set of extensions to the Real-Time Operating System incorporating features for managing real-time capabilities.

3.1.2. Integration of a CBP-based planner in ARTIS. This section shows how a new bounded CBP-based planner technique has been integrated into the ARTIS agent architecture. This planner allows a more efficient execution time management, depending upon the agent's goals. In this system, the planner activates tasks that will fulfil the agent's goals, and these tasks will be performed by real-time schedulers working within the given real-time constraints. CBR-based planner (or CBP) has been included as a sporadic in-agent that will be activated when a new plan needs to be generated for a new goal. Moreover the in-agent will also be activated when replanning because the environment evolution makes it impossible to finish the current plan. The in-agent's initial job is to read the planning or replanning event that activated it. According to this event, it checks if the existing current plan is still feasible. If it is not, it builds a new plan or modifies the existing one. As an option, it tries to improve the new plan. Lastly, the action part of this in-agent begins the plan.

The CBR-based planner provides planning based on previous experiences. CBR systems use memories (past experiences) to solve new problems. The main concept when working with CBR systems is the concept of case. A case is a past experience that can be represented as a 3-tuple $< P, S(P), R >$. Thus, a case is composed of a problem description (initial state), the solution applied to solve the problem (in CBP the solution is a plan or a set of plans, in other words, the sequences of actions executed in order to achieve the objectives) and the result obtained after applying the solution (the final state being an evaluation of the plan executed). The planner needs to maintain a case memory that will be used to solve new problems. When a new problem is presented the planner executes a CBR cycle to solve it. The CBR cycle is composed of four sequential stages: Retrieve, where those cases with the most similar problem description to the current problem are recovered from the cases memory; Reuse, in which the plans (solutions) corresponding to the similar cases retrieved in the previous stage are reused to construct a new plan; Revise, where the proposed plan is evaluated; and Retain, where the planner learns from the new experience. One of the key points in CBR-based planning is the notation used to represent the solution (the plans). A solution can be seen as a sequence of intermediate states in transition from an initial state to the final state. States are usually represented as propositional logic sets. The set of actions can be represented as a set of operators together with an order relationship. Furthermore Carbonell (Carbonell 1986) indicates that additional information is needed on the decisions taken during the plan execution.

A deliberative CBP-BDI agent is specialized in generating plans and incorporates a case-based planning (CBP) reasoning mechanism. The purpose of a CBR agent is to solve new problems by adapting solutions that have been used to solve similar problems in the past [1], and the CBP agents are a variation of the CBR agents, based on the plans generated from each case. An innovative technique that allows replanning during execution time has been incorporated in order to construct an efficient planner. Next, the CBP planner is presented. Let $E = \{e_0, ..., e_n\}$ the set of the possible tasks that have to be completed.

$$a_j : \begin{array}{ccc} E & \rightarrow & E \\ e_i & \rightarrow & a_j(e_i)=e_j \end{array} \quad . \tag{1}$$

An Agent plan is the name given to a sequence of actions (1) that, from a current state e_0, defines the path of states through which the agent passes in order to offer a better path according to the initial problem description. Below, in (2), the dynamic relationship between the behaviour of the agent and changes in the environment is modelled. The behaviour of agent A can be represented by its action function $a_A(t)$ $\forall t$, defined as a correspondence between one moment in time t and the action selected by the agent,

$$Agent\ A = \{a_A(t)\}_{t \in T \subseteq N}. \tag{2}$$

From the definition of the action function $a_A(t)$ a new relationship that collects the idea of an agent's action plan (3) can be defined,

$$p_A(t_n) = \int_{t_0}^{t_n} a_A(t)dt.$$

(3)

The variation of the agent plan $p_A(t)$ will be provoked essentially by: the changes that occur in the environment and that force the initial plan to be modified, and the knowledge from the success and failure of the plans that were used in the past, and which are favoured or discarded. O indicates the objectives of the agent and O' the results achieved by the plan. R represents the total resources and R' are the resources consumed by the agent. The efficiency of the plan (4) is the relationship between the objectives attained and the resources consumed

$$E_{ff} = \frac{\#(O' \cap O)}{\#R'},$$

(4)

Where $\#$ means cardinal of a set. The objective is to introduce an architecture for a planning agent that behaves and selects its actions by considering the possibility that the changes in the environment block the plans in progress. This agent is called MRPI (most re-planable Intention agent) because it continually searches for the plan that can most easily be re-planned in the event of interruption. Given an initial point $e0$, the term planning problem is used to describe the search for a way of reaching a final point $e_i = e* \in E$ that meets a series of requirements. Given a problem E and a plan $p(t)$, the functions Ob and Rc accumulated are constructed from the objectives and costs of the plan (5). For all time points ti two variables are associated:

$$Ob(t_i) = \int_a^{t_i} O(t)dt \quad Rc(t_i) = \int_a^{t_i} R(t)dt.$$

(5)

This allows us to construct a space representing the environment for planning problems as a vectorial hyper-dimensional space where each axis represents the accumulative variable associated with each objective and resource. In the planning space, defined in this way, conform to the following properties:

1. Property 1: The representations of the plans within the planning space are always monotonously growing functions. Given that $Ob(t)$ and $Rc(t)$ are functions defined as positive, function $p(t)$ expressed at these coordinates is constant or growing.
2. Property 2: In the planning space, the straight lines represent plans of constant efficiency. If the representations of the plans are straight lines, the slope of the function is constant, and coincides with the definition of the efficiency of the plan. $\frac{d}{dt}p(t) = constant \Leftrightarrow \lim_{\Delta \to 0} \frac{\Delta O(t)}{\Delta R(t)} = constant.$

In an n-dimensional space, the extension of the straight concept line is called a geodesic curve. In this sense, the notion of geodesic plans can be introduced, defined as those that maintain efficiency at a constant throughout their development.

This way, only plans of constant efficiency (geodesic plans) are considered, due to the fact that they are the ones of minimum risk. In an environment that changes unpredictably, to consider any plan that is different from the geodesic plan means to accept a certain risk. The agent must search for a plan that determines a solution with a series of restrictions $F(O;R)=0$. The alternative plans sought are those that are initially compatible with the problem faced by the agent, with the requirements imposed on the solution according to the desires, and in the current state. If all the possible plans $\{p_1, ..., p_n\}$ are represented within the planning space, a subset of states that the agent has already created in the past will be obtained in order to resolve similar problems. With the mesh of points obtained (generally irregular) within the planning space and using interpolation techniques, we can obtain the working hyperplan $h(x)$ (that encapsulates the information on the set of restrictions from restored experiences, by definition leading to a hyperplan since it verifies $h(x_j) = p_j j = 1, ..., n$ and the planning space is the dimension n). From this, geodesic plans can be calculated and the variation calculation is applied. Suppose, for simplicity's sake, a planning space of dimension 3 with coordinates $\{O, R1, R2\}$. Between point $e0$ and objective points $f_s f = \{e1, ..., em\}$ and over the interpolation surface $h(x)$, the Euler Theorem [30] [26] guarantees that the expression of the geodesic plans will be obtained by resolving the system of equations in (6), where R_i is the function accumulated R, O is the function of accumulated O and L is the distance function on the hyperplan $h(x)$, $L = \int_h dl$.

In order to obtain all the geodesic plans that, on the surface $h(x)$ and beginning at $e0$, allows us to reach any of the points $e* \in (f_s f)$, a condition of the surrounding must be imposed: the initial point will be $e_0 = (O_0, R_0)$. Once an efficient plan is developed, the plans around it (along its trajectory) are used to create a denser distribution of geodesic plans. The tool that allows us to determine this is called the minimum Jacobi field associated with the solution set [27]. Let $g_0 : [0, 1] \rightarrow S$ be a geodesic over a surface S. Let $h : [0, 1]x[-\varepsilon, \varepsilon] \rightarrow S$ be a variation of $g0$ so that for each $t \in (-\varepsilon, \varepsilon)$, the set $\{ht(s)\}t \in (-\varepsilon, \varepsilon)$: $ht(s)$ for all $t \in (-\varepsilon, \varepsilon)$ are geodesic in S and they begin at $g_0(0)$; in other words, they conform to $h_t(0) = g_0(0)$ for all $t \in (-\varepsilon, \varepsilon)$. In these conditions, taking the variations to a differential limit (7),

$$\begin{cases} \frac{\partial L}{\partial R_1} - \frac{d}{dO}\frac{\partial L}{\partial R_1'} = 0, \\ \frac{\partial L}{\partial R_2} - \frac{d}{dO}\frac{\partial L}{\partial R_2'} = 0. \end{cases}$$

(6)

$$\lim_{t \to 0}\{h_t(s) = g_0(s + t)\} = \lim_{t \to 0}\{h(s,t)\} =$$
$$\frac{\partial g_0}{\partial t}\Big|_{(s,0)} = \frac{dg_0}{ds} \equiv J_{g_0}(s).$$

(7)

The term $Jg_0(s)$ is given to the Jacobi field of the geodesic g_0 for the set $\{gn(x)\}n \in N$, and in the same way that the definition has been constructed, it is possible to give a measurement for the distribution of the other geodesics of

$\{gn(x)\}n \in N$ around g_0 throughout the trajectory. Given a set of geodesics, some of them are always $g*$ that, in their environment, have a greater distribution than other geodesics in a neighbouring environment. This is equivalent to saying that it presents a variation in the distribution of geodesics lower than the others and therefore the Jacobi field associated with $\{ gn(x) \}$ $n^a N$ reaches its lowest value at J_g*. Let's return to the MRPI agent problem that, following the recuperation and variation calculation phase, contains a set of geodesic plans $\{ p1,...,pn \}$. If the $p*$ is selected with a minimum Jacobi field value, it can be guaranteed that in the event of interruption it will have around it a greater number of geodesic plans in order to continue. This suggests that given a problem with certain restrictions $F(O;R)=0$, the geodesic plan $p*$ with minimum associated Jacobi field associated with the set $\{gn(x)\}n \in N$ is called the most re-plan-able solution. The behaviour model G for the MRPI agent is (8).

$$G(e_0, p_1, \ldots, p_n) = p* \Leftrightarrow \exists n \in N / J_{g_n}$$
$$\equiv J_{g*} = \underset{n \in N}{Min} \, J_{g_n} \tag{8}$$

If the plan $p*$ is not interrupted, the agent will reach a desired state $ej = e* \in fsf, j \in \{1, \ldots, m\}$. In the learning phase, a weighting $wf(p)$ is stored. With the updating of weighting $wf(p*)$, the planning cycle of the CBP motor is completed. In Figure 4, it is possible to see what happens if $p*$ is interrupted. Let's suppose that the agent has initiated a plan $p*$ but at a moment $t > t0$, the plan is interrupted due to a change in the environment. The geodesic planning meets the conditions of the Bellman Principle of Optimality [6]; in other words, each one of the plan's parts is partially geodesic between the selected points. This guarantees that if $g0$ is geodesic for interrupted $e0$ in $t1$, because $e0$ changes to $e1$, and $g1$ is geodesic to $e1$ that is begun in the state where $g0$ has been interrupted, it follows that: $g = g0 + g1$ is geodesic to $e = e0 \, (t1 - t0) + e1 \, (t2 - t1)$

The dynamic process follows the CBP cycle recurrently: each time a plan finds itself interrupted, it generates from the state reached so far, the surroundings of the plans from the case base and adjusts them to the new problem. With this it calculates the geodesic plans and selects the one which meets the minimum conditions of the associated Jacobi field. A minimum global Jacobi field J(t) also meets Bellman's conditions of optimality [6]; in other words, a minimum global Jacobi field, must select minimum Jacobi fields "in pieces" (9).

$$J_{\min}(t) = \{J_{\min}(t_1 - t_0), J_{\min}(t_2 - t_1), \ldots,$$
$$J_{\min}(t_n - t_{n-1})\}. \tag{9}$$

If on the one hand, successive Jacobi fields generate one Jacobi field, and on the other hand, minimum Jacobi fields generate a minimum Jacobi field, the MRPI agent that follows a strategy of replanning $G(t)$ as indicated to survive a dynamic environment, generates a global plan $p*(t)$ that, faced with all possible global plans $\{pn(t)\}n \in N$, presents a minimum value in its Jacobi field $J_g * (t) = J_p * (t)$. An

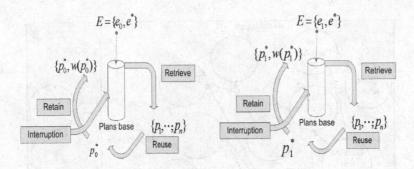

FIGURE 4. Model for behaviour G(t).

agent has been formally defined that in a dynamic environment seeks plans that lend it greater capacity for replanning.

4. Applications

This section illustrates the above concepts with three applications. The first one, a grill robot developed by Universitat de Girona, describes a multi-agent architecture developed to control a single robot (along with an ad-hoc FIPA compliant platform). The second application, also by Universitat de Girona, shows the submarine robot designed to participate in an international competition. Finally, Universidad Politécnica de Valencia presents an industrial application, with hard real-time constraints, that is, a multi-agent system for solving the automatic allocation problem in a container terminal.

4.1. The Grill robot. A multi-agent control architecture

One of the current challenges of robotics is to make completely autonomous robots capable of modifying their performance in complex and changing environments. So, distributed control systems should be used to develop the robot control architecture, in order to provide mechanisms to distribute, coordinate, adapt and extend the control system of the robots. On the other hand, robots require high-level cognitive capacities, and multi-agent architectures provide the appropriate way to define them. Merging both research lines, distributed control and multi-agent systems, a multi-agent architecture to control a single robot, an ActivMedia Pioneer 2DX mobile robot has been developed by the EXIT Research Group at the Universitat de Girona [21].

In order to implement the multi-agent control architecture, an ad-hoc multi-agent platform has been built to deal with real-time issues. This platform follows the FIPA (the Foundation for Intelligent Physical Agents) standards [18], but avoids some communication overheads, a key issue in robotics when a real-time response is expected.

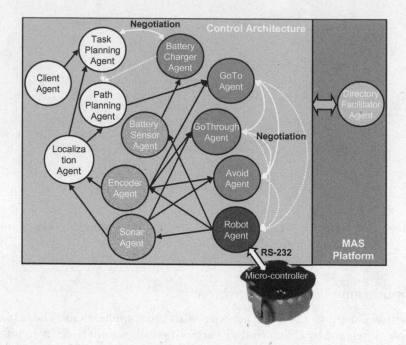

FIGURE 5. MAS Architecture.

In Figure 5,the agents of the MAS architecture are shown, as well as some platform specific agents and the information flow among them. Agents of the Control Architecture can be grouped in perception, behavioral, deliberative and actuator agents. Solid lines among agents means that there are no restrictions in message passing, while dotted lines indicate that only one agent at a time can send the message (after coordination). White solid lines denote conflicting agents.

Perception agents obtain information about the environment and about the internal conditions of the robot, as they collect data from the sensors and transform it to provide the suitable information to other agents. There are as many perception agents as there are sensors or groups of them in the robot. Particularly for the available robot the perception agents are the following:

- **The encoder agent** that is in charge of obtaining the position and heading of the robot with reference to a fixed frame.
- **The sonar agent** which collects all the sonar readings and creates a local map of obstacles.
- **The battery sensor agent** which monitors the battery charging in order to prevent permanent damage.

Behavioral agents carry out specific actions, such as avoiding obstacles. There are as many agents as necessary to describe the behavior of the robot. Based on the information received from perception agents, they react to changes in the environment and in the robot itself. Particularly, behavioral agents are the following:

- **The goto agent** that is in charge of driving the robot to the target position, based on the information provided by the encoder agent.
- **The avoid agent** that must go around obstacles found in the path of the robot.
- **The battery charger agent** that asks for replanning when the battery is going under a threshold in order to guide the robot to the recharging area.
- **The gothrough agent** that is in charge of going through narrow places like doors, based on the information received from the sonar and the localization agents.

Deliberative agents implement high-level complex tasks as for example, planning. These agents are the following:

- **The localization agent** that must localize the robot in the global map.
- **The path planning agent** that calculates the trajectory to the goal, free of non-moving obstacles.
- **The task planning agent** that plans the sequence of tasks to perform in order to reach the goal.
- **The client agent** which interacts with the user.

Actuator agents are in charge of controlling the linear and angular speed of the robot interacting directly with motors. There is an actuator agent per each possible actuator. Particularly only one agent is needed because of the limitations of the Pioneer 2DX operating system. This agent is:

- **The robot agent** which communicates, each 100 ms, with the robot microcontroller and gets the actual position and sonar readings and sends the desired linear and angular speeds to the onboard controllers. The role of the actuator agent has been reduced to a mere interface between the robot and the whole architecture, due to the robot constraints mentioned above.

Platform agents: They implement the basic services that have to be in the platform in order to guarantee the correct functioning of the community of agents. Particularly, there is only one agent that provides several basic services. This agent is:

- **The directory facilitator agent (DFA):** knows which agents are active in the community, their location in the net, the services they provide and the resources they need. It also informs the agents when a new one joins the community, the resources it uses and the services it provides.

As can be seen in Figure 5, there are several agents trying to use the same resource at a given time, so some coordination is necessary. For example, conflicts can arise among the avoid, the goto and the gothrough agents when trying to send conflicting actions to the robot agent and between the battery charger and the task planning agents when demanding a trajectory to the path planning agent.

One solution to this problem is to define a central coordinator agent which, having knowledge of the agents in conflicts imposes one decision. However, we believe that such centralized coordination mechanism can be a bottleneck when dealing with architectures with a lot of agents. Conversely, we think that conflicts are local and a distributed coordination approach can be more appropriate. Particularly, a peer-to-peer coordination mechanism among the agents involved in one conflict is proposed. Coordination process is carried out locally based on utilities values computed by the agents in conflict.

All the agents in the architecture have their own utility function, known only by themselves, but all normalized between [0,1] (they are comparable). Agents that can have conflicting decisions exchange their utility value. In case of conflict, the agent who has a higher value of utility wins the decision. This agent gets the control of the conflicting activity. For example, suppose that the goto agent has a utility value of 0.5, the gothrough agent of 0.3 and the avoid agent of 0.7; being 0.7 the higher value, the avoid agent takes the control of the situation, and it is the only one that sends messages to the robot agent (see [22, 23]).

In order to reduce communication among agents, the last agent who has had the control broadcasts its utility value. If there is no response, meaning that it has the higher value, the agent uses the resource. On the other hand, if there is an agent with a higher utility value, then it informs all the agents with its utility value, indicating that the agent is going to use the resource. In this way, communication process is reduced and centralization of coordination is avoided.

4.2. The $ICTINEU^{AUV}$ submarine robot

¿From 1990, the Association for Unmanned Vehicle System International (AUVSI) has promoted the design and development skills of Autonomous Underwater Vehicles (AUV) by means of an annual competition. Inspired by this competition, the Defence Science and Technology Lab (DSTL), the Heriot Watt University and the National Oceanographic Centre of Southampton organized the first Student Autonomous Underwater Challenge Europe (SAUC-E) [38]. In January 2006, a team of students collaborating with the Underwater Robotics Lab of the University of Girona decided to form the VICOROB-UdG Team [41] to face the challenge by designing its own submarine robot, $ICTINEU^{AUV}$.

4.2.1. Design. The SAUC-E [38] mission takes place in a small space in which a high maneuverability is required. In this situation a hover-type vehicle propelled and steered by thrusters is the most desirable configuration. A classical open frame design, together with a modular design of the components conveniently housed in pressure vessels, has been considered [36] the simplest and most reliable approach for the physical design of the $ICTINEU^{AUV}$ robot. The robot is propelled by four thrusters that make it a fully actuated vehicle in four degrees of freedom: surge, sway, heave and yaw, while being passively stable in roll and pitch as its meta-center is above the center of gravity. The robot chassis is made of Delrin material. Three pressure vessels are used for holding the electronics. One of them houses the computers, another the thruster controllers and the batteries, and the last encapsulates the Motion Reference Unit (MRU).

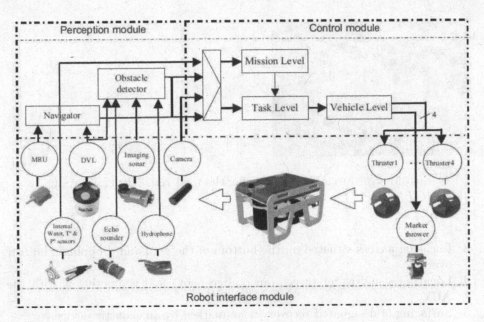

FIGURE 6. $ICTINEU^{AUV}$ software architecture.

The robot uses two PCs, one for control and one for image and sonar processing. It is also equipped with a complete sensor suite composed of a forward-looking color camera, a downward looking b&w camera, an imaging sonar, an echo sounder, a transducer for acoustic device detection and an Argonaut Doppler Velocity Log which also includes a compass/tilt sensor.

The software architecture of the robot can be seen in Figure 6. There are three main modules: robot interface module, perception module and control module. Following the principles of hybrid control architectures, the control module is organized in three layers: vehicle level, task level and mission level. The vehicle level controls the speed of the robot; the task level is a conventional behavioral layer [3] including a library of behaviors that can run alone or in parallel. During the execution of a mission, more than one behavior can be enabled simultaneously; hence, a coordinator module is used to fuse all the responses corresponding to the enabled behaviors into a single response to be sent to the velocity controller (vehicle level). Finally, the upper layer (mission level) is responsible for the sequencing of the mission tasks, selecting for each mission phase the set of behaviors that must be enabled as well as their parameters.

4.2.2. The SAUC-E Competition. The SAUC-E competition takes place in a water tank environment of 20 meters by 10 meters and a depth of 6 meters. The mission consists of (see the left side of Figure 7 for a graphical representation):

1. Moving from a launch/release point and submerging.
2. Passing through a 3x4 meter validation gate.

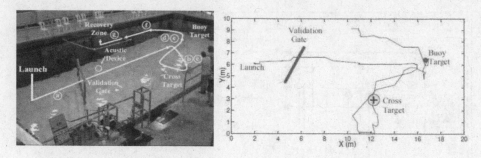

FIGURE 7. LEFT: The mission for the final run. RIGHT: Plot of $ICTINEU^{AUV}$'s trajectory

3. Locating a cross situated on the bottom of the pool and dropping a marker over it.
4. Locating a mid-water target (an orange buoy) and contacting it with the AUV.
5. Surfacing at designated recovery zone marked by an acoustic device.

The mission starts facing the validation gate. We can see in the right side of Figure 7 the trajectory made by $ICTINEU^{AUV}$ during the final run of the competition. This plot has been obtained by the localization data logged in the vehicle during the mission. As can be seen, the result is similar to what we can expect from the mission planning. First, the vehicle went through the validation gate (until it detected the far end of the water tank) with only minor perturbations in the heading. Next, the vehicle started the search procedure for the bottom target. At the first sight of the target, $ICTINEU^{AUV}$ released one marker at 56 cm from the center. Unfortunately, while the vehicle was trying to make a second shot, it got stuck near a wall because of the peculiarities of the competition environment. The zone boundary between the black walls and the white bottom of the tank caused the vision algorithm to get confused. After the timeout expired, the vehicle proceeded with the mission going to the next waypoint. When $ICTINEU^{AUV}$ found the buoy, it was too close. This made it harder to aim at the target. As a result, the vehicle missed the target by just a few millimeters. Finally, the vehicle moved to the recovery zone to end the mission. $ICTINEU^{AUV}$ proved its capability to undertake a preprogrammed mission. It did two tasks and almost completed the other two, being the only entry of the competition able to link all the tasks. This performance gave the final victory to the VICOROB-UdG team.

4.3. An industrial application: A Port Container Terminal

A multi-agent system for solving the automatic allocation problem in a container terminal is presented in this section. This proposal has been developed by the Universidad Politécnica de Valencia. This section only presents a brief explanation of the proposal. A more detailed explanation can be found at [35] and [34]. The operations carried out in this terminal are included in the most complex tasks of the transport industry. This is due to:

- The great diversity of entities acting in the container import and export processes.
- Interaction with a dynamic environment.
- The distributed nature of the problem which is formed by a set of independent systems, but whose individual decisions directly affect the performance of the others.

The traditional centralised and sequential applications for Container Terminal Management are being found to be insufficiently flexible to respond to changing management styles and highly dynamic variations in loading/unloading requirements. With the traditional centralised approaches to management and control, the entire terminal is generally controlled by central software, which limits the expandability and reconfiguration capabilities of the systems. Using hierarchical organization forces the grouping of resources into permanent, tightly coupled subgroups, where information is processed sequentially by a centralised software supervisor. This may result in much of the system being shut down by a single point of failure, as well as plan fragility and increased response overheads. The multi-agent system model seems to be an adequate framework to overcome such problems and for dealing with the design and development of an application which is flexible, adaptable to the environment, versatile and robust enough for the efficient management of a container terminal. It is very important for the turn-around time of a cargo ship which is in port container terminals to be as short as possible. An average cargo liner spends 60% of its time in port and has a cost on the order of U.S. $1000 for each hour it spends in port. The whole container allocation process must be directed towards minimising the containership stowage time. This is the main objective of the optimisation of the global performance allocation process.

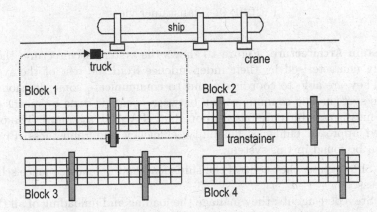

FIGURE 8. General view of a port container terminal.

4.3.1. Problem Description. The traditional solutions to Container Terminal Management are addressed by means of a modular decomposition of the problem into several sub-problems, each one representing a specialized aspect of it. The set of operations to be conducted in the terminal is very extensive, but the existing approaches share some common systems:

- Marine Side Interface. This system focuses on loading/unloading containers to/from ships. Normally two or three gantry cranes (GC) are used to move containers for each ship.
- Transfer System. It transfers containers from/to the apron to/from the container storage yard. The method used in the terminal is to employ yard trucks (YT) to make the transports. Transtainers are used to pick up or to put down a container on the storage area of the yard (Figure 8).
- Container Storage System. Its purpose is to allocate and to control the containers in the yard (Figure 9).
- Land Side Interface. It focuses on handling the interactions with the land transportation modes.

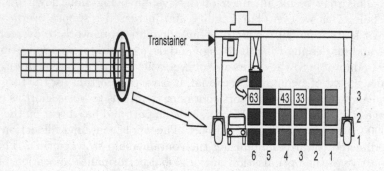

FIGURE 9. Transtainer view.

4.3.2. System Architecture. Figure 10 shows the system architecture; the agents are mainly characterised by their independence from the rest of the system elements. They are able to coordinate and to communicate some decisions to the rest of the system. The communication between agents is done by means of asynchronous messages, which are based upon the FIPA-ACL standard. The proposed distributed approach enhances flexibility, efficiency and robustness. Five agent classes can be found in this system:

- The Ship agents: they control the ships load and unload sequence scheduling process.
- The Stevedore agents: they manage the loading and unloading of all the ships docking in the port.
- The Service agents: they distribute the containers in the port terminal.
- The Transtainer agents: they optimise the use of these machines.

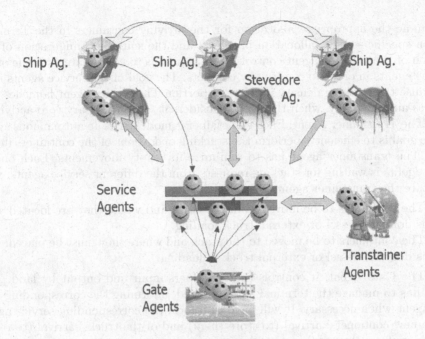

FIGURE 10. System Architecture.

- The Gate agents: they interact with the land transport (I/O of containers by land).

4.3.3. Agent Description. This section presents the above commented agents which forms the multi-agent approach:

The Ship Agent: In response to the arrival of a ship the system will create a new Ship agent instance for this ship and its load profile. Its goals are: to minimize the gantry crane idle time, to maximize its utilization, to minimize the ships load/unload time, and to minimize the derived costs from the stowage process. This work is closely related to the Stevedore agents involved, with which the Ship agent will have to co-ordinate. The different Ship agents active at any given moment must co-ordinate with each other as a whole to minimise the possible blockages between the assigned cranes. The goal of this minimisation is to maximise the active time of all the cranes and to reduce the load/unload time of each ship.

The Stevedore Agent: When a gantry crane is active loading or unloading containers from a specific ship, the Stevedore agent will try to obtain the most appropiate scheduling to manage the container stowage in the ships load/unload sequences. To develop these goals, the agent is co-ordinated with the rest of the active Ship agents and the suitable Service agents.

The Service Agent: The Terminal has been divided into services. Each service has assigned some specific stacking ranges. The main goal of a service agent is to determine the appropriate allocation for the arriving containers in the Terminal from a specific service (allocation problem) and the suitable configuration of the portion of the yard the agent controls. The agent has to coordinate with the other service agents in order to resolve any conflicts. The goal of the service agents is to maximise the stacking density in its yard portion The service agent launches this process automatically, when the agent considers it to be necessary (pro-activity).

The Transtainer Agent: Each transtainer is modelled as an autonomous agent whose goal is to efficiently perform the stacking operations of the containers in the yard. The transtainer agent has to minimize its empty movements. Each one of these agents is waiting for stacking requests from the different service agents, who facilitate the transtainer agent with:

- The containers to be moved from the stack and where they are located: this is done for vessel or external truck loading.
- The containers to be moved to the stack and where they must be placed: this is done for vessel or external truck unloading.

The Gate Agent: it controls the containers input and output by land. The agent has to manage the terminal gate assigned, informing the corresponding service agent when necessary. It will have to inform the corresponding service agent of the new containers' arrival (to store them) and of the trucks' arrival (to retire containers from the yard).

This section has presented a multi-agent system architecture for the automatic allocation problem in a port container terminal . Apart from the benefits obtained from a multi-agent approach, the independence which is obtained in all of the presented subsystems must be pointed out. This architecture provides a maintenance of the necessary co-operation in order to minimize the time the ships are in the container terminal. A first version of the system is currently implemented, which models the container terminal function of a real port. This prototype has been integrated with a yard simulator developed at the same time.

5. Conclusions

A physical agent is an agent with some peculiarities that have been analyzed along this chapter. Some of them are the need for a previous simulation in the development process, a direct interaction with physical devices, and other problems like access to continuous data, real-time communication, or hard resource management. This chapter has analyzed in detail how we can achieve high-level multi-agent planning processes with physical agents taking into account related restrictions as, for instance, the time. Specifically, a bounded deliberative technique has been presented. This technique introduces a Case Base Planning proposal into a specific agent architecture for this kind of environment, the ARTIS agent architecture. The proposal has been tested with significant benefits. Moreover, nowadays some interesting advances have been made when applying agent technology to control physical processes. Physical agents allow better performance and coordination of autonomous robots in complex and changing environments. It favours the design and development of complex missions in very restricted environments, like the ocean. And, it can be considered a good abstraction to be employed in the development of industrial applications which include the interaction between physical devices.

Finally, it is important to underline that only through working in a real physical environment may be carried out one of the main purposes of any research, the transference of technology.

References

[1] Aamodt A. and Plaza E. Case-based reasoning: foundational issues, methodological variations, and system approaches. *AICOM*, 7:39–59, 1994.

[2] Martens A. and Uhrmacher A.M. Adaptative tutoring processes and mental plans. *In Proceedings of Intelligent Tutoring Systems-ITS 2002, Cerri S.A., Gouardères G. and Paraguaçu F. (Eds). Springer*, pages 71–80, 2002.

[3] R. C. Arkin. *Behavior-Based Robotics*. MIT Press, 1998.

[4] N.C. Audsley, A. Burns, Davis R.I, Tindell K.W., and A.J. Wellings. Fixed priority pre-emptive scheduling: An historical perspective. *Real-Time Systems*, 8:173–198, 1995.

[5] F. Barber, V. Botti, E. Onaindía, and A. Crespo. Temporal reasoning in reakt: An environment for real-time knowledge-based systems. *AICOMM*, 7(3):175–202, 1994.

[6] R.E. Bellman. Dynamic programming. *Princeton University Press*, 1957.

[7] V. Botti, C. Carrascosa, V. Julian, and J. Soler. Modelling agents in hard real-time environments. *Proc. of the MAAMAW'99. LNCS, vol. 1647*, pages 63–76, 1999.

[8] R.A. Brooks. A robust layered control system for a mobile robot. In *IEEE Journal of Robotics and Automation*, 1986.

[9] S. Bussmann and K. Schild. Self-organising manufacturing control: an industrial application of agent technology. *Proc. 4th international Conference Multi-Agent Systems, Boston*, pages 87–94, 2000.

[10] C. Carrascosa, J. Bajo, V. Julian, J.M. Corchado, and V. Botti. Hybrid multi-agent architecture as a real-time problem-solving model. *Expert Systems With Applications*, 34, 2007.

[11] C. Carrascosa, A. Terrasa, A. García-Fornes, A. Espinosa, and V. Botti. A meta-reasoning model for hard real-time agents. *Selected Papers from the 11th Conference of the Spanish Association for Artificial Intelligence (CAEPIA 2005)*, 4177:42–51, 2006.

[12] Javier Palanca Cámara, Gustavo Aranda Bada, Carlos Carrascosa Casamayor, and Luis Hernández López. Hybrid mas to solve problems with different temporal constraints. In *New Trends in Real-Time Artificial Intelligence (NTeRTAIn 2006 / ECAI 2006)*, pages 19–28, 2006.

[13] Darren Cofer, Eric Engstrom, Robert Goldman, David Musliner, and Steve Vestal. Applications of model checking at honeywell laboratories. In *Lecture Notes in Computer Science, Vol. 2057*, pages 296–303. Springer-Verlag, 2001.

[14] F. Cristian. Understanding fault-tolerant distributed systems. In *Comm. ACM*, pages 57–78, 1991.

[15] F. Cristian and C. Fetzer. Probabilistic internal clock synchronization. In *Proc. of 12th Symposium on Reliable Distributed Systems. IEEE Computer Society Press*, pages 22–31, 1994.

[16] R.I. Davis, K.W. Tindell, and A. Burns. Scheduling slack time in fixed priority preemptive systems. In *Proc. R-T Systems Symposium, North Carolina*, pages 222–231. IEEE Comp. Society Press, 1993.

[17] G. Ekberg. Benefits of autonomous agent approach to manufacturing systems control. *Proc. of Third Annual Chaos East Technical Conference*, 1997.

[18] FIPA Foundation for Intelligent Physical Agents. http://www.fipa.org. *FIPA Abstract Architecture Specification*, 2002.

[19] A. Garcia-Fornes, A. Terrasa, V. Botti, and A. Crespo. Analyzing the schedulability of hard real-time artificial intelligence systems. *EAAI*, pages 369–377, 1997.

[20] A. Garvey and V. Lesser. A survey of research in deliberative real-time artificial intelligence. *The Journal of Real-Time Systems*, 6:317–347, 1994.

[21] B. Innocenti, López. B., and J. Salvi. How MAS support distributed robot control. *37th International Symposium on Robotics, ISR'06 ISBN.3-18-091956-6.*, 2006.

[22] B. Innocenti, B. López, and J. Salvi. A multi-agent collaborative control architecture with fuzzy adjustment for a mobile robot. *Proceedings of Third International Conference on Informatics in Control, Automation and Robotics. ISBN.972-8865-60-0.*, pages 523–526, 2006.

[23] B. Innocenti, B. López, and J. Salvi. A multi-agent system with distributed coordination for controlling a single robot. *7th Portuguese Conference on Automatic Control (CONTROLO), CDROM: Article 126*, 2006.

[24] N.R. Jennings, J.M. Corera, and I. Laresgoiti. Developing industrial multi-agent systems. In *First International Conference on Multi-agent Systems, ICMAS-95*, pages 423–430, 1995.

[25] N.R. Jennings, E. Mamdani, J. Corera, I. Laregoiti, F. Perriolat, P. Skarek, and L.Z. Varga. Using archon to develop real-world dai applications. *IEEE Expert*, 11:64–70, 1996.

[26] J. Jost and X. Li-Jost. Calculus of variations. *Cambridge University Press*, 1998.

[27] J.M. Lee. Riemannian manifolds. an introduction to curvature. *Springer-Verlag, New York, Inc*, 1997.

[28] A. Lucas. Decision support systems for arrivals flow management. *ATCA International Technical Conference, Prague*, 1997.

[29] Corchado J. M. and Laza R. Constructing deliberative agents with case-based reasoning technology. *International Journal of Intelligent Systems.*, 18:1227–1241, 2003.

[30] Glez-Bedia M. and Corchado J. M. A planning strategy based on variational calculus for deliberative agents. *Computing and Information Systems Journal*, 10:2–14, 2002.

[31] D. Mackenzie. A design methodology for the configuration of behavior-based mobile robotics. In *PhD Dissertation. University of Georgia Institute of Technology*, 1996.

[32] D. Mills. Improved algorithms for synchronizing computer network clocks. In *IEEE Transactions Networks*, pages 245–254, 1995.

[33] Kanna Rajan. Autonomy from the ground up bridging the gap between theory and practice for nasa missions. In *VI Workshop de Agentes Físicos (WAF 2005) - Invited Speech*, pages 3–5. CEDI 2005, 2005.

[34] M. Rebollo, V. Julian, C. Carrascosa, and V. Botti. A mas approach for port container terminal management. In *Proceedings of the 3rd Iberoamerican Workshop on DAI - MAS*, pages 83–94, 2000.

[35] M. Rebollo, V. Julián, C. Carrascosa, and V. Botti. A multi-agent system for the automation of a port container terminal. *Proc. of Agents in Industry Workshop, Autonomous Agents, Barcelona*, 2000.

[36] D. Ribas, N. Palomeras, E. Hernandez, P. Ridao, and M. Carreras. $ICTINEU^{AUV}$ wins the first SAUC-E competition. Scheduled for presentation during the Regular Sessions "Field Robotics: Systems and Applications" (WeA5). 2007 IEEE International Conference on Robotics and Automation, 10-14 April, 2007, Rome, Italy.

[37] S. Russell and P. Norvig. *Artificial Intelligence: A Modern Approach*. Prentice Hall International Editions, 1995.

[38] SAUC-E. Available at http://www.dstl.gov.uk/news events/competitions/sauce/.

[39] J. Soler, V. Julian, C. Carrascosa, and V. Botti. Applying the artis agent architecture to mobile robot control. In *Proceedings of IBERAMIA'2000. Atibaia, Sao Paulo, Brasil*, volume I, pages 359– 368. Springer Verlag, 2000.

[40] J. Soler, V. Julian, M. Rebollo, C. Carrascosa, and V. Botti. Towards a real-time mas architecture. In *Proceedings of Challenges in Open Agent Systems. AAMAS'02. Bolonia, Italia,*, 2002.

[41] VICOROB-UdG Team. Available at http://eia.udg.es/sauce.

[42] A. Terrasa, A. García-Fornes, and V. Botti. Flexible real-time linux. *Real-Time Systems Journal*, 2:149–170, 2002.

[43] K. Tindell and A. Burns. Guaranteeing message latencies on control area network (can). In *Proc of the 1st International CAN Conference*, 1994.

[44] A. Van Breemen. Agent-based multi-controller systems – a design framework for complex control problems. In *PhD Dissertation. University of Twente*, 2001.

[45] M. Wzorek and P. Doherty. Reconfigurable path planning for an autonomous unmanned aerial vehicle. In *New Trends in Real-Time Artificial Intelligence (NTeR-TAIn 2006 / ECAI 2006)*, pages 12–18. Università di Trento - Italy, 2006.

Vicente Julián
Departamento de Sistemas Informáticos y Computación
Universidad Politécnica de Valencia
e-mail: vinglada@dsic.upv.es

Carlos Carrascosa
Departamento de Sistemas Informáticos y Computación
Universidad Politécnica de Valencia
e-mail: carrasco@dsic.upv.es

Whitestein Series in Software Agent Technologies, 145–177
© 2007 Birkhäuser Verlag Basel/Switzerland

Artificial Social Intelligence in MAS: From Swarms to Electronic Institutions

Esteve del Acebo

Abstract. Artificial Social Intelligence (ASI) studies ways to model and implement the skills that allow agents to cope with their social environment in an efficient manner. This study has to play a major role in MAS research and development in the years to come and can be tackled from different points of view depending upon the kind of social environment under consideration, the nature of the modeled social phenomena and the characteristics and capabilities of the individual agents involved. This chapter presents the research work of the Social Intelligence cluster of AgentCities.ES concerning two fields as diverse but as strongly related to Artificial Social Intelligence as Swarm Intelligence and Electronic Institutions.

1. Artificial Social Intelligence

The wide ensemble of abilities that allows humans to, among other things, reason, learn, communicate with each other, deal with new situations and apply knowledge to manipulate our environment, which is called collectively intelligence, is a multiple faceted phenomenon. Edward L. Thorndike gave to this notion the shape of a scientific theory as early as 1920 [63, 55], when he drew an important distinction among three broad classes of intellectual functioning: *abstract intelligence* (the one measured by standard intelligence tests), *mechanical intelligence* (the ability to visualize relationships among objects and understand how the physical world works) and *social intelligence* (the ability to function successfully in interpersonal situations). In spite of this, historically, the bulk of the research effort made by both Psychology and Artificial Intelligence communities has headed toward the study of the abstract, classical, part of intelligence, to the point of most authors reducing social intelligence just to general intelligence applied to social situations. The reason for this can, perhaps, be found in the lack of adequate instruments (in the style of IQ tests) for the measurement of the less conventional aspects of

---

Co-authors of this chapter: Josep Lluís Arcos, Josep Lluís Marzo and Eduard Muntaner.

intelligence and, on the other hand, in the relative success of early AI research in the development of modeling mechanisms for classes of tasks directly related to abstract intelligence (i.e., reasoning, planning and problem solving).

However, this situation has changed over the last years. In Psychology, the appearance of the *Machiavellian Intelligence Hypothesis* [9, 43], according to which primate intelligence originally evolved to solve social problems and was only later extended to problems outside the social domain, has rapidly increased interest in the study of social aspects of intelligence. A similar phenomenon happened in the AI field after the shift to the agent paradigm. The agent paradigm contemplates the physical situation of agents, the tight coupling between the agent and its environment, as an unavoidable requirement in building intelligent agents[1]. An agent's environment contains typically other agents with whom it has to interact. This defines a social environment and justifies the necessity of situation from the social point of view. Following Edmonds [23]:

> "In a physical situation the internal models may be insufficient because of the enormous computation capacity, amount of information and speed that would be required by an agent attempting to explicitly model its environment. In a social situation, although the speed is not so critical, the complexity of that environment can be overwhelming and there is also the obvious external computational resources provided by the other agents and their interactions. This means that an agent can be said to be socially situated by analogy with being physically situated. In both cases the balance of advantage lies in using external causal processes and representations rather than internal ones."

A consequence of embedding the agent into the social environment is the necessity to develop a set of skills which allow the agent to perform efficiently within it. As usual, there is no universal agreement about the precise meaning of Social Intelligence (SI) and Artificial Social Intelligence (ASI) (in fact, Edmonds remarks in [30] that the term social intelligence is ambiguous in the sense that it can either indicate the intelligence that an individual needs to effectively participate in a society, or the intelligence that a society as a whole can exhibit). Duffy [21] defines social intelligence as "the intelligence that underlies behind group interactions and behaviours" while Cantor and Kihlstrom [42] redefine the term to refer to "the individual's fund of knowledge about the social world". Edmonds [22] proposes the Turing Test as a criteria for determining the achievement of truly social intelligence while Hoggs and Jennings [34] prefer to talk about social rationality[2]. Kerstin Dautenhahn [13], finally, gives perhaps the most cited definition of social intelligence as:

---

[1]See, for example, in [30], Franklin and Graesser's definition of agent as "a system situated within and a part of an environment that senses that environment and acts on it, over time, in pursuit of its own agenda and so as to effect what it senses in the future".

[2]Extending Newell's *Principle of Rationality* to state the *Principle of Social Rationality* : "If a socially rational agent can perform an action whose joint benefit [for the whole society] is greater than its joint loss, then it may select that action."

"the individual's capability to develop and manage relationships between individualized, autobiographic agents which, by means of communication, build up shared social interaction structures which help to integrate and manage the individual's basic ("selfish") interests in relationship to the interests of the social system at the next higher level. The term artificial social intelligence is then an instantiation of social intelligence in artifacts."

Neither is there a general agreement about the way ASI has to be implemented or even what its final goal has to be. Researchers coming from "classic" AI mostly focus on the human-agent social interaction (i.e., the "human in the loop" approach [15]). From this point of view ASI has to serve a double purpose: on one hand, to facilitate the interaction between agents and humans and, on the other hand, to study human social processes through the development of suitable social models. The architecture of this type of social agents uses to be an extension of some form of BDI architecture (e.g., [52]) and its design tends to follow the *Life-Like Agents Hypothesis*[3] [14]. Two examples of this type of social agents are the AURORA Project [13], a remedial tool for getting children with autism interested in coordinated and synchronized interactions with the environment and the *Let's Talk!* socially intelligent agents for language conversation training [56].

On the other side, research coming from the social sciences community is focused on social simulation. That is, the design of synthetic societies of agents in physical or virtual environments in order to study the emergence and evolution of social phenomena like cooperation, competition, trust, reputation, markets, social networks dynamics, norms and languages. The interested reader can find a classical introduction to the field in [31]. The significance of this aspect of ASI has to be expected only to increase due to the growing importance that electronic markets and virtual societies will have in the years to come.

Finally, a third aspect of ASI research has its roots arguably in Artificial Life and Distributed Problem Solving. It is the "Engineering with Social Metaphors" approach to ASI, which tries to devise socially inspired problem solving techniques and algorithms. Perhaps the most representative class of such techniques are those based in Swarm Intelligence [5].

Whichever point of view is chosen, the field of Socially Intelligent Agents is a fast growing and increasingly important area that comprises highly active research activities and strongly interdisciplinary approaches coming from as diverse fields as Organizational Science, Philosophy, Cognitive Science, Artificial Intelligence, Cybernetics and Social Simulation.

In this chapter the work of the Social Intelligence cluster of AgentCities.ES is presented. It covers two areas strongly related to the ASI field: Swarm Intelligence

---

[3] "Artificial social agents (robotic or software) which are supposed to interact with humans are most successfully designed by imitating life, i.e., making the agents mimic as closely as possible animals, in particular humans."

and Electronic Institutions. The Agents Research Lab and the Broadband Communication and Distributed Systems (BCDS) groups of the University of Girona present two of their research lines on Swarm Intelligence. The ArLab Group introduces Bar Systems, a class of reactive multi-agent systems whose behavior is loosely inspired by that of a staff of bartenders. The BCDS Group presents AntNet-QoS, a Quality of Service routing approach for DiffServ Networks using Ant Colony Optimization. The Artificial Intelligence Research Institute (IIIA-CSIC) gives an introduction to Electronic Institutions, describing several tools for Electronic Institution design and development and presents its Fish Market and Electricity Market research work. Finally the ARLab group introduces the novel concept of Dynamic Electronic Institutions.

2. Swarm Intelligence

A commonly accepted and used definition of the term Swarm Intelligence is: "the property of a system whereby the collective behaviors of (unsophisticated) agents interacting locally with their environment cause coherent functional global patterns to emerge". The origin of the term is to be found in the observation of social insect colonies and its paradigm is an ant colony. In it, individual ants' behavior is controlled by a small set of very simple rules, but their interactions (also very simple) with the environment allow them to solve complex problems (such as finding the shortest path from one point to another one). Ant colonies (and the same could be said about human beings) are intelligent systems with great problem solving capabilities, formed by a quantity of relatively independent and very simple subsystems which do not show individual intelligence. It is the "many dummies make a smart" phenomenon of emergent intelligence.

A bunch of Swarm Intelligence-inspired problem solving techniques have appeared over the last few years. Three of the most successful such techniques currently in use are Ant Colony Optimization [20], Particle Swarm Optimization [53] and Stochastic Diffusion Search [4]. Ant Colony Optimization techniques, also known as Ant Systems, are based in ants' foraging behavior, and have been applied to problems ranging from determination of minimal paths in TSP-like problems to network traffic rerouting in busy telecommunications systems. Particle Swarm Optimization techniques, inspired by the way a flock of birds or a school of fish moves, are general global minimization techniques that deal with problems in which a best solution can be represented as a point or surface in an n-dimensional space. Stochastic Diffusion Search is another generic population-based search method in which agents perform cheap, partial evaluations of a hypothesis (a candidate solution to the search problem) and then share information about hypotheses (diffusion of information) through direct one-to-one communication. As a result of the diffusion mechanism, high-quality solutions can be identified from clusters of agents with the same hypothesis.

Swarm Intelligence techniques present several advantages over more traditional ones. On one hand, they are cheap, simple and robust; on the other hand, they provide a basis with which it is possible to explore collective (or distributed) problem solving without centralized control or the provision of a global model. Over recent years they have found application in a wide variety of domains: collective robotics, vehicle navigation, planetary mapping, streamlining of assembly lines in factories, coordinated robotic transport, banking data analysis and much more. The interested reader can find a lot of useful references about self-organization and Swarm Intelligence theory and applications in [3], [44], [58], [5], [1], and [6].

3. Swarm Intelligence Applications: Bar Systems

Anybody who has tried to get served a pint in a bar crowded with customers will have had more than enough time to wonder about the method used by waiters, if there is any, to decide which customer to pay attention to at each time. Sometimes there is not much point, in order to be served before others, in having been waiting for long or in yelling at the waiter. Details like the bar area where the customer is, his/her sex, whether the waiter knows him/her or whether the waiter likes the customer's face determine to a high extent the way in which orders are served.

The situation can be examined, though, from the bartenders' point of view: a bevy of customers are ordering drinks all at once, new customers arrive all the time, and the bartenders have to make their best effort to serve all of them. Of course, they cannot do it in an random way; they have to try to maximize some kind of utility function which will typically take into account aspects such as average serving time, average serving cost or average customer/boss satisfaction. Thus, they will have to pay attention to facts such as that some of them can prepare certain drinks more quickly or better than others, that the order in which the drinks are served influences the time or the total cost of serving them, and also that moving from one place in the bar to another costs time. All of this without forgetting, on one hand, that the order in which orders take place has to be respected as much as possible and, on the other hand, that they have to try to favor the best customers by giving them preferential attention and keeping them waiting for a shorter time.

The problem is not at all trivial, actually it has been shown to be NP-hard [16]. Bartenders have to act in a highly dynamic, asynchronous and time-critical environment, and no obvious greedy strategy (e.g., serving first the best customer, serving first the nearest customer or serving first the customer who has arrived first) gives good results. Nevertheless, a staff of good bartenders usually can manage to serve a lot of customers in such a way that the vast majority of them were, more or less, satisfied. The way they accomplish the task seems to have little to do with any global planning or explicit coordination mechanisms but, rather, with trying to maximize some local utility function which takes into account aspects

like the importance of the customer, the cost for the waiter of serving her/him and
the time that he/she has been waiting for service.

Based on this behavior, the ARLab Group at the University of Girona has
developed a general formalism for optimization problems in real-time environments
which has been named Bar Systems [17].

3.1. Definition

A Bar System is a quadruple (E, T, A, F) where:

1. E is a (physical or virtual) environment. The state of the environment at
   each moment is determined by a set of state variables V_E. One of those
   variables is usually the time. S is defined as the set of all possible states of the
   environment E, that is, the set of all the possible simultaneous instantiations
   of the set of state variables V_E.
2. $T = \{t_1, t_2, ..., t_M\}$ is a set of tasks to be accomplished by the agents within
   the environment E. Each task t_i has associated:
   - $pre(t_i)$. A set of preconditions over V_E which determine whether the
     task t_i can be done.
   - $imp(t_i)$. A nonnegative real value which reflects the importance of the
     task t_i.
   - $urg(t_i)$. A function of V_E which represents the urgency of task t_i in the
     current state of the environment E. It will be usually a nondecreasing
     function of time.
3. $A = \{a_1, a_2, ..., a_N\}$ is a set of agents situated in the environment E. Each
   agent a_i can have different problem-dependent properties (i.e., weight, speed,
   location, response time, maximum load, etc.). Agents have also capabilities
   which allow them to carry out tasks and adapt the environment to tasks'
   preconditions. For each agent a_i and each task t_j, $cost(a_i, t_j)$ reflects the cost
   for agent a_i to execute the task t_j in the current state of the environment.
   This cost can be divided in two parts: on one hand, the cost for a_i to make
   the environment fulfill the preconditions of task t_i and, on the other hand,
   the cost for a_i to actually execute t_j. If an agent a_i is unable to adapt the
   environment to the preconditions of the task t_j, or if it is unable to carry the
   task out by itself, then $cost(a_i, t_j)$ is defined as infinite. It is worth remarking
   that the cost functions associated to each agent are not equal for all the
   agents. That is, a task may have different costs for different agents. That
   fact introduces heterogeneity among the set of agents and makes possible the
   appearance of specialized groups of agents (casts).
4. $F : S \times A \times T \to \Re$ is the function which reflects the degree to which agents
   are "attracted" by tasks. Given a state s of the environment, an agent a_i
   and a task t_j $F(s, a_i, t_j)$ must be defined in a way such that it increases with
   $imp(t_j)$ and $urg(t_j)$ and it decreases with $cost(a_i, t_j)$.

In Bar Systems, agents operate concurrently in the environment in an asynchronous manner, thus eliminating the typical operation cycles of other Swarm Intelligence systems (e.g., Ant Systems, Particle Swarm Optimization Systems, Cellular Automata, etc.). That fact makes very easy the implementation of Bar Systems by means of distributed architectures and makes them widely applicable to the resolution of distributed problems. The general individual behavior of agents is given by Algorithm 1. The crucial step in it is the choice of the task which the agent

---

Algorithm 1 Individual agents' behavior algorithm

1: **procedure** BARSYSTEMAGENT
2:     **repeat**
3:         Find the most attractive free task M
4:         **if** the agent is doing M **OR** trying to fulfill $pre(M)$ **then**
5:             Keep doing it
6:         **else**
7:             Stop doing the current task, if any
8:             **if** $pre(M)$ holds **then**
9:                 Start doing M
10:            **else**
11:                Do some action in order to fulfill $pre(M)$
12:            **end if**
13:        **end if**
14:    **until** no tasks left
15: **end procedure**

---

has to try to execute for the next timestep. In its simplest form, it can consist in choosing the one which maximizes the attraction function F. It can also involve some kind of negotiation between agents and even some kind of local planning.

3.2. Inter-agent communication

Even if Bar Systems don't require from the agents any communication skills, they are indispensable in order for the system to attain the coordinated and self-organized behavior typical of Swarm Intelligence Systems. In order to increase Bar Systems' problem solving capabilities, there are three main purposes to which communication can serve:

- *Conflict resolution and negotiation.* The way Bar Systems are defined makes unavoidable the occurrence of conflicting situations in which two or more agents choose the same task to carry out. A lack of communication will lead to a waste of resources because of several agents trying to fulfill the preconditions of the same task, even if only one of them will finally carry it out. In such situations it would be convenient to have some kind of negotiation method, which can be as simple as "the first one to see it goes for it".

- *Perception augmentation*. In the case that agents have limited perception capabilities (this means capability to perceive the tasks), communication can allow an agent to transmit to the others information about pending tasks they are not aware of.
- *Learning*. The attraction function f defined in Section 3.1 does not need to be fixed in advance. Agents can learn it through their own activity and their communicative interactions with other agents. For example, an agent can find out that a certain kind of task has a high cost and communicate this fact to the other agents. Not only that, agents can even learn from other agents the way of carrying out new tasks.

On the other side, It is worth differentiating two main classes of inter-agent communication processes:

- *Direct*. Agents establish direct communication with each other via some channel and following some kind of agreed protocol.
- *Indirect* or *stigmergetic*. Agents communicate with each other through their actions, which cause changes in the environment. In the Bar Systems framework, it can be seen as agents generating "communicative tasks" which, when carried out by other agents, increase the information they possess (about the environment, the task set, etc.).

3.3. Local planning

Although there is nothing like global planning in the way a set of bartenders work, they have tricks which allow them to spare time and effort. For example if two customers are asking for a pint and they are close enough to each other in the bar, the bartender will usually serve them at once. In a similar way, a taxi driver who is going to pick up a passenger will surely take advantage of the opportunity if he finds in his way a new passenger and he can transport him without deviating too much from his original route. The inclusion of this sort of very simple, problem-dependent, local planning techniques in the choice of tasks is not difficult and can be done through different methods ranging from a local search to the use of expert rules.

3.4. The CONTS problem

A class of problems frequently found in "real life" involves some kind of scheduling in the transport of goods or people from one place to another. The problem presented as a framework for the study of Bar Systems applicability and efficiency is inspired by the problem which has to be solved by a group of loading robots in a commercial harbor. The task of these robots is to transport containers from their storage place to the docks where the corresponding ships have to be loaded. Of course, this transport has to be done in such a way that the containers arrive in time to be loaded and with the lowest possible cost.

3.4.1. Definition of the problem. Let $C = \{c_1, c_2, ..., c_n\}$ be a set of containers, let $L = \{l_1, l_2, ..., l_m\}$ be a set of loading robots and let $P = \{(x, y) \in \{0..MaxX\} \times$

$\{0..MaxY\}\}$ be a set of positions. Each container c_i has the following associated properties:

- $p(c_i) \in P$. The position where the container lies.
- $dest(c_i) \in P$. The position to which the container has to be carried.
- $weight(c_i) \in \Re^+$. The weight of the container.
- $dline(c_i) \in \Re^+$. The latest instant of time in which the container can arrive at the dock in order to be loaded in time onto the ship.

In order not to complicate the problem too much, constant importance for all the containers will be assumed. There are also several properties associated to each loading robot l_i:

- $p(l_i) \in P$. The place where the robot is at each time instant.
- $maxload(l_i) \in \Re^+$. The maximum weight the robot is able to carry.
- $maxdist(l_i) \in \Re^+$. The distance beyond which the robot can't "hear". It permits the modelling of the perceptual limitations of the robot.
- $speed(l_i) \in \Re^+$. The speed at which the agent can move.

Robots can perform different actions, they can move towards any position, load (if container and robot are in the same position) containers which weigh less or the same as its $maxload$ value and download containers.

The problem consists in finding, if it exists, a sequence of actions that allows the robots to transport every container to its destination point in such a way that no container arrives after its deadline. In order to simplify the problem, it is assumed that the robots always move at the same speed, that uploading and downloading operations are instantaneous and that robots can only carry one container at a time.

3.4.2. A Bar System for solving the CONTS problem.

The idea upon which the Bar System is based is very simple: to simulate an environment where the containers "shout" to the agents asking for somebody to take them to their destination. The intensity of the shout of each container depends on the remaining time before its deadline and the distance between its position and the delivery position (it could also depend on the importance of each container but, the way the problem is defined, they are all equally important). The robots hear the calls of the containers diminished by the distance, so they go and take the ones they hear better. In order to achieve this behavior in the robots a linear attraction function will be used. Following the notation introduced in Section 3.1, for each container c and for each robot l, the attraction function F is defined as follows:

$$F(c,l) = \begin{cases} -\infty, & \text{if } c \text{ has been delivered,} \\ -\infty, & \text{if } c \text{ is being delivered for a} \\ & \text{robot other than } l, \\ K_1 \cdot urg(c) - K_2 \cdot cost(c,l), & \text{ow,} \end{cases} \qquad (3.1)$$

where K_1 and K_2 are adjustable parameters. The urgency function $urg(c)$ is defined as inversely proportional to the time which remains to c's deadline and takes into account the time required for transporting the container to its destination point:

$$urg(c) = curtime + \frac{d(p(c), dest(c))}{meanspeed} - dline(c), \qquad (3.2)$$

where d is the Euclidean distance, *curtime* is the current time and *meanspeed* is an environmental constant which averages agents' speeds. The *cost* function is defined as follows:

$$cost(c, l) = \begin{cases} \infty, & \text{if } weight(c) \geq maxload(l), \\ \infty, & \text{if } d(p(l), p(c)) \geq maxdist(l), \\ \dfrac{d(p(l), p(c)) + d(p(c), dest(c))}{speed(l)}, & \text{ow.} \end{cases} \qquad (3.3)$$

The election of this attraction function F is quite arbitrary. A nonlinear function would probably better reflect the "hearing" metaphor. In the same way, a more sophisticated urgency function could be defined (e.g., nonlinearly increasing depending on the time to the containers' deadline). Bar Systems are general enough to use any attraction, cost or urgency functions. The choice of the attraction function F is based on its simplicity, in spite of which, it has allowed the system to obtain very good results.

The behavior of the robots will be very simple and will obey Algorithm 1. Each robot will choose a container to go for and will go towards its position, will load it (unless anther robot has arrived first) and will take it to the delivery point. After that, it will repeat the cycle until no containers are left to transport.

3.4.3. Inter-agent communication and local planning for the CONTS problem. In order to study the utility of interagent communication, two different methods for the choice of the next container to go for have been investigated. If no communication between agents is allowed, each agent will simply choose the one which maximizes the attraction function. On the other hand, if the possibility of communication between agents is activated, each robot will ask the others (perhaps not all of them but only those for which communication is feasible) which containers they prefer and, in the case of a conflict (that is, another robot preferring the same container), a small negotiation process will start, the goal of which is to give preference to the agent who will be able to carry the container faster to its delivery position. The agent that finds itself in the situation where other agents have priority over it to transport its favorite container will try with the next best container, in order of preference according to its point of view, until if finds one for which it will have more priority than any other agent. It would be easy to devise more sophisticated negotiation processes taking into account the second-best options of the agents in conflict in such a way that one agent could resign carrying its preferred container, even if it has the higher preference over it, whenever the preference difference between the best and the second-best containers was small enough.

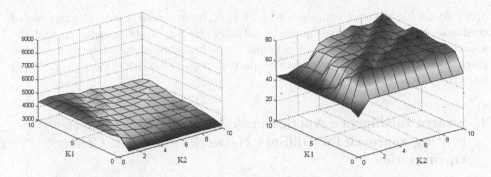

FIGURE 1. Left: Total time needed by the system to deliver all
the containers for different values of the parameters $K1$ and $K2$.
Right: Number of containers delivered before their deadlines.

A very straightforward planning-like strategy has also been implemented in
our Bar System. Whenever a robot has a container to go for, it tries to see whether
another container exists such that it is possible to transport it without deviating
too much from the robot's original way to the first container's position. If so, the
agent transports it before resuming its original way to the first container position.

3.4.4. Results. A graphical simulator for the problem has been developed in order
to analyze the efficiency of the method and experiment with different settings and
parameter values. Experiments have been done with an instance of the problem
with eighty containers randomly scattered on a 300×300 rectangular area with
random delivery points and deadlines and four carrier robots with different speeds.

Figure 1 shows a graph representing the results of the simulation for different
values of the parameters. Each row represents a series of 121 simulations (for
values of the $K1$ and $K2$ parameters ranging from 0 to 10 in increments of 1). The
chart in the left column shows the time used to deliver all the containers and the
chart in the right column shows the number of containers delivered before their
deadlines. It is clear from the figure that, for some values of the parameters $K1$
and $K2$, the system finds much better solutions than those which can be obtained
by using nearest neighbor-like methods. The performance of those methods can
be observed in Figure 1. When $K1 = 0$ the preference function F depends only
on the *cost* function and the system behaves in the "nearest container" way. The
results are a low total delivery time and a considerable number of containers being
delivered after its deadline. The case $K2 = 0$ is even worse. The system follows
the "most urgent container" behavior, resulting in very long displacements which
cause a big total delivery time and, consequently, a large number of containers
delivered with delay. It is worth noting that the improvement over those greedy
methods achieved by our Bar System for some values of the parameters $K1$ and
$K2$ is not attained in exchange for a greater complexity; in fact, the complexity
of the system, understood as the amount of work which each agent has to do in

order to decide the next container to go for, increases linearly with the number of containers. Although the comparison between the Bar Systems solution and the solutions found by the greedy algorithms is vastly favorable to the former, further work has to be done in order to compare it with other techniques (e.g., ACO based).

4. Swarm Intelligence Applications: A Quality of Service (QoS) routing approach for DiffServ Networks using Ant Colony Optimization

Over the last years, Swarm Intelligence has served frequently as a basis for different approaches in solving distributed system optimization problems. In the area of network routing, some proposed algorithms have taken inspiration from the notion of stigmergy, which describes the indirect communication taking place among individuals through modifications induced in their environment. Most of those algorithms are inspired by natural ant colonies because of their ability to find shortest paths by using pheromone trails deposited by individual ants.

4.1. ACO Routing Algorithms

It has been observed that ants in a colony can converge on moving over the shortest path connecting their nest to a food source [10]. The main catalyst of this colony-level shortest path behavior is the use of a chemical substance called pheromone. Ants moving back and forth between nest and food deposit pheromone, and preferentially move towards areas of higher pheromone intensity. Shorter paths can be completed quicker and more frequently by the ants, and are therefore marked with more pheromone. These paths attract more ants, which in turn increase the pheromone level. This behavior is shown in Figure 2.

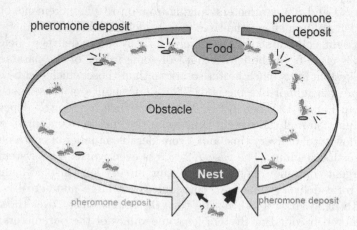

FIGURE 2. Ant's shortest path discovery and reinforcement.

The overall effect is a distributed reinforcement learning process which eventually allows the majority of the ants to converge onto the shortest path. This behavior has attracted attention as a framework for optimization and has been reverse-engineered in the Ant Colony Optimization (ACO) meta-heuristic.

In ACO algorithms for routing, nodes obtain routing information using ant-like agents (referred to in the following as ants) which repeatedly sample and reinforce good paths. These ants are in fact small control packets similar to probes. The role of pheromones in nature is played by the routing tables, which are therefore also called pheromone tables. The pheromone table of a node contains for each destination a number of different routing options, each with an associated goodness value, also called a pheromone value. Two types of ants (routing packets) are used: forward ants and backward ants. Forward ants are explorers that discover new routes and constantly evaluate the state of existing ones, analyzing (memorizing) the delay and the sequence of visited nodes. They use routing tables as data packets, i.e., stochastically selecting the next node according to the probability value (higher pheromone deposit). When a forward ant reaches its goal, another ant is activated, a backward ant, which returns to its source node using the reverse path taken by the forward ant and updates the routing table at each node along the return path. In consequence, the pheromone values are updated by the ants according to the quality of the paths they have sampled. A stochastic routing decision is taken at each node, giving higher probability to routing options associated with higher pheromone values. As a result of this process, up-to-date quality information is available for the different possible paths between each pair of nodes. Data packets are stochastically spread over these paths, with higher preference for the best paths. In this way, automatic load balancing and optimization of network resource utilization is obtained.

Several ACO routing algorithms have been developed so far, many of them showing very good performance in dynamic environments. The first two were Ant-Based Control (ABC) for circuit-switched networks [60] and AntNet for best-effort traffic in IP networks [11]. Current ACO routing algorithms include algorithms for a variety of networks and applications (see [19] for an overview).

4.2. The AntNet-QoS System

AntNet-QoS is based on the Di Caro and Dorigo's AntNet routing system [11], which was originally designed to route best-effort traffic across IP networks. AntNet-QoS attempts to extend it to provide high Quality of Service (QoS) routing in DiffServ (Differentiated Services) networks. In opposition to best-effort routing, QoS routing algorithms also consider the performance characteristics of links (e.g., available bandwidth, delay, delay variation (jitter), packet loss, etc).

In a DiffServ network, ingress nodes classify incoming flows into n predefined Classes of Services (CoS) (e.g., Platinum, Gold and Silver) that can be provided by the network, and network core nodes handle each packet according to its QoS label. AntNet-QoS extends AntNet by using n different and independent Classes of Ants (CoAs) to sample and find paths that can provide the QoS associated to the specific CoS managed by its specific CoA. AntNet-QoS considers configurable parameters for every CoA according to the ones set up in previous studies for traditional AntNet routing. See the QoS statistics table in Figure 3.

AntNet provides on-line adaptive load-balancing through repeated sampling of end-to-end path delay and stochastic data load spreading across multiple paths. In AntNet-QoS, the AntNet path sampling approach can be extended to measure QoS metrics such as available bandwidth and delay. These different QoS metrics are combined in a weighted formula to calculate the routing tables used for AntNet's stochastic data load spreading (see [36]).

The combination of ant-based probing and stochastic data load spreading allows the design of DiffServ classes and the differentiation between the services provided to each class, so that a good exploitation of network resources can be provided using a purely proactive approach without any strict reservation schemes.

AntNet has been compared with other state-of-the art routing algorithms, and has showed superior performance in terms of delay and robustness to load changes. Moreover, AntNet performs well in periods of congestion, one of the issues inside a DiffServ domain when provisioning is not carefully performed. Considering DiffServ as a scalable architecture and AntNet as a scalable routing algorithm, AntNet-QoS is a scalable QoS-Routing approach that can be employed in large networks.

5. Electronic Institutions

Multi-agent systems (MAS) are systems composed of autonomous agents which interact in order to satisfy their common and/or individual goals. A main feature of MAS is that the communication occurs at knowledge level and that they use flexible and complex interactions among their components. Thus, the design and development of MAS suffer from all the problems associated with the development

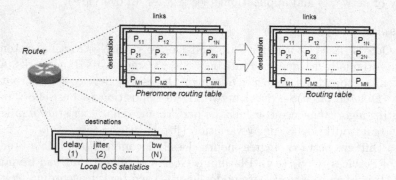

FIGURE 3. Routing tables extension to cope QoS per node.

of distributed concurrent systems and the additional problems which arise from having flexible and complex interactions among autonomous entities [38].

The complexity of designing multi-agent systems increases when the focus is on open systems [33]. Open multi-agent systems are those in which the participants are unknown in advance and can change over time. These systems are populated by heterogeneous agents, generally developed by different people using different languages and architectures, representing different parties and acting to maximise their own utility. In order to cope with these problems, appropriate methodologies that allow the analysis and design of agent systems and software tools that support their development life cycle are needed [32, 38, 37].

Human societies successfully deal with similar issues by deploying institutions [51] that establish how interactions of a certain sort will and must be structured within an organization. Institutions represent the rules of the game in a society, including any (formal or informal) form of constraints that human beings devise to shape human interaction. Therefore, they are the framework within which human interaction takes place, defining what individuals are forbidden and permitted and under what conditions. Furthermore, human institutions not only structure human interactions but also enforce individual and social behavior by obliging everybody to act according to the norms.

It seems important, therefore, to advocate for the introduction of their electronic counterpart, namely electronic institutions, to establish the rules of the game in agent societies. Electronic institutions provide a computational analogue of human organizations in which intelligent agents playing different organizational roles interact to accomplish individual and organizational goals. In this scenario agent technology helps enterprises reduce their operational costs and speed-up the time-to-market by helping distributed business parties, represented by the agents, run smoother and in a more coordinated fashion. Electronic institutions appear as the glue that puts together self-interested business parties, coordinating, regulating, and auditing their collaborations. The concept of electronic institutions was first introduced in 1997 [50] and it has been mainly developed in the context of three Phd theses [50, 59, 25] at the Artificial Intelligence Research Institute (IIIA-CSIC).

5.1. Fundamental Concepts

Loosely speaking, electronic institutions are computational realizations of traditional institutions (cf. North [51] pp. 3 ss.); that is, coordination artifacts that establish an environment where agents interact according to stated conventions, and in such a way that interactions within the (electronic) institution would *count as* interactions in the actual world.

According to the basic definition of an electronic institution (see [25]), an electronic institution is composed of three components: a dialogical framework that establishes the social structure, the ontology, and a communication language to be used by participating agents; a performative structure defining the activities along with their relationships; and a set of norms defining the consequences of agents' actions.

5.1.1. Dialogical Framework. The first component of the dialogical framework (DF) is the *social structure*. The social structure defines the set of participating roles and the relationships among them (e.g., roles that can not be played at the same time). From the set of roles that can participate in an electronic institution, it is possible to differentiate between internal (staff) roles and external (non-institutional) roles. Internal roles are those in charge of the electronic institution services and tasks, and that guarantee some of the institutional rules. A social information model is associated to each role, establishing what information will be kept by the institution for those agents playing the role.

The second component of the DF is the *ontology*. The ontology contains the formalization of the relevant concepts of the institution domain. An object oriented approach has been taken for the ontology definition. Hence, the domain is formalized as a set of classes representing the different domain concepts and a hierarchy relationship among them.

The third component of the DF is the *communication language*. Agents interact with each other by means of illocutions. Similar to other agent communication languages, illocutions contain an illocutionary particle, expressing the intention when uttering an illocution, the sender and addresse(s), the message content, which must be an ontology term, and a time term to capture the instant at which an illocution is uttered. The communication language allows one to specify that an illocution is addressed to an individual agent, to all the agents playing a given role or to all the agents in a conversation.

5.1.2. Performative Structure. The performative structure (PS) models the relationships among dialogic activities, each one involving different groups of agents playing different roles. The PS defines the causal dependencies among activities, establishes the role flow policy among activities, and provides agent synchronization/choice mechanisms. From a structural point of view, performative structures must be regarded as networks of activities. For example the performative structure depicted in Figure 4 defines the relationships between the usual activities during the enactment of an auction. In this case —in addition to the initial and final scenes that are necessary in all e-Institutions— there are four basic scenes: `Admission`, `ItemRegister`, `Auctioninfo`, `Auction`, all depicted as boxes. Causal dependencies and the role flow policy are represented by directed arcs and transition gates.

For each activity, interactions between agents are articulated through well-defined protocols, which are called scenes. Scene protocols are patterns of multi-role conversation specified by a finite state directed graph where the nodes represent the different states of the conversation and the labels of the directed arcs contain the actions that make the scene state evolve.

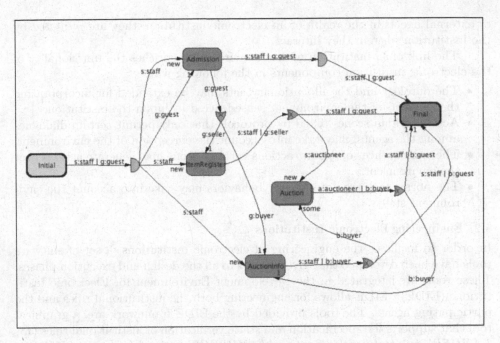

FIGURE 4. An ISLANDER specification of the Performative
Structure of an institution for simultaneous auctions.

5.1.3. Norms. Agent actions in the context of an institution have consequences, usually in the shape of compromises which impose obligations or restrictions on dialogic actions of agents in the scenes wherein they are acting or will be acting in the future. The purpose of normative rules (Norms) is to affect the behavior of agents by imposing obligations or prohibitions. Notice that since dialogic institutions are being considered, the only actions under consideration are the utterance of illocutions. Therefore, it is possible to refer to the utterance of an illocution within a scene or when a scene execution is at a concrete state. The intuitive meaning of normative rules is that if illocutions are uttered in the corresponding scene states, and some predefined expressions are satisfied, then other illocutions satisfying other expressions must be uttered in the corresponding scene states in order to fulfill the normative rule.

5.1.4. Environment. MAS applications are usually concerned with some external environment. The environment is application-specific and refers to the part of the world that is relevant to the MAS application. In [2] is presented the way an environment can be linked to an electronic institution. Environments are plugged into electronic institutions as institutional services. In our approach, agents cannot directly sense and act over the environment. Instead, and likewise for all interactions of external agents in the realm of an electronic institution, they are *mediated* by the institution wherein they interact.

The link of an institution with an environment enriches the functionality of the electronic institution components in the following way:

- The ontology and the illocutionary acts may be extended for incorporating the elements of the environment sensed/acted by/upon the institution.
- Actions within scenes, fixed by protocols that only permit certain dialogues among the agents, may take into account the perception of the environment.
- The consequences of agents' actions within a scene may generate actions over the environment.
- The norms that regulate agents' behaviors may take into account the environment state.

5.2. Engineering Electronic Institutions

In order to facilitate the engineering of electronic institutions, a set of software tools have been developed that give support to all the design and execution phases. These tools are integrated in the Development Environment for Electronic Institutions (EIDE)[4]. EIDE allows for engineering both the institutional rules and the participating agents. The tools provided by the EIDE framework are: a graphical tool that supports the specification and static verification of institutional rules (*IS-LANDER*), an agent development tool (*aBUILDER*), a simulation tool (*SIMDEI*), and a software platform to run electronic institutions (*AMELI*).

5.2.1. ISLANDER. *ISLANDER* is a tool for Electronic Institution design [26] that allows one to make a graphical specification of the Electronic Institution components and produces an XML file with the specification. That specification is used to enact instances of the institution by agent designers to build agents that conform to the institutional conventions and to design and run experiments with different agent populations.

An example of the graphical specification of the performative structure modeling an auction house is shown in Figure 4. Boxes represent scenes and directed arcs inter-connect scenes through transition gates. Arcs are labeled by agent-variables and the roles these are to play. Moreover, arcs entering a scene are also labeled with a legend that indicates if transient agents may enter one scene, or one or more scenes of that type, or if a staff member may create new scenes of that type.

5.2.2. aBUILDER. EIDE provides a software tool, *aBUILDER* [40], for agent development that supports the graphical specification of agent skeletons based on *ISLANDER* specifications. Specifically, *aBUILDER* takes an *ISLANDER* specification and produces for each role that may be played in the institution an "agent skeleton". Those skeletons comply with all the conventions of the specified institution, in particular with its dialogical framework and the performative structure.

---

[4]Software available at http://e-institutions.iiia.csic.es/

Hence, external agents may be built from scratch —based on the XML specification of the Electronic Institution— but they may also be readily built —on top of the *aBUILDER* skeletons— by programming the decision means associated with illocutions and having the skeleton take care of navigation and communication within the Electronic Institution.

5.2.3. SIMDEI. Validating the desired behavior of an Electronic Institution is a highly intricate and computationally expensive task, as illustrated by [65, 64, 41, 28]. Such validation becomes even more complicated when an environment with a partially observable behavior is incorporated into the Electronic Institution. *SIMDEI* [40] allows one to run discrete event simulations of *AMELI* along the lines of multi-agent simulations produced with the aid of libraries like Repast [57]. Similar to environment simulations, the modeling simulation tool must be chosen (e.g., Simile [61], Simulink [62], EJS [24]) which best fits the domain features. After choosing a simulation tool, it is necessary to glue it with *AMELI* so that agents in an Electronic Institution can sense and act upon the simulated environment. This required *simulation bridge* is a software component whose main purpose is: (i) to synchronise both simulators; (ii) to forward environment variables' values to *SIMDEI*; and (iii) to translate actions within the simulated Electronic Institution into environment actions. At present, there exist implementations of the simulation bridge to connect *SIMDEI* simulations to either Simulink [62] or EJS [24] simulations.

SIMDEI can exploit parametrised agent skeletons to generate agent populations by setting the number of agents to create from a given skeleton, along with the means to set up values for their parameters. An agent's action can be parametrised in two ways: (i) by defining whether an action is carried out or not as a parameter; (ii) by defining (some of) the actual values of each action as parameters. Figure 5 illustrates how to generate a population of energy producers whose production capacity will be randomly generated by a normal distribution.

5.2.4. AMELI. The core of EIDE is *AMELI* [27], an institutional engine that provides a run-time middleware for the agents that participate in the enactment of a given institution. The middleware is deployed to *guarantee* the correct evolution of each scene, to *warrant* legal movements between scenes, and to *control* the obligations or commitments that participating agents acquire and fulfill. Furthermore, the middleware *handles* the information agents need within the institution. The *AMELI* generated middleware *mediates* between agents in order to facilitate agent communication within scenes. Broadly speaking, *AMELI* achieves those functions because, on the one hand, it generates the staff agents and the institutional *governors* that mediate all communications with external agents, and, on the other hand, it handles all the institutional communication traffic by wrapping illocutions as messages that are handled by a standard agent-communication layer.

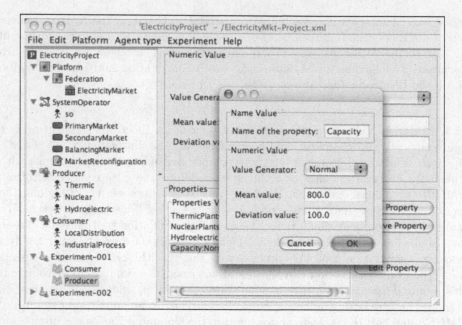

FIGURE 5. Generating Agent Populations for the Electricity Market with SIMDEI.

Additionally, *AMELI* provides a set of monitoring facilities that allow a graphical depiction of all the events that occur during the enactment of an Electronic Institution (Figure 6 shows a snapshot of the monitoring tool for the electricity market application). Fairness, trust and accountability are the main motivations for the development of a monitoring tool that registers all interactions in a given enactment of an electronic institution [50, 59]. Giving accountability information to the participants increases their trust in the institution. This is especially important for electronic institutions where people delegate their tasks to agents. Furthermore, the tool permits them to analyse their agents' behaviour within the institution in order to improve it. From the point of view of the institution designers, the tool is useful for testing the system and the staff agents before making the institution available to external agents. Furthermore, when the institution is running it can be used to detect unexpected situations and fraudulent behaviours of external agents.

6. Electronic Institutions Application: The Fish Market

Along the Mediterranean coast, fresh fish has been traditionally sold through downward bidding auctions operating in auction houses in fishing towns. Fish is presented in collections of boxes, called lots, and put up for auction following a Dutch-like protocol: price is progressively and quickly lowered—4 quotes per

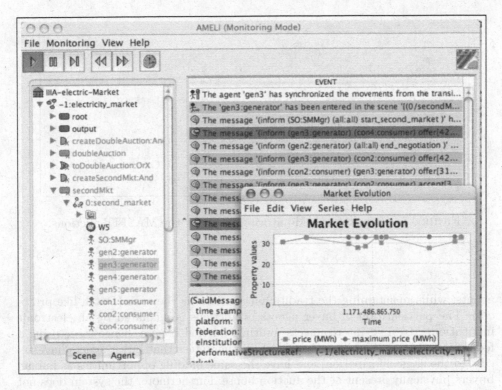

FIGURE 6. Monitoring the Electricity Market with AMELI.

second—until a buyer submits a bid or the price descent reaches the reservation price. The buyer submitting the bid can decide to buy the complete lot or just some boxes. In the later case, the remaining boxes are put back up for auction in the next round. When the last box of the last lot is sold, the auction is over.

Some fishmarkets are adapting their selling methods to new technologies and most auctions are nowadays somewhat automated, although the presence of human buyers in the auction houses is still necessary. This has two significant drawbacks. First, it restricts potential buyers to those present in the auction house. Second, it makes simultaneous participation in several auctions costly, since companies have to send a representative to each one. The elimination of such limitations would be profitable for both buyers and sellers. Increasing the number of buyers makes the market more competitive, and thus increases the buying price to the benefit of sellers. It also permits the participation of buyers without intermediaries saving costs to the buyers.

Agent technologies may be used to eliminate these limitations. The Multi-agent System for FIsh Trading (MASFIT) [12] allows buyers to remotely and simultaneously participate in several wholesale fish auctions with the help of software

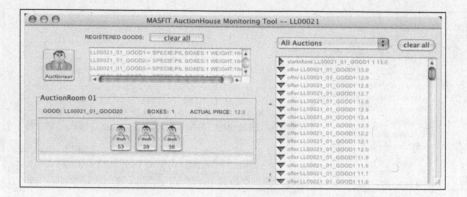

FIGURE 7. Snapshot of a Monitoring panel for the MASFIT auctions.

agents, while maintaining the traditional auctions as they are (Dutch-like protocol). The participation of buyer agents in auctions is mediated by an electronic institution. MASFIT interconnects multiple auction houses, hence structuring a federation of them. Significantly, MASFIT guarantees that buyer agents have access to the same information, and have the same bidding opportunities as human buyers physically present at the auction house. Furthermore, the system does not alter the current operation of the auction houses. In order to permit buyer agents to participate in the auctions, the auction systems running in the (physical) auction houses have been extended to connect with the electronic institution. Thus, the auction systems send to the MASFIT electronic institution information about all the events occurring at the corresponding auction house that are relevant for the buyers.

As reported in [12], the EIDE tools played a key role in the design and development of the MASFIT system. On the one hand, the MASFIT electronic institution was specified using ISLANDER. On the other hand, agents in the institution have their interactions mediated by AMELI. Figure 7 shows a monitoring panel developed for the MASFIT institution extending the monitoring facilities of AMELI.

Finally, notice that the participation in a market scenario as created by MASFIT, a federation of auction houses, is a complex decision-making task, as buyer agents are participating simultaneously in several auctions [8]. Buyer agents receive information from different auction houses and they should decide the most suitable place to buy. Agents have to manage huge amounts of information—even uncertain information—and their reasoning and processing time must be short enough to react to changes. To support this complex design, MASFIT makes available tools to create, customise, manage and train software buying agents.

7. Electronic Institutions Application: The Electricity Market

The main goal of an electricity market is to provide a set of rules for conciliating the demand for electricity and its generation. There are two issues that must be avoided: a lack of production that can leave customers without supply and an unwanted overproduction. Moreover, these goals have to be achieved while maintaining a reasonable electricity price.

The players of the market are the producers, the consumers and the system operator. Producers and consumers are external roles in the institution whereas the system operator is a staff role. The producers use different technologies (thermic, nuclear or hydroelectric) for electricity generation in order to satisfy the demand. The consumers who participate in an electricity market are large industrial companies and local energy wholesalers that sell the energy to smaller or domestic consumers. The main goal of the consumers is to buy energy for half hour periods. The task of the system operator is to guarantee the voltage level and the dynamic security of the electricity network. Specifically, the system operator controls that the power deficit is never greater than 10% of the total production, which is the obliged safety power that each power station must fulfill.

The electricity market is organized in three different markets: the primary market, the secondary market and the balancing market: The primary market performs periodic auctions of transmission rights, in the form of tickets valid for the injection or extraction of energy over half hour periods and was modeled as a double auction protocol. The goal of the secondary market is to provide an additional round for the trading of transmission tickets. The balancing market permits the system operator to adapt the plans of production to the quality and security restrictions.

8. New Trends in Electronic Institutions: Dealing with Openness, Dynamicity and Autonomy

It is a fact that real-world applications are becoming increasingly complex, mainly as a result of the ever more significant role of the Internet in our lives and the emerging model of electronic business. There are many application domains in which autonomous and heterogeneous agents (enterprises, nodes, groups of people, etc.) have to collaborate and make temporary alliances that should change dynamically according to their environment (market, topology, etc.). Open multi-agent systems can map these situations, and coalition formation mechanisms facilitate them forming, but in these kinds of systems the emergent behaviour of the global system can become chaotic and unexpected. In critical applications this can be a significant problem, and it is evident that it is necessary to introduce regulatory measures which determine what the agents can do, and what they cannot.

Electronic institutions could be an effective solution to this problem. The idea to use organizational metaphors to model systems was proposed in [54]. This approach suggested structuring the agent society with roles and relationships between agents. However, the study of electronic institutions is a relatively recent field (the first approach was [50]). The main idea is simple, and it could be summarized by imagining groups of intelligent, autonomous and heterogeneous agents, which play different roles, and which interact with each other under a set of norms, with the purpose of satisfying individual goals and/or common goals. The different approaches to electronic institutions have demonstrated how organisational approaches are useful in *open agent systems*, but in some application domains that require norm-regulated short to medium-term associations of agents, classical electronic institutions still have several problems and limitations: they are based on medium to long-term associations between agents, they require a design phase performed by humans, and they have no mechanisms for reconfiguration and dissolution processes.

Recent approaches are trying to solve these problems by studying new concepts like *dynamic electronic institutions* or *autonomic electronic institutions*.

8.1. Dynamic Electronic Institutions

There is little previous work on *dynamic electronic institutions*: this idea has just recently been introduced as a challenge for agent-based computing. It first appeared when the term *dynamic electronic institution* appeared in a roadmap for agent technology [45].

As stated in [47], *dynamic electronic institutions* (DEIs from here on) arise from the convergence of two research lines: electronic institutions and coalition formation; and can be described as follows: emergent associations of intelligent, autonomous and heterogeneous agents, which play different roles, and which are able to adopt a set of regulatory components (norms, missions, coordination protocols, etc) in order to interact with each other, with the aim of satisfying individual goals and/or common goals. These formations are dynamic in the sense that they can be automatically formed, reformed and dissolved, in order to constitute temporary electronic institutions on the fly.

There are several application domains that require short-term agent organisations or alliances, in which DEIs could be applied. Some of them are: Digital Business Ecosystems, B2B Electronic Commerce, Mobile Ad-Hoc Networks, simulation of Operations Other Than War, etc.

In [47] a DEI's life cycle made up of by three phases is proposed: Formation (the coalition formation phase), Foundation (the process of turning the coalition into a temporary electronic institution) and Fulfilment (the dissolution phase). This life cycle is called *3F cycle*. Figure 8 depicts this cycle.

One of these three phases has been poorly studied in the past: the foundation phase. This phase is the real challenge because the process of turning the coalition into a temporary electronic institution is not a trivial problem. It requires the agents to adopt a set of components that regulate their interactions. This must be an automated process, without any human intervention, so agents must be able to reason and negotiate at a high level. To construct an institution from zero without human intervention may be too difficult, so an approach based on using knowledge from previous cases (like Case Based Reasoning, CBR) could be interesting and useful for solving this issue.

With a CBR approach to the Foundation phase (see Figure 9), a stored case (*institution case*) refers to a problem situation and contains a description of a problem, and its solution (the *institutional elements* to be adopted), and a new case (*coalition case*) contains the description of the problem to be solved. Therefore, when a coalition has been formed and needs to turn itself into an institution, agents should consult their case database (K) in order to find the stored institution's specification that adapts best to the present situation, and should then make the pertinent reforms to the selected specification in order to obtain an institution that works correctly.

The first step in this process is to build a *coalition case CC* from the coalition C that has been formed. The components of the *coalition case* are the elements that need to be taken into account when we search the institution that adapts best to the present coalition. These components are:

- *Ty (types):* this component is the set of types of the agents in the coalition.
- *Tk (tasks):* this component is the set of tasks of the agents in the coalition.
- *Ob (objectives):* this component is a set of objectives. These are not the objectives of the coalition (coalition has no objectives; each agent has its own objectives). These are a subgroup of the objectives of all the agents. More specifically, *Ob* is the set of shared objectives, extracted from the intersection of the different sets of objectives.
- *n (number of agents):* this component is the number of agents in the coalition.

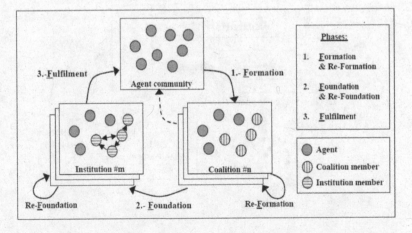

FIGURE 8. DEI construction phases (3F cycle).

- *div (diversity measure):* this component is the diversity within the coalition with respect to the objectives of the agents. This value is measured using an adaptation of Shannon's entropy function.
- *tr (internal trust):* this component is the mean trust value.

When we have the coalition case (*CC*), the next step is to start the CBR process. We need a *previous-institutions base*, which contains the knowledge of the system. This institutions base is called *K*. Each case of this base is an *institution case (IC)* which contains a *CC* and the *institutional elements (IE)*, that is, the elements that have to be adopted to turn the coalition into a dynamic institution.

To initialise the system, an initial set of *institution cases* must be introduced into the case base. Therefore, in the first CBR iterations the coalitions can reuse previous *institution cases*. This set is important, and should capture some general and typical associations among agents in the specific application domain. This process has to be performed by humans, before starting up the system, and then the rest of the processes should be automatic.

The *institutional elements IE* are:

- *M (Missions):* sets of specific objectives for each agent, where each objective is an expression.
- *N (Norms):* these are the norms to be adopted by the coalition. These can be obligations (*obl*), permissions (*per*), or prohibitions (*pro*).

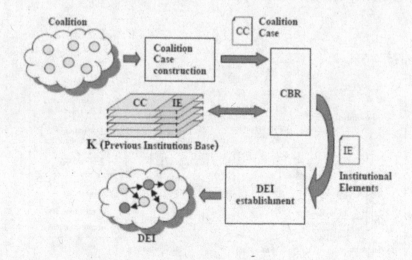

FIGURE 9. Foundation phase.

- *F (Fulfilment Requirements):* this component refers to future requirements for the fulfilment phase. It includes: *Fulfilment Conditions* (that allow the execution of the fulfilment process) and *Fulfilment Norms* (obligations, permissions and prohibitions that have to be followed during the fulfilment phase).
- *pr (Protocol):* this is the protocol to be adopted by the coalition. It will steer the communication processes within the dynamic institution.
- *ont (Ontology):* an ontology to be adopted by all agents in the coalition (of course if an agent already has the ontology there is no need to adopt it).

The CBR process compares the present *coalition case* (CC) with the *coalition case* included in each *institution case* (IC). This process requires some similarity rules. Each component of the CC has a specific similarity measure, and there is global similarity that corresponds to a weighted sum of partial similarities.

When the *institution case* (IC) that best adapts to the *coalition case* (CC) is found, an adjustment of the *institutional elements* (IE) is required in order to allow the agents of the new coalition to re-use them. This is not a simple process; in fact it can become very complicated, and it depends partially on the specific implementation of the model.

The Agents Research Lab (ARLab, University of Girona) has been focusing on the CBR approach to the Foundation phase. A preliminary exploratory work was carried out focusing on the simulation of Operations Other Than War (OOTW) [46]. These first experiments were very simple, but the preliminary results were encouraging. They used a centralized CBR approach on the OOTW domain, and showed that the foundation phase is feasible, and that the DEI life cycle can be fully implemented. This first work used the JADE/Agent-0 framework [49], and the agents had a BDI architecture with a mental state composed of three mental categories: *Beliefs*, *Commitments* and *Capabilities*. In this first approach, norms were adopted by taking on new commitments.

At this moment there is work in progress in the Digital Business Ecosystems application domain [48]. The idea is to allow the spontaneous composition and adaptation of the different services and software components within digital environments. In the business domain, these temporary business unions are called UTEs (from the spanish expression *Union Temporal de Empresas*). A UTE is a legal form of temporary business cooperation set up for a specified period of time or for a specified project or service. UTEs allow several companies to operate together in one common project. This form of association is commonly used in engineering and construction projects.

The ARLab is focusing its work on the study of the foundation process (turning coalitions into dynamic institutions), but there are several open issues in DEIs. These include works on the institutions' adaptivity and on the dissolution process (fulfilment phase). However, the CBR approach is not the only one feasible, and alternative approaches like meta-institutions or genetic algorithms should be studied. A Meta-Institution could provide general modules (norms, ontologies, protocols, etc.), which have to be instantiated in order to build specific dynamic electronic institutions. It could act as a shell for generating specific institutions for particular application domains.

8.2. Autonomic Electronic Institutions and Other Approaches

Currently the IIIA (The Artificial Intelligence Research Institute, Spanish Scientific Research Council) has a work in progress [7] that is focused on the extension of electronic institutions with autonomic capabilities (*autonomic electronic institutions*, AEIs) to allow them to yield a dynamical answer to changing circumstances, through the adaptation of their norms. In fact, the same happens in real human institutions; they are not static and they evolve over time by adapting their norms. In this work, a genetic algorithm is suggested to learn the best parameters for a population of agents. Current frameworks for Electronic Institutions do not support norm adaptation, so this work could have a significant impact on Electronic Institutions.

Both DEIs and AEIs are closely related to the concept of Contractual Agent Societies [18], a metaphor for building open information systems where agents configure themselves automatically through a set of dynamically negotiated social contracts. In this approach, social contracts define the shared context of agent interactions including ontologies, joint beliefs, joint goals, normative behaviours, etc.

Another related work is [29] which studies the dynamic selection of coordination mechanisms among autonomous agents. The authors presented a framework that enables autonomous agents to dynamically select the mechanism they choose to employ in order to coordinate their inter-related activities. They use a grid world scenario to empirically evaluate their framework.

Recently, there is an increasing interest on reorganisation and *organisational self-design*. However, although there are many practical applications being developed, there is need for formal theories to describe dynamic organisational structures.

In [39], a general view of the reorganisation problem within a multi-agent system is presented. The authors propose an organisation-centred model for controlling the reorganisation process. In their model, a special group of agents have autonomy to change their organisations (and thus their behaviour) using reinforcement learning for choosing an appropriate organisation. Their approach is based on the MOISE+, which is an organisational model for multi-agent systems based on notions like roles, groups, and missions.

Another interesting approach to organizational design is proposed in [35], where the authors conceive organizational designs as patterns of organizing multi-agent system with a view to classifying their performance characteristics. In this article, the authors present a survey of the major organizational paradigms used in multi-agent systems. These include hierarchies, holarchies, coalitions, teams, societies, federations, markets, etc. They provide a description of each, discuss their advantages and disadvantages, and provide examples of how they may be instantiated and maintained.

9. Conclusions

Artificial Social Intelligence, the study of the ways of building software or hardware systems capable of performing efficiently within a social environment, is a fascinating subject which can be tackled from different points of view depending upon the precise kind of social environment under consideration.

This chapter has presented the recent research work of the Artificial Social Intelligence cluster of the AgentCities.ES network covering two areas within Artificial Social Intelligence: Swarm Intelligence and Electronic Institutions. These two areas differ greatly both from the point of view of their purpose and from the point of view of the communication, reasoning and representation capabilities of the individual agents involved. Swarm Intelligence systems are mainly headed toward the resolution of optimization problems, and their problem solving capabilities emerge from the interactions that a set of very simple agents maintain with each other and with their environment. Electronic Institutions, on the other hand, are dialogical frameworks (with a social structure, an ontology and a communication language) in the form of higher-level MAS that integrate complex and possibly heterogeneous agents in the realization of a traditional institution. As we have seen in this chapter, both approaches have shown themselves useful in the development of a broad range of applications.

References

[1] Engelbrecht A.P. *Fundamentals in Computational Swarm Intelligence*. John Wiley and Sons, 2006.

[2] J.L. Arcos, P. Noriega, J.A. Rodríguez-Aguilar, and C. Sierra. E4mas through electronic institutions. In D. Weyns, H.V.D. Parunak, and F. Michel, editors, *Environments for Multiagent Systems III*, volume 4389 of *Lecture Notes in Artificial Intelligence*, pages 184–202. Springer-Verlag, 2007.

[3] R. Beckers, O.E. Holland, and Deneubourg J.L. *From Local Actions to Global Tasks: Stigmergy in Collective Robotics*, pages 181–189. Artificial Life IV. MIT Press, Cambridge, MA, 1994.

[4] J.M. Bishop. Stochastic searching networks. In *Proc. 1st IEE Conf. on Artificial Neural Networks*, pages 329–331, London, 1989.

[5] E. Bonabeau, M. Dorigo, and G. Théraulaz. *Swarm Intelligence. From Natura to Artificial Systems*. Oxford University Press, 1st edition, 1999.

[6] E. Bonabeau and G Théraulaz. Swarm smarts. *Scientific American*, March 2000:72–79, 2000.

[7] E. Bou, M. López-Sánchez, and J.A. Rodriguez-Aguilar. Norm adaptation of autonomic electronic institutions with multiple goals. *International Transactions on Systems Science and Applications*, 1(3):227–238, 2006.

[8] A. Byde, C. Preist, and N. Jennings. Decision procedures for multiple auctions. In *Proceedings of the First International Joint Conference on Autonomous Agents and Multi-Agent Systems*, pages 613–620, 2002.

[9] R. Byrne and A. Whiten. *Machiavellian Intelligence : Social Expertise and the Evolution of Intellect in Monkeys, Apes, and Humans (Oxford Science Publications).* Oxford University Press, USA, September 1989.

[10] S. Camazine, N.R. Franks, J. Sneyd, E. Bonabeau, J.L. Deneubourg, and G. Theraulaz. *Self-Organization in Biological Systems.* Princeton University Press, Princeton, NJ, USA, 2001.

[11] G. Di Caro and M. Dorigo. Antnet: Distributed stigmergetic control for communications networks. *J. Artif. Intell. Res. (JAIR)*, 9:317–365, 1998.

[12] G. Cuní, M. Esteva, P. Garcia, E. Puertas, C. Sierra, and T. Solchaga. Masfit: Multiagent systems for fish trading. In *16th European Conference on Artificial Intelligence (ECAI 2004)*, pages 710–714, Valencia, Spain, August 2004.

[13] K. Dautenhahn. Embodiment and interaction in socially intelligent life-like agents. *Lecture Notes in Computer Science*, 1562:102–142, 1999.

[14] K. Dautenhahn. Socially intelligent agents and the primate social brain –towards a science of social minds. In *Socially Intelligent Agents: The Human in the Loop, AAAI Fall Symposium*, North Falmouth, MA, 2000. AAAI Press.

[15] K. Dautenhahn. Socially intelligent agents. the human in the loop. *IEEE Transactions on Systems, Man, and Cybernetics-Part A:Systems and Humans*, 31:345–348, 2001.

[16] E. del Acebo. Sistemes multiagent i solució distribuida de problemes. Research Report. Departament d'Informàtica i Matemàtica Aplicada. Universitat de Girona, 2006.

[17] E. del Acebo and J.Ll. de la Rosa. Bar systems. a class of optimization algorithms for reactive multi-agent systems in real time environments. In *eNTeRTAIn'06 Workshop: New Trends in Real-Time Artificial Intelligence. ECAI 2006.*

[18] C. Dellarocas. Contractual agent societies: Negotiated shared context and social control in open multi-agent systems. In *Autonomous Agents-2000. Proceedings of the WS on Norms and Institutions in Multi-Agent Systems*, 2000.

[19] G. Di Caro. *Ant Colony Optimization and its application to adaptive routing in telecommunication networks.* Phd thesis, Faculé des Sciences Appliquées, Université Libre de Bruxelles, Brussels, Belgium, 2004.

[20] M. Dorigo and T. Stützle. *Ant Colony Optimization.* MIT Press, 2004.

[21] B.R. Duffy. Towards social intelligence in autonomous robotics: A review. In *Robotics, Distance Learning and Intelligent Communication Systems 2001 (RODLICS 2001)*, 2001.

[22] B. Edmonds. The constructibility of artificial intelligence (as defined by the turing test). *Journal of Logic, Language and Information*, 9(4):419–424, 2000.

[23] B. Edmonds and K. Dautenhahn. Social embeddedness: Origins, occurrence and opportunities. In *SAB'02: From Animals to Animats 7. The Seventh International Conference on the simuation of adaptive behavior*, Cambridge, MA, 2002. MIT Press.

[24] Ejs, easy java simulations. http://www.um.es/fem/Ejs.

[25] M. Esteva. *Electronic Institutions: from specification to development. PhD Thesis Universitat Politècnica de Catalunya (UPC), 2003.* Number 19 in IIIA Monograph Series. IIIA, 2003.

[26] M. Esteva, D. de la Cruz, and C. Sierra. ISLANDER: an electronic institutions editor. In W. Lewis Johnson Cristiano Castelfranchi, editor, *Proceedings of the First International Joint Conference on Autonomous Agents and Multiagent Systems, (July 15-19, 2002, Bologna, Italy)*, volume 3, pages 1045–1052. ACM PRESS, 2002.

[27] M. Esteva, B. Rosell, J.A. Rodríguez-Aguilar, and J.L. Arcos. AMELI: An agent-based middleware for electronic institutions. In N. et al. Jennings, editor, *Third international joint conference on autonomous agents and multiagent systems (AAMAS 2004)*, volume I, pages 236–243, New York, USA, July 19-23 2004. ACM.

[28] M. Esteva, W. Vasconcelos, C. Sierra, and J.A. Rodríguez-Aguilar. Norm consistency in electronic institutions. In *Proceedings of the XVII Brazilian Symposium on Artificial Intelligence (SBIA'04)*, number 3171 in Lecture Notes in Artificial Intelligence, pages 494–505. 2004.

[29] C.B. Excelente-Toledo and N.R. Jennings. The dynamic selection of coordination mechanisms. *Journal of Autonomous Agents and Multi-Agent Systems*, 9(1-2):55–85, 2004.

[30] S. Franklin and A. Graesser. Is it an agent, or just a program?: A taxonomy for autonomous agents. In *ECAI '96: Proceedings of the Workshop on Intelligent Agents III, Agent Theories, Architectures, and Languages*, pages 21–35, London, UK, 1997. Springer-Verlag.

[31] N. Gilbert and K.G. Troitzsch. *Simulation for the Social Scientist*. Open University Press, 2005.

[32] J.J. Gómez and J. Pavón. Methodologies for developing multi-agent systems. *Journal of Universal Computational Science*, 10(4):359–374, 2004.

[33] C. Hewitt. Offices are open systems. *ACM Transactions of Office Automation Systems*, 4(3):271–287, 1986.

[34] L.M. Hogg and N.R. Jennings. Socially rational agents. In *Proc. AAAI Fall symposium on Socially Intelligent Agents*, pages 61–63, Boston , Mass., 1997. Springer-Verlag.

[35] B. Horling and V. Lesser. A survey of multi-agent organizational paradigms. *The Knowledge Engineering Review*, 19(4):281–316, 2005.

[36] N. Hu and P. Steenkiste. Evaluation and characterization of available bandwidth probing techniques. *IEEE JSAC Special Issue in Internet and WWW Measurement, Mapping, and Modeling 21, 6.*, August 2003.

[37] C.A. Iglesias, M. Garijo, and J.C. Gonzalez. A survey of agent-oriented methodologies. In J. P. Muller, M. Singh, and A. S. Rao, editors, *Intelligent Agents V*, Lecture Notes in Artificial Intelligence. Springer-Verlag, 1999.

[38] N.R. Jennings, K. Sycara, and M. Wooldridge. A roadmap of agent research and development. *Autonomous Agents and Multi-agent Systems*, 1:275–306, 1998.

[39] O. Boissier J.F. Hübner, J.S. Sichman. Using the moise+ for a cooperative framework of mas reorganisation. In *SBIA 2004. Proceedings of the XVII Brazilian Symposium on Artificial Intelligence*, pages 506–515, 2004.

[40] J.L.Arcos, M. Esteva, P. Noriega, J.A. Rodríguez-Aguilar, and C. Sierra. Environment engineering for multiagent systems. *Engineering Applications of Artificial Intelligence*, 18(1):191–204, January 2005.

[41] I. Khalil-Ibrahim, G. Kotsis, and R. Kronsteiner. Substitution rules for the verification of norm-compliance in electronic institutions. In *Proceedings of the 13th IEEE International Workshops on Enabling Technologies: Infrastructure for Collaborative Enterprises (WET ICEâ04)*, pages 21–26. IEEE Computer Society, 2004.

[42] J.F. Kihlstrom and N. Cantor. *The Handbook of Intelligence*, chapter Social Intelligence, pages 359–379. Cambridge University Press, Cambridge, U.K., 2000.

[43] H. Kummer, L. Daston, G. Gigerenzer, and J. Silk. *The social intelligence hypothesis*, pages 67–81. Human by Nature: Between Biology and Social Sciences, vol. 47. Erlbaum Associates, Hillsdale, NJ, 1991.

[44] M.A. Lewis and G.A. Bekey. *The Behavioral Self-Organization of Nanorobots Using Local Rules*. Proceedings of the 1992 IEEE/RSJ International Conference on Intelligent Robots and Systems. 1992.

[45] M. Luck, P. McBurney, and C. Preist. Agent technology: Enabling next generation computing. a roadmap for agent based computing. AgentLink II, 2003.

[46] E. Muntaner-Perich, J. L. de la Rosa, C. Carrillo, S. Delfín, and A. Moreno. Dynamic electronic institutions for humanitarian aid simulation. In *AI Research and Development*, volume 146 of *Frontiers in AI and Applications*, pages 239–246. IOS Press, 2006.

[47] E. Muntaner-Perich and J.L. de la Rosa. Towards dynamic electronic institutions: from agent coalitions to agent institutions. In *Innovative Concepts for Autonomic and Agent-Based Systems*, volume 3825 of *Lecture Notes in Computer Science*, pages 109–121. Springer-Verlag, 2006.

[48] E. Muntaner-Perich and J.L. de la Rosa. Using dynamic electronic institutions to enable digital business ecosystems. In *COIN'06 Workshop: Coordination, Organization, Institutions and Norms in Agent Systems, ECAI 2006*, 2006.

[49] E. Muntaner-Perich, E. del Acebo, and J.L. de la Rosa. Rescatando agent-0. una aproximación moderna a la programación orientada a agentes. In *II Taller de Desarrollo en Sistemas Multiagente, DESMA'05. Primer Congreso Español de Informática, CEDI*, 2005.

[50] P. Noriega. *Agent-Mediated Auctions: The Fishmarket Metaphor*. Number 8 in IIIA Monograph Series. 1997.

[51] D.C. North. *Institutions, Institutional change and economic performance*. Cambridge Universisy press, 40 west 20th Street, New York, NY 10011-4211, USA, 1990.

[52] P. Panzarasa and N.R. Jennings. Collective cognition and emergence in multi-agent systems. In R. Sun, editor, *Cognition and Multi-Agent Interaction: From cognitive modeling to social simulation*, pages 401–408. Cambridge University Press, 2006.

[53] K.E. Parsopoulos and M.N. Vrahatis. Recent approaches to global optimization problems through particle swarm optimization. *Neural Computing*, 1 (2-3):235–306, 2002.

[54] H. Pattison, D.D. Corkill, and V.R. Lesser. *Distributed Artificial Intelligence*, chapter Instantiating Descriptions of Organizational Structures, pages 59–96. Pitman Publishers, 1987.

[55] J.A. Plucker. Human intelligence: Historical influences, current controversies, teaching resources. Retrieved 3-3-2007, from http://www.indiana.edu/ intell, 2003.

[56] H. Prendinger and M. Ishizuka. Let's talk! socially intelligent agents for language conversation training. *IEEE Transactions on System, Man and Cybernetics - Part A. Systems and Humans*, 31(5), September 2001.

[57] Repast. http://repast.sourceforge.net.

[58] M. Resnick. *Turtles, Termites and Traffic Jams, Explorations in Massively Parallel Microworlds*. MIT Press, 1997.

[59] J.A. Rodríguez-Aguilar. *On the Design and Construction of Agent-mediated Electronic Institutions,*. Number 14 in IIIA Monograph Series. 2003.

[60] R. Schoonderwoerd, O.E. Holland, J.L. Bruten, and L.J.M. Rothkrantz. Ant-based load balancing in telecommunications networks. *Adaptive Behavior*, 5:169–207, 1996.

[61] Simile. http://simulistics.com.

[62] Simulink. http://www.mathworks.com/products/simulink/.

[63] E.L. Thorndike. Intelligence and its use. *Harper's Magazine*, 140:227–235, 1920.

[64] W. Vasconcelos. Norm verification and analysis of electronic institutions. In Joao Leite, Andrea Omicini, Paolo Torroni, and Pinar Yolum, editors, *Declarative Agent Languages and Technologies II: Second International Workshop, DALT*, volume 3476 of *Lecture Notes in Computer Science*, pages 166–182. Springer-Verlag, 2005.

[65] F. Viganò. A framework for model checking institutions. In *Proceedings of the ECAI Workshop on Model checking and Artificial Intelligence (MOCHART IV)*, 2006.

Esteve del Acebo
ARLAB group
Universitat de Girona
Lluís Santaló s/n
Girona 17071. Spain
e-mail: esteve.acebo@udg.edu

Whitestein Series in Software Agent Technologies, 179–206
© 2007 Birkhäuser Verlag Basel/Switzerland

Agent Applications in Tourism

Antonio Moreno

Abstract. Agent technology has been applied in recent years to solve different problems that are common to many applications in Tourism, such as dynamic service discovery, automatic management of user profiles, personalisation of cultural information or planning of touristic activities. This chapter shows different contributions of Spanish research groups in the following areas: personalised access to cultural information from mobile devices, planning of complex touristic activities, service discovery in Tourism applications and dynamic location tracking.

Keywords. Tourism, mobile devices, user profile management, personalisation, recommendation, service discovery, planning, dynamic location tracking.

1. Introduction

Agent technology is especially amenable to be applied to domains in which information is physically distributed and a set of autonomous entities have to join their efforts and coordinate their activities to solve a complex task. Tourism is a domain with such characteristics, as a tourist needs to search for information related to the cultural and leisure activities available in a given city (which is usually distributed in different places all around the city, as it depends on different stakeholders), filter those that fit with his personal interests, and try to build a plan in which the selected activities may be performed within a given time span. There are diverse research fields within agent technology that can be directly applied to the provision of cultural information to tourists:

- Implementation of agents in mobile devices.

    Tourists are keen on accessing cultural information directly from their mobile devices, at any point of the city at any time, without having to go to tourist offices or specific places in the city.

Co-authors of this chapter: Javier Bajo, Vicente Botti, Juan M. Corchado, Arantza Ilarramendi, Sergio Ilarri, Vicente Julián, Miguel A. López Carmona, Iván Marsá, Eduardo Mena, Antonio Moreno, Juan Pavón and Aïda Valls.

- Automatic management of user profiles, and personalised proactive recommendations.

    It is very interesting that systems that provide information to tourists are able to automatically learn and maintain a profile with the interests of every particular user, so that they can filter the cultural information that is relevant for each person and can offer that information proactively to the user at the appropriate moment.

- Dynamic discovery and access to tourist e-services.

    Tourists should be able to easily discover the available e-services and be able to access them in a transparent way.

- Planning of touristic activities.

    An intelligent agent-based system with planning capabilities may help a tourist to select those activities that are more relevant for him during his stay in a city and to arrange a temporal sequence of movements within the city in order to optimize the time that the tourist has to enjoy his holidays.

The following sections of this chapter provide some examples of agent-based systems related to the Tourism domain which have been developed by Spanish research groups in recent years:

- `Turist@` is a multi-agent system developed at University Rovira i Virgili that is focused on the intelligent personalised proactive recommendation of cultural activities to tourists visiting Tarragona.
- `TourAgent`, developed at the Technical University of Valencia, allows users to make structured searches of tourist information, make reservations in restaurants, and plan the activities in a given day.
- The University Complutense of Madrid and the University of Salamanca designed, developed and made a trial with real tourists of an agent-based system that uses Case Based Reasoning techniques to provide personalised plans to tourists visiting Salamanca.
- The University of Alcalá has proposed the idea of having a hierarchy of *smart spaces* in order to approach the problem of dynamic service discovery.
- Finally, `Loqomotion` is a system designed at the University of Zaragoza that solves the problem of dynamic location tracking in Tourism applications.

2. `Turist@`: agent-based proactive and personalised recommendation of cultural activities

Big cities attract tourists due to the large amount of activities that they offer. However, despite being an advantage, that huge offer also has a negative side: the tourist must select the activities he wants to do from an immense set.

The multi-agent system `Turist@`, developed at University Rovira i Virgili (URV, Tarragona), tries to remedy this difficulty. The system is context-aware, and the user may receive touristic information at any point of the city by interacting with a *Personal Agent* that is executing in his mobile phone. The system keeps a dynamic profile of the interests of each user, and uses both fuzzy logic and novel content-based and collaborative recommendation techniques to make personalised and proactive suggestions of cultural events that may interest the user.

The system is composed of a set of agents that have information about different types of cultural activities, such as museums, itineraries, conferences or exhibitions. This idea makes the approach very scalable, since it is very easy to dynamically add agents that manage new kinds of events. Figure 1 depicts the structure of Turist@ (showing only a subset of the cultural activities). In addition to the agents that manage different types of events, there is a *Broker Agent* that facilitates the mediation between the *Personal Agent* (which belongs to each tourist that logs into the system) and the cultural activities agents, and a *Recommender Agent* responsible for making (on demand or proactively) personalised recommendations to the users as well as maintaining a database with their profiles. As will be described below, both content-based and collaborative techniques are used to make the recommendations.

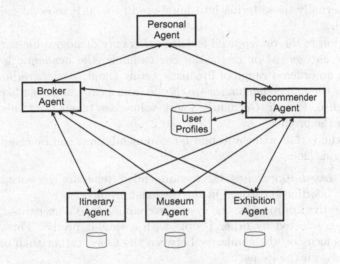

FIGURE 1. Turist@ multi-agent system architecture.

2.1. Personalised recommendation of cultural events

The main feature of Turist@ is the existence of a personalized recommendation system. The purpose of this system is to select, from a large set of activities, the ones that are most suitable for a particular person according to his personal characteristics and preferences. Each activity is described by a set of variables that include descriptive information about the activity, such as the place, timetable or price, and information about the features of the activity that can match with the interests of the tourist. To make this matching, the *Recommender Agent* keeps a dynamic profile of the user's interests.

An activity is represented with a vector a_i, in which each component indicates to what extent the activity fits with a specific property (e.g., the artistic or historical relevance of the activity). In the same way, the user's profile u_i is described in terms of numerical preference degrees with respect to the variables that describe the activities.

Any recommender system must consider at least the following three issues: (1) how to initialize the user's profile,(2) how to use the profile to make recommendations and (3) how to adapt the user's profile dynamically (explicitly vs. implicitly).

The user profile in Turist@ is initialized with the information provided by the user the first time he accesses the system. One of the weaknesses of recommender systems is that people usually do not want to spend much time providing data to computer applications. To ease this task the tourist is allowed to describe his interest in each of the variables considered in the system by selecting a linguistic term from a fixed vocabulary: {none, little, medium, quite, a lot}. The system translates internally those terms into numbers in the [0,1] interval using a fuzzy logic approach.

In addition to the preferential features, there are demographic variables that can be either categorical or linguistic. For example, the academic level can be selected from an ordered range of linguistic terms {none, basic, graduate, university}, whereas the spoken languages are chosen from a categorical set like {Catalan, Spanish, English, French, German}. These values are taken from this closed set and stored in the profile.

The methods that make automatic recommendations can be classified in two broad paradigms [26]:

- *Content-based approaches*: the recommended items are the ones that match with the information stored in the personal profile.
- *Collaborative approaches*: the system recommends to a user those items that have been selected by other people with a similar profile. Thus, those approaches focus on the similarity between the users, rather than on the similarity between the items.

A pure content-based system has several shortcomings. Considering only the similarities in the features stored in the personal profile, one can omit other aspects of the items that also influence user decisions. Moreover, the user is restricted to seeing items similar to his profile, without having the opportunity to explore new activities, with different unexplored features. The pure collaborative approach can deal with any kind of content and the user can receive items with content dissimilar to those seen in the past. However, this pure approach has other drawbacks: a large number of users is needed to be able to start making recommendations; when a new item appears, there is no way to recommend it before any user has selected it; and for a user whose tastes are unusual compared with the rest, it will be difficult to find similar users, which will lead to poor recommendations. By combining content-based and collaborative techniques, one can eliminate some of the weaknesses of each approach. Turist@ applies a content-based and a collaborative method separately and then aggregates the results to obtain the final list of recommended items.

Turist@ makes content-based recommendations using only the user's preferences stored in the profile. A similarity measure is used to compare the user's profile u_i with each activity profile a_i. Several classical similarities were implemented within the system.

When a minimum number of user profiles has been stored in the database, the *Recommender Agent* can start to make collaborative recommendations. Unsupervised clustering techniques are used to generate a partition of the users into clusters of users with similar tastes [27]. However, those clusters must be periodically updated in order to take into account the changes in the user profiles. The clusters are computed considering the users' preferences and also the demographic variables. To make a recommendation to a tourist, the system selects those items that have been positively evaluated by the people that belong to the same cluster as him.

Finally, the automatic adaptation of the user's profile has also been studied in Turist@. Both explicit and implicit adaptation procedures have been incorporated into the system.

- *Explicit profile adaptation*: the user indicates which of the recommended activities he likes and which day he will do it. When the system detects that the activity has been finished, it sends a message to the user asking for an evaluation of this activity. The user must pick up one of the terms {*horrible, bad, good, very-good, excellent*}, which is used by the system to modify the vector of user's preferences accordingly (reducing or increasing the preference value stored in the profile).

- *Implicit profile adaptation*: this is done when the tourist makes searches in Turist@ through the *Broker Agent*. The search parameters are used to detect if the user is looking for activities with interests in features different from the ones that he used to be interested in. If that is the case, his profile is updated. The change in the user preferences depends on the actual preference values in the profile and the main characteristics of the activity (e.g., if the user searches for art exhibitions, his interest in the *art* feature will be slightly increased).

2.2. Dynamic location of users

To provide touristic information to users, Turist@ features a *Personal Agent* that is executed in a mobile phone. The main advantages of this technology in the Tourism domain are:

- It is not necessary for tourists to acquire new specific hardware to access the system.
- The tourist can receive at any place information on new activities that are uploaded to the system.

- The system can know the position of the tourist in the city and can provide personalised information about the sites of interest that are near this position.

This agent is implemented using JADE-LEAP. To know the position of the tourist, the GSM technology is used. The reasons for not using GPS are the following: it is not always possible in a city to locate the satellites needed to calculate the position (for example, if the device is in a pocket or inside a building), it requires some start-up time, and not all the phones include this feature.

The GSM network is the natural way of communicating in mobile phones, so no extra device is needed. This network divides the territory into small cells of some hundreds of meters, which is a good approximation to the location of the tourist inside the city. This precision is necessary and sufficient to know what interesting cultural activities are available in the vicinity (inside that cell). So, each time that a new activity is loaded to the system, it is located in one of those cells, which are uniquely identified in the GSM network. To work in this way, the *Personal Agent* must read the configuration of the cells in the city that the user is visiting before starting to use the system. Figure 2 shows the interface of the *Personal Agent* when the user is looking at his position on the city map.

Once the position of the user has been automatically discovered by the agents, the possibility of making proactive recommendations is straightforward. The *Recommender Agent* is notified about the position of the tourist, and it uses a similarity measure to filter which of the activities in the corresponding cell coincide with the preferences of the person. If any activity matches, it is automatically recommended to the tourist.

FIGURE 2. Visualizing the user location.

2.3. Integration of Turist@ components

The different aspects of the Turist@ system (the basic multi-agent system, the *Personal Agents* running in mobile devices, the recommendation techniques and the planning capabilities) have been developed in the last four years independently, mainly by Computer Science students at URV. This temporal span has fostered the use of different versions of the underlying development framework (JADE and

JADE-LEAP). Currently all the different parts are being integrated in a single system, and trials of the whole system in the city of Tarragona are scheduled for summer 2008.

3. TourAgent

The main goal of this research is to develop an open system, capable of incorporating as many agents that can provide useful services to the tourist as necessary. To provide personalised services, the system needs to identify tourists in a transparent and ubiquitous manner. In this sense, the growing use of handheld devices is a great opportunity to interact with the clients in a simple way and to manage the tourist profiles.

The TourAgent system [25] is a multi-agent system architecture which offers services in the Tourism industry. It gives the possibility to different users (mainly tourists in a city) to obtain up-to-date information about the places they will visit and to plan activities in a specific day. Users can access and employ these services using a Java-enabled mobile phone or PDA.

From a tourist point of view, it would be of great help to have all the updated information, in a dynamic and flexible way, about the different places of interest in the city, such as a cheap restaurant, or a restaurant that serves a particular type of food, giving them the opportunity to make reservations in those restaurants; or if they want to know if there is any art showroom open; or simply know to which cinema they can go and receive information about which movies are playing. Because of all of these aspects, the advantages of having a resource for tourists that allows them to search and plan different activities of interest during a given day are noticeable.

3.1. System architecture

This section presents the developed application in which the applicability of agent technology integrating different devices has been evaluated. In the implemented version of this system, a tourist can find information about places of interest like restaurants, cinemas, museums, theatres and other places of general interest like monuments, churches, beaches, parks, etc., according to his preferences using his mobile phone or PDA. Once a specific place has been selected, the tourist can establish a process to make a reservation in a restaurant, buy tickets for a film, etc, in a given time period proposed by the tourist.

The system is basically formed by four classes of agents: the *BrokerAgent*, the *UserAgent*, the *SightAgent* and the *PlanAgent*. The main functionalities of these agents are:

- The *BrokerAgent* has updated information about the registered *SightAgents*. It is in charge of establishing a communication between the user and the *SightAgents*.

- The *SightAgent* manages all the information about the characteristics and activities of one specific place of interest in the city. It is exclusive to one place of interest and has all the information efficiently up-to-date.
- The *UserAgent* allows the tourist to use the different services by means of a GUI on his mobile device. This agent is exclusive to one interested tourist.
- The *PlanAgent* is in charge of establishing and managing all the planning processes offered by the system, taking into account the preferences previously established by the users, and/or different searches users made previously within the system.

As agents need to communicate with each other, it was indispensable to establish a common conceptual vocabulary as a representation of the information for establishing and controlling tasks. The implemented ontology gives detailed descriptions of touristic places, contains information about scheduling (necessary for the planning service), etc. Besides, the developed ontology has some actions and predicates that help to control and establish tasks in the system.

Figure 3 shows the architecture of the implemented MAS system, illustrating the communication between the different agents commented above.

3.2. Basic functionalities

In the proposed system, if the user (tourist) is anywhere in the city, using the GPRS connection he can take advantage of the tourism information system, sending questions or actions to the *BrokerAgent*. The *BrokerAgent* will interact with the corresponding *SightAgents* trying to find the desired information about the sites that fall into the parameters the user has chosen. Then, the *BrokerAgent* will send the appropriate answer to *UserAgent*. After the user gets an answer to his search, he will establish automatically a communication with the corresponding *SightAgent*. Users can establish the required connection using GPRS. The wireless option can be set up and established (from a PDA or a smartphone supporting this kind of connection) to access the system, if the user has the proper infrastructure to do it. The main functionalities of the system are the following:

Search (see Figure 4). This service is offered by the *BrokerAgent* and it is invoked by the *UserAgent*. In order to be employed, the *UserAgent* must send a *Request* message (according to FIPA-ACL) with the preferences as the message content. The result of this service will be a list formed by all the places that match the user requirements containing the relevant information about each specific site. To check the detailed information of a specific place, the user can perform a search by different types of places like restaurants, cinemas, museums, theaters, and other places of general interest like monuments, churches, beaches, parks, etc. This search can be filtered according to the user's preferences. As a result of this service, the *UserAgent* will receive a list of elements that fulfil its search parameters. By choosing one of the elements of the list, the *UserAgent* will get detailed information about the place.

Reserve (see Figure 5). This service is offered by the *SightAgent* and can be invoked by the *UserAgent*. In order to be used, the *UserAgent* must send a *Propose*

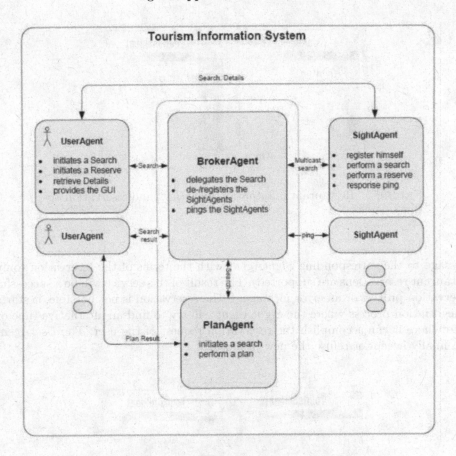

FIGURE 3. TourAgent general architecture.

FIGURE 4. Main options view (left) and basic restaurant search options (right).

FIGURE 5. Restaurant information view (left) and reservation options (right).

message to the corresponding *SightAgent* with the terms of the reservation (only restaurant reservations are supported). The result of this service will be a successful reservation process or an error message. If the reservation is not possible, it starts a negotiation process where the *SightAgent* will try to find an alternative time or date where it can accomplish the reservation request of the user. The *UserAgent* can finally accept or refuse the new proposal.

FIGURE 6. Main plan options (left) and tentative plan result (right).

Plan a Specific Day (see Figure 6). This service is offered by the *PlanAgent* and can be invoked by the *UserAgent*. In order to be used, the *UserAgent* must send a *Request* message to the *PlanAgent* with some parameters to take into account for the plan. The result of this service will be a list of places or activities forming the plan. This important service makes it possible for users to plan a specific day with a series of activities where reservations for lunch, dinner or both can be included. The *PlanAgent* tries to arrange the activities in such a way that time can be managed efficiently throughout the day.

3.3. Implementation details

The Tourism Information System has been implemented using JADE. The agents running on the mobile devices were implemented using JADE-LEAP. The graphic interface (GUI) was developed using J2ME, that combines the Mobile Information Device Profile (MIDP) with the Connected Limited Device Configuration (CLDC). Different controlled experiments were conducted to evaluate different parameters in order to assess the proposal. The main set of experiments investigates the performance of the system according to the number of tourists requesting services at the same time. As an example, Figure 7 illustrates how the average response time increases in proportion to the number of agents. However, the system maintains a good performance, taking into account the great number of services requested concurrently in each test.

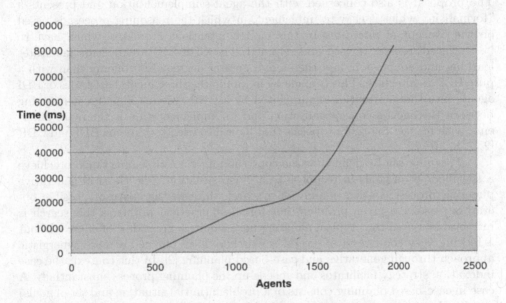

FIGURE 7. Average time test.

4. A CBR-planning based Tourism application

Agents are usually classified depending on the set of capabilities that they support, such as autonomy, reactivity, proactivity, social ability, reasoning, learning, and mobility, among others [11]. One of the possibilities is the development of deliberative agents using *case-based reasoning* (CBR) systems, as a way to implement adaptive systems in open and dynamic environments. Agents in this context must be able to reply to events, take the initiative according to their goals, communicate with other agents, interact with users, and make use of past experiences to find the best plans to achieve goals.

Deliberative agents are usually based on a BDI model [9], which considers agents as having certain *mental attitudes*: Beliefs, Desires, and Intentions (BDI). Under this model, agents have a *mental state* that consists of informational, motivational, and deliberative states respectively. Case-based reasoning systems solve new problems by adapting solutions that have been used in the past. A classical CBR reasoning cycle consists of four sequential phases: retrieve, reuse, revise, and retain [1]. The structure of the CBR system has been designed around the concept of a *case*. A case is made of three components: the problem, the solution, and the result obtained when the proposed solution is applied [1]. The CBR-BDI proposal defines a direct mapping from the concept of an agent to the reasoning model. In this model, the CBR system is completely integrated into the agent's architecture. The proposal is also concerned with the agent's implementation and presents a "formalism" which is easy to implement, in which the reasoning process is based on the concept of *intention*. In this model, intentions are cases, which have to be retrieved, reused, revised and retained. The CBR-BDI architecture facilitates learning and adaptation, and therefore a greater degree of autonomy than with a pure BDI architecture. This is made by mapping the three mental attitudes of BDI agents into the information manipulated by a CBR system. This direct mapping between the agent's conceptualisation and its implementation is the main difference with respect to other proposals that have also tried to combine BDI and CBR [2, 7, 8, 10].

Planning can be defined as the construction of a course of actions to achieve a specified set of goals in response to a given situation. The classical generative planning process consists mainly of a search through the space of possible operators to solve a given problem, but for most practical problems this search is intractable. Given that typical planning may require a great deal of effort without achieving very good results, several researchers have pursued a more synergistic approach through generative and case-based planning [2]. In this context, the case indexation strategy facilitates and speeds up the planning process substantially. A case in case-based planning consists of a problem (initial situation and set of goals) and its plan. Given a new problem, the objective of the retrieval and reuse phase is to select a case or a number of cases from the case-base whose problem description is most similar to the description of the new problem and to adapt it/them to the new situation. In case-based reasoning, two different approaches to reuse can be distinguished: transformational and derivational adaptation. Transformational adaptation methods usually consist of a set of domain dependent concepts that directly modify the solution that was obtained in the retrieved case. For derivational adaptation, the retrieved solution is not modified directly, but is used to guide the planner to find the solution.

There are different ways to integrate generative and case-based planning. The method chosen in the work described in this section is the *Variational Calculus*

Based Planner (VCBP) [5]. Although VCBP is domain dependent, it introduces a new interesting strategy to efficiently deal with the adaptation stage. Variational Calculus-based Planner guarantees the planning and re-planning of the intentions in execution time. This planning strategy is divided into two steps:

1. identify cases that are similar to the problem case (retrieval stage), and
2. adapt them to the problem case (reuse stage).

Variational calculus automates the reasoning cycle of the BDI agents, and guarantees the identification of an efficient plan, close to the optimum. Although different types of planning mechanisms can be found in the literature, none of them allows replanning in execution time, and agents inhabit changing environments in which replanning in execution time is required if goals are to be achieved successfully in real-time.

The proposed system has been used to improve an agent based wireless system developed for guiding tourists around the city of Salamanca (Spain). The integrated, multi-platform computer system is composed of a guide agent (*Planner Agent*) that assesses the tourists and helps them to identify tourist routes in a city with a given visiting time period and under a number of restrictions related to cost, tourist interest, etc. There is one assistant agent for each user of the system, the *Performer Agents*. Each user willing to use the system has to register and solicit one of these agents. Finally, there is a third type of agent, the *Tracker Agent*, which maintains updated information about the monuments, the restaurants, public transport conditions, etc. This agent maintains horizontally and vertically compiled information on hotel accommodation, restaurants, the commercial sector and transport, in order to meet the needs of the potential visitor on an individually customized basis, and responds to requests for information, reservations and purchases as soon as they are expressed.

The user may decide whether to install the corresponding *Performer Agent* on a mobile phone or PDA, or run it on the server and interact with it via its mobile device. Users may interact either with their *Performer Agents* installed in their wireless devices or in an internet server. The *Performer Agents* interact with the *Planner Agent* looking for plans, and the *Tracker Agent* interacts with the *Planner Agent* to exchange information. The *Planner Agent* is the only CBR-BDI agent in this architecture. The *Performer Agents* can be considered assistant agents and the *Tracker Agent* is a reactive agent. Tourists may use a mobile device to contact their agents and to indicate their preferences (monuments to visit, visits duration, dinner time, amount of money to spend, etc.).

The *Planner Agent* is the only deliberative agent in this system. This agent deals with *cases*. There are different types of cases. The cases store information about the environment, for example the opening and closing times of monuments. This type of information can be seen as an agent belief, for example, the Museum of Contemporary Art opens from 9:00 to 14:00 and from to 16:30 to 20:00. Cases may also be previous successful routes (plans), as shown in Figure 8(a), that includes the monuments to visit, the time to spend visiting each monument, information

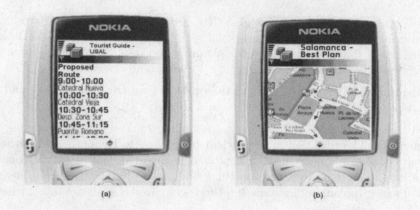

(a)   (b)

FIGURE 8. Textual and graphical presentations of plans.

about the cost of the visit, the time required for going from one place to another, the characteristics of the route (museum route, family route, university route, roman route, gothic route), etc. Once a tourist contacts the system he has to describe his profile, select the type of visit in which he is interested, determine how much money he wants to spend and for how long, and the type of restaurants he prefers. This information is used to construct the *problem case*. Then the reasoning mechanism of the planning agent generates the plan. This reasoning mechanism is the previously mentioned CBR system using VCBP [5, 6].

The *Planner Agent* generates a plan that fulfils the given conditions. This plan is easy to modify at execution time if the user changes his mind. The retrieval stage must be carried out using a method that guarantees the retrieval of a reasonably small number of cases that are related to the current problem case. A number of different retrieval methods have been analysed, such as Sparse Kernel Principal Component Analysis [3] or a K-nearest neighbour algorithm based strategy [6]. The best results have been obtained with a variational calculus based strategy. Once the most similar cases have been retrieved, VCBP adapts them to the problem case (reuse stage). Basically, for the solutions (plans) corresponding to the similar retrieved cases, the following procedure is executed. The new optimum plan is constructed in such a way that the planner proposes the plan in sections. The optimum plan is the one with a greatest density of plans around it, that is, the one that offers the best alternative for replanning if an interruption happens. Figure 8(b) shows a graphical view of a generated plan. The plan is presented in sections to the user. If the plan is interrupted, the user can choose the replanning option.

As can be seen in [4], the system was tested during 2003. The system needed initial knowledge, so the case base was initially filled with information collected during a recent five month period. Local tourist guides provided the agent with a number of standard routes. Three city hotels offered the option to their 6217 guests to use the help of the agent or a professional tourist guide; 14% of them decided to use the agent based system and 23% of them used the help of a tourist guide. The rest of the tourists visited the city by themselves. On arrival at the hotel the tourists were asked to evaluate their visit and the route. The tourists that used the help of the agent-based tourist guide provided the answer directly to the agent. The system was tested for 135 days and the obtained results were very encouraging [4].

5. A hierarchical approach to service discovery in touristic *Smart Spaces*

One of the technical solutions to the problem of service discovery from mobile devices is defining a Service-Oriented Architecture where physical locations are given a key role. In particular, SETH (Smart EnvironmenT Hierarchy) approaches this problem by defining a hierarchical, modular architecture for smart spaces, which are specific, self-contained locations within the environment able to adapt themselves to the user needs and to provide customized interfaces to the services available at each moment. There are vastly different research lines regarding service provision in smart environments, like i-Room [30] or Gaia [29]. Some of them use multi-agent systems, as they have been revealed as a good technology for developing distributed, autonomous, and intelligent systems [28]. The hierarchical approach devised in SETH allows one to create complex smart environments by combining, for instance, a certain number of smart rooms to create a smart building and a certain number of smart buildings and smart outdoor spaces to create a smart touristic city. Detailed description of the SETH architecture is beyond the scope of this chapter, and can be found in [14]. In this section the most relevant characteristics of the architecture needed to follow the rest of the description are outlined. Then, the section focuses on the mechanisms for service discovery and access to services.

5.1. SETH: a hierarchy of *Smart Spaces*

SETH relies on the concept of *smart spaces* (SSs), which are specific, self-contained locations within the environment. From a functional point of view, a given *smart space* is characterized by a set of devices, a set of available services, and a given context. Smart spaces may be hierarchically arranged if the specific characteristics of the environment require so. This hierarchical approach allows one to provide different layers of services, context information, and security. The demonstration scenario which will be referred to through the rest of the section considers a *city* smart space, which contains four indoor smart spaces, *home*, *restaurant*, *hotel* and *touristoffice* and an outdoor smart space *monument*. The *hotel* smart space contains the *secondFloor* space, which also contains the *hotelRoom* and *meetingRoom* spaces.

Inheritance rules may be established in the hierarchy to govern from which context information, services and devices from higher levels in the hierarchy are available at a specific location. Aggregation rules may also be established, so that a smart space may export context information, services and devices to other spaces located at higher levels in the hierarchy. Inheritance and aggregation rules may be combined to allow, for example, that users within the *home* space have access through inheritance to the reservation service, which is provided at the *restaurant* space, but has been made available to users in the *city* space by means of aggregation.

5.2. SETH devices

To meet its goals, the architecture relies on a set of devices distributed throughout the environment. The *Smart Space Agent Platform (SSAP)*, mandatory in any SETH smart space, contains the agent platform which supports the existence of all other agents in the smart space, hosting the higher-level agents of the system and also those agents used to control non-intelligent devices. *Devices with Agents* are sensors and effectors with a certain degree of autonomy, usually provided by agents running over an embedded Java Virtual Machine. *Devices without Agents* are sensors and effectors without autonomy or intelligence, controlled from the SSAP. Furthermore, each user must carry a portable *Identification Device*, which is used to identify the user and determine the user location within the smart environment. Finally, users may carry handheld, mobile *Personal Devices* (cell phones, PDAs) which not only may provide the functionality of the identification devices above, but may also host the necessary agents to learn, maintain and try to satisfy user preferences, and to display adequate interfaces to the available services when needed.

5.3. SETH software agents

In a typical SETH smart space, different kinds of software agents may be found. The *Smart Space Coordination Agent (SSCA)*, residing in the SSAP, provides device, service and context discovery to all other users or agents in the smart space, and to SSCAs of other smart spaces. *Device Agents* provide a common interface to devices, so that other agents in the system may use them regardless of specific hardware issues. *System Agents*, like context and security agents, reside in the SSAP, and add an additional layer of intelligence on top of the devices in the environment through control and coordination mechanisms. *Personal Agents (PAs)*, usually residing in the user personal device, are the very representatives of users to the environment, since they are in charge of enforcing user preferences. Finally, *Service Agents* are intended to provide services directly to the user, and they may be *persistent*, if they are always active at a given SSAP, and *non-persistent or mobile*, if they are created by the SSCA for each request of the service, move from one SSAP to another when user location changes, and are destroyed once the use of the service has concluded. For the *Service Agents* to be able to provide their services to the users, the *Personal Agents* need to be aware of the services available at every moment. This is where the problem of service discovery appears.

5.4. Service discovery

Since *Personal Agents* are transported within the user personal devices, they move through the different SSAPs following the movements of their associated users to provide personalized services at each location. But in order to provide this personalization, PAs need to know which are the available services, and how to access them. Service discovery functionality is provided by the *Smart Space Coordination Agents* (SSCAs). As the coordinator of a given smart space, an SSCA must be aware of all agents present in the space, and all the services they may provide. This may be accomplished through any registration process, such as the ones provided by CORBA, the IEEE FIPA DFs [15] or by architectures based on Web Services. In this way, the SSCA knows all devices, agents and services available at its associated smart space. The address of the SSCA of a given smart space is provided by the context agents when the *Personal Agent* enters the associated SSAP, so the PA may know the addresses of all relevant SSCAs in the hierarchy.

At any given time, a PA can query the SSCA at its SSAP for a list of available services. Queries may be general or specific (i.e., request a list of all available services which meet certain characteristics). The returned list of services includes the name of the service, the service agents that provide them, and the service description, which in turn contains the information needed by the personal agent to know how to access the service.

As stated above, services may be inherited from higher levels in the hierarchy or aggregated from lower levels. Services may be inherited or aggregated at the SSCA level or at the personal agent level, and thus service discovery may be *SSCA-driven* or *PA-driven*. Inheritance or aggregation at the SSCA level occurs when an SSCA is interested in providing a service available at another SSAP. In this case, the SSCA adds the service to its list of available services, providing the address of the agent which provides the service at the remote SSAP. Service inheritance at the SSCA level is provided automatically, that is, all SSCAs query regularly their upper level SSCAs to see which services are available for inheritance. Service aggregation is provided by a subscription mechanism. Lower-level service agents subscribe to higher-level SSCAs to have their services made available to users at the upper levels of the hierarchy.

In scenarios with many levels in the hierarchy, automatic inheritance and aggregation may result in huge lists of available services. This is solved by limiting automatic inheritance and aggregation to a small subset of services, and providing extended search services at the SSCAs only when specific service discovery queries yield void results (i.e., a given service is not found within the list of available services, and the search is propagated to selected SSCAs at higher and lower levels to see if the service may be provided at another SSAP). In SETH, this is called *SSCA-driven service discovery*. *PA-driven service discovery* can be performed at any time by issuing direct queries from the PA to the corresponding SSCAs.

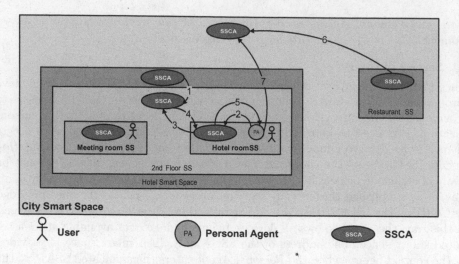

FIGURE 9. Inheritance, aggregation and service discovery.

To illustrate the mechanisms described above, we can refer to a typical use case shown in Figure 9. User *Alice* is in her hotel room, and her associated PA knows she has an appointment to have lunch with user *Bob* at the restaurant in an hour. The *Personal Agent* decides to notify *Bob*, but it does not know where he is. We can see examples of service aggregation, service inheritance and service discovery in the following process:

- *Service Inheritance:* there is a user location service at the *hotel* smart space which is provided at the floor level (1).
- *SSCA-driven Service Discovery:* to locate *Bob*, Alice's personal agent queries $SSCA_{hotelroom}$ for a location service (2). It has no such service in its list, but it propagates the query up in the hierarchy (3), receives from $SSCA_{secondfloor}$ (4) the requested information, and finally forwards it to the PA (5).
- *Service Aggregation:* the *SSCA* at the restaurant has eventually advertised its reservation service to $SSCA_{city}$, which has aggregated it to its list of available services (6).
- *PA-driven Service Discovery:* after being able to locate *Bob* and remind him of the meeting, *Alice*'s personal agent decides to make a reservation in a restaurant. None of the SSCAs of the building has inherited that service, nor are they willing to propagate service discovery requests for this kind of services (e.g., it may be against their business policy). So, perhaps after a series of unsuccessful searches at floor and hotel level, *Alice*'s personal agent will have to send its query directly to $SSCA_{city}$ (7) to find the agents who are providing restaurant reservation services.

5.5. Access to services

To access a given service, a PA only needs to send a request message to the agent providing that service. The *Service Agent* will then attempt to provide the service, usually by requesting actions to other service, system or device agents. However, the process may be slightly more complex depending on the kind of service requested. As we mentioned in Section 5.3, there are services directly related to each specific smart space, such as climatization, lighting, or interfaces which are required to be available at any moment to every user in the space, and so they are provided by *persistent* service agents. These agents are always active in the SSAP, and their addresses are specified in the service lists returned by the SSCA, so that any PA can request services directly to these agents at any time.

However, there are other services, such as content access or unified messaging, which are more directly related to the user who requests them, and they are provided by *non-persistent* service agents, which are created for each specific request for the service and destroyed once the service has been provided. The SSCA uses a special address value in the list of available services to indicate which services are provided by non-persistent agents. If a PA wants to access a service provided by a non-persistent agent, it must first request the *SSCA* to create the agent. The non-persistent agent is created and its address returned to the PA, so that it can issue the service request as in the previous case.

Figure 10 illustrates a typical service access case in the SETH system. User *Alice* enters the *hotelRoom* smart space. The personal agent arrives at the hotel room SSAP through one of the processes described in [12]. Context agents notify both the PA and $SSCA_{hotelRoom}$ of this event (1). The personal agent, knowing that its user is planning to go sightseeing for a while, and after checking Alice's user preferences, concludes that she would like to watch a presentation about the city's main monument. According to that, Alice's PA asks $SSCA_{hotelRoom}$ for an agent providing a presentation service (2). No such agent is persistently active in the SSAP, so $SSCA_{hotelRoom}$ creates an instance of a Non-persistent Presentation Service Agent (NPPSA) (3) and returns its address to the PA (4). The personal agent then contacts the NPPSA and requests it to present a slideshow of some touristic contents known to be stored in the tourist office (5). Then, the NPPSA contacts $SSCA_{touristoffice}$ to learn who to ask for the document (6). He is given the address of a persistent *File Transfer Service Agent* (FTSA) (7), which the NPPSA contacts to request the file (8). The FTSA obtains the file from the *Device Agent* (DA) associated to the content server in the tourist office (9) and transfers it to the NPPSA (10). Finally, the NPPSA requests the *device agent* of the TV in the hotel room to display the presentation (11).

Any typical interaction such as the one described above may involve service discovery requests to different SSAPs, requests to service and device agents, and even access to resources within the user's desktop computer. This flexibility of the interaction mechanism provided by agents greatly improves the functionality

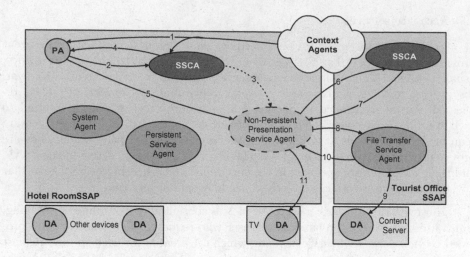

FIGURE 10. Access to services.

of the smart space, but also raises some relevant security concerns that must be addressed in order to ensure there is no misuse of the provided infrastructure [13].

5.6. Experimental results

For the evaluation and validation of the developed system, three services were implemented on top of the SETH architecture. The first was an interactive tourist guide that used GPS over a PDA to locate the user in the city map and was able to suggest touristic routes according to user preferences and user previous movements throughout the city, leading the user to the most suitable points of interest. Integrated with this service was a content service, which presented to the users personalised contents on their PDAs regarding the different points of interest in their vicinity at each moment. The contents were hosted in a centralised touristic content server. Finally, the negotiation system described in [24] was adapted and integrated with the SETH architecture to provide a recommendation service for restaurant reservations. When lunchtime approached, the personal agents residing on users' PDAs contacted the reservation agents at the different restaurant smart spaces and used the information received to make weighted recommendations to the users. The city smart spaces were simulated in our campus, using the wireless network infrastructure available to provide connectivity for the user PDAs and the servers representing the different smart spaces (points of interest, tourist office, and restaurants). The experiment yielded promising results, and we expect to be able to test the system on a real-world scenario, making a limited deployment of the SETH architecture in the touristic city of Alcalá de Henares by 2008.

6. Dynamic location tracking for Tourism applications

When considering data services for tourism, an important aspect is to provide the mobile user with information relevant to his current location (e.g., information about nearby attractions or the locations of his travel guides). In this section, the challenges that this goal presents are first analyzed, from the point of view of location tracking, through the concept of location-dependent queries. Then, LOQOMOTION [18], an architecture that benefits from agent technology to overcome such challenges, is presented.

6.1. Challenges for location-dependent query processing

In a tourism context, a user could specify his interests by issuing (e.g., with the help of a graphical user interface) *location-dependent queries*, which are queries whose answer depends on the location of relevant *objects* (interesting entities). As an example, a tourist guide could want to track the locations of his customers (calling them if they get too far away), or a tourist may want to track the nearby tourist buses. These queries must be handled as *continuous* queries [23], that is, their answers must be continually refreshed because they depend on the locations of the involved objects. For example, the answer to a query issued by a tourist guide to track his nearby customers will change as the tourist guide and/or customers move around. Moreover, it would be very interesting to continuously show the updated locations of those customers to the user, locating them on a map. Therefore, the answer to the query must be updated with new location data even if the set of customers satisfying the query condition does not change (as their locations do change continuously).

As the previous examples show, the most frequent types of location-dependent queries in the context of Tourism applications are those about entities that are near the current user's location. Those entities may be static (monuments, restaurants, etc.) or moving (other tourists, tourist buses, tourist guides, etc.). A user querying about the surrounding area of a different entity (e.g., a tourist agency manager asking about tourists near the tourist guides working for his company) is less frequent, although also useful in some situations.

In these contexts where users with mobile devices must be provided with context-aware information, two important challenges arise. On the one hand, the most evident difficulty is derived from the mobility aspect. As the user moves, the interesting entities (*objects*) around him can change continually. Moreover, the user may be interested in monitoring nearby entities that are themselves mobile (*moving objects*), such as the people or friends they travel with. On the other hand, in a wireless network an object can be detected only by the *base station* that provides it with coverage; in other words, the data about the objects are naturally distributed. This is also a requirement from the point of view of performance. Thus, a single computer storing all the relevant data and also processing all the requests of data would easily become a bottleneck: such a solution would not scale with the number of users, the volume of data (number of objects), or the frequency of data changes (which would be very high for location data). Instead, several computers are needed to manage data and queries related to different geographic areas. Along with its clear advantages, a distributed architecture introduces some difficulties from the point of view of data processing; for example, a request about nearby objects could span several geographic areas and, therefore, involve several computers.

6.2. An agent-based approach for dynamic location tracking

Existing commercial products only allow queries about static objects whose attributes do not change with time (e.g., information about nearby restaurants, whose information and location do not change); in that way, they can safely assume that the interesting information is available on the mobile device itself. In a more general context, a different solution is required. In this section, the system LOQOMOTION (*LOcation-dependent Queries On Moving ObjecTs In mObile Networks*) [18], an agent-based architecture which benefits from the use of mobile agents to efficiently support general query processing in a distributed environment, is presented.

The underlying infrastructure of LOQOMOTION is a set of computers that manage data (location and other attributes) about objects within their areas. It is based on a layered hierarchy of mobile agents that move autonomously over the mobile network in order to track efficiently the relevant moving objects (they keep themselves close to the interesting data in order to carry out the processing tasks wherever they are needed), correlate partial results and, finally, present and continually update the answer to the user's query.

The agent-based query processing approach in LOQOMOTION follows a divide-and-conquer strategy, with agents that cooperate to process the queries in the distributed environment and keep the answers up-to-date. The main component of a user device is a graphical application that allows the user to launch queries whose answer will be shown (and automatically updated) on the screen. Six steps can be distinguished in the query processing. The following paragraphs briefly explain how those steps are executed on a distributed environment of computers which manage data about objects within different geographic areas:

1. *Obtaining the query.* In a context where the user could be driving or walking while posing queries, it is important to require minimum user interaction. The ideal user interface would consist of: 1) a voice recognition system to allow the user to orally express a query, and 2) a convenient way to return the answers to the user (depending on the type of answers required, they could be provided through a graphical user interface, a text-to-speech engine, etc.).

2. *Analysis of the query.* The application creates a *QueryMonitor* agent in charge of the query. The *QueryMonitor* will identify the class of objects and geographic area that are interesting to the user. For example, suppose that a user wants to track the tourist buses that are close to him. In this case, the class of interesting objects would be the set of tourist buses. Regarding the

query condition, as *closeness* is a relative attribute, it must be defined previously by the user. For example, he can consider that all the tourist buses within an area of one mile are close: this is called the *relevant area*. The goal of the query processing is therefore to retrieve the objects (of a certain class) within the relevant area. Notice that this area moves with the user.

3. *Translate into a database query.* The previous query cannot be executed over a traditional Database Management System because it depends on the continuously changing location of the user. Therefore, the location-dependent query is transformed into a *database query*, that is, a query where the user is not mentioned or referenced explicitly: instead, his current location is used as part of the query conditions.

4. *Deployment of a network of agents.* Processing the query in a distributed environment is challenging because the location data that the system must correlate are handled by different computers (depending on the current location of the user) and those data are constantly changing. A suitable mechanism to perform distributed monitoring is a major concern of LOQOMOTION. To overcome this difficulty, the system deploys a network of agents to perform the query processing in a distributed and cooperative manner:

   (a) The *QueryMonitor* agent creates a *MonitorTracker* mobile agent which travels to the computer in charge of the user's location (see Figure 11, step 1). The *MonitorTracker* represents the mobile user in the fixed network (in a similar way to the idea of *user agent* in the *Mobile Shadow* project [21]), and plays the role of *mediator* between the mobile user and the fixed network. It follows the monitor wherever it goes, according to the approach proposed in works such as [22, 20]. Moreover, it tracks the current location of the user and processes his queries[1].

   (b) The *MonitorTracker* creates one *Updater* agent on each computer whose area intersects (totally or partially) with the area of the query (see Figure 11, step 2), which are the computers relevant to the query, in order to detect objects that satisfy the query constraints. Every *Updater* keeps track of a portion of the interesting area, so any object entering such an area will be detected by one of the *Updaters*.

5. *Execution of traditional database queries and obtaining of an initial answer.* In this step, the different types of agents in our architecture work cooperatively in order to obtain an initial answer to the location-dependent query. Firstly, each *Updater* executes its database query against the computer where it resides, with the goal of retrieving data about the relevant target objects, which it communicates to its *MonitorTracker*, which correlates the results

---

[1]For the sake of clarity, many aspects of LOQOMOTION have been simplified in this explanation. In the real architecture, the *MonitorTracker* creates a network of *Tracker* agents to process the query. Such an additional step is needed in order to process queries where an entity different from the user is explicitly mentioned in the query, which may be not so important in the context of Tourism.

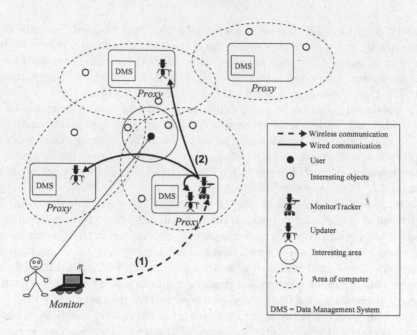

FIGURE 11. Deployment of the agent network.

it receives, and so on until the *QueryMonitor* obtains an initial answer and shows it to the user.

Notice that the only wireless data transfers needed to obtain an answer to the query occur: 1) at query initialization, when the *QueryMonitor* creates a *MonitorTracker* which must travel to the computer that manages the user's data; and 2) when the *MonitorTracker* sends an answer to the *Query-Monitor*. Any other communication occurs among fixed computers using the wired network. Thus, fixed networks are used whenever possible, following the recommendations of [19].

6. *Continuous Processing.* The previous process must be repeated periodically in order to keep the answer up-to-date. For that, two related tasks must be performed: 1) to keep the network of agents ready to obtain a new answer according to the current locations of the interesting objects (e.g., the set of relevant computers and associated *Updaters* change as the interesting area moves), and 2) to update automatically the answer to the query. During the query processing, the agents must synchronize among themselves in order to obtain the necessary data at the right time. The proposed synchronization approach [17, 16] can deal with situations where some agents cannot communicate (e.g., due to disconnections).

One of the main difficulties is that the previous steps must be executed in a distributed environment, correlating location data managed by different computers. As mentioned before, this is a basic requirement because a centralised solution to manage all the data and process all the queries is not possible at medium or large scale. Moreover, a distributed query processing approach brings important benefits; for example, objects and queries regarding different geographic areas do not compete for the same resources.

6.3. Conclusions and future trends

Processing location-dependent queries is important for Tourism applications. The use of mobile agents is very interesting in this context because they provide the right mechanisms to process location-dependent queries in a distributed and efficient manner. The different query processing tasks must *move* from computer to computer following their relevant data, which is naturally achieved by packaging those processing tasks as mobile agents. An alternative *client/server* approach could lead to a non-flexible and more difficult to implement solution. Thus, there should be a server process on each computer with the capability of launching new threads encapsulating the behaviours of the agents, and agent migrations across computers would be simulated by invoking remote procedures that create and destroy threads. Moreover, the programmer should keep track of where each relevant thread is executing (e.g., to communicate with them). This implies a significant programming effort, that can be saved using a mobile agent platform. Moreover, a mobile agent platform is also expected to perform better. Thus, the use of an architecture based on mobile agents is very interesting in this scenario.

Besides the difficulties of designing an efficient mechanism for dynamic location tracking for Tourism applications, testing the proposed solutions is also challenging. Existing alternatives are usually evaluated by means of simulations. Although they are expected to perform similarly in a real environment, some difficulties will undoubtedly arise to validate them in a wireless network (e.g., currently there is no real interoperability between different mobile agent platforms, so all the devices would need to use the same agent platform). Existing wireless network protocols could also be improved in the future to facilitate the transmission of location data from moving objects.

7. Summary and conclusions

The agent-based systems described in this chapter, albeit having mainly an academic focus, prove how the properties of agents (autonomy, proactiveness, social capability, intelligent behaviour with high level reasoning and planning) seem to fit quite nicely with the needs of Tourism service providing systems. Furthermore, the current trend towards ever more affordable and computationally powerful PDAs and mobile phones permits us to predict a mid-term future in which tourists will have *Personal Agents* running in their pockets, and these agents will be able to effortlessly communicate with agents providing touristic information on the fly.

Thus, tourists undoubtedly will demand the possibility of requesting information, making reservations or getting proactive personalised recommendations at any point of the city at any time, paving the way for the development of new styles of e-business in touristic destinations.

References

[1] Aamodt A. and Plaza E. *Case-Based Reasoning: Foundational Issues, Methodological Variations, and System Approaches.* AI Communications **7**. No 1, March 1994.

[2] Bergmann, R., Muñoz-Ávila, H., Veloso, M. and Melis, E. *CBR Applied to Planning.* In Lenz, M. Bartsch-Sporl, B., Burkhard, H. and Wess, S. (Eds.) Case-Based Reasoning Technology: From Foundations to Applications. Lecture Notes in Computer Science 1400, Springer, 1998, 169–200.

[3] Corchado J. M. And Laza R. *Constructing Deliberative Agents with Case-based Reasoning Technology,* International Journal of Intelligent Systems. **18**, No. 12, December 2003.

[4] Corchado J.M., Pavón J., Corchado E.S, Castillo L.F. *Development of CBR-BDI Agents: A Tourist Guide Application.* ECCBR 2004. LNAI vol. 3155, Springer Verlag. (2005), 547–559.

[5] González-Bedia M. and Corchado J. M.*A planning strategy based on variational calculus for deliberative agents.* Computing and Information Systems Journal. **10**, No 1, (2002), 2–14.

[6] González-Bedia M., Corchado J. M., Corchado E. S. and Fyfe C. *Analytical Model for Constructing Deliberative Agents,* Engineering Intelligent Systems, **3**, (2002), 173–185.

[7] Martín F. J., Plaza E., Arcos J.L. *Knowledge and experience reuse through communications among competent (peer) agents.* International Journal of Software Engineering and Knowledge Engineering, **9**, No. 3, (1999), 319–341.

[8] Olivia C., Chang C. F., Enguix C.F. and Ghose A.K. *Case-Based BDI Agents: An Effective Approach for Intelligent Search on the World Wide Web,* AAAI Spring Symposium on Intelligent Agents, Stanford University, USA, 1999.

[9] Rao, A. S. and Georgeff, M. P. *BDI Agents: From Theory to Practice.* First International Conference on Multi-Agent Systems (ICMAS-95). San Francisco, USA, 1995.

[10] Wendler J. and Lenz M. *CBR for Dynamic Situation Assessment in an Agent-Oriented Setting.* Proc. AAAI-98 Workshop on CBR Integrations. Madison (USA), 1998.

[11] Wooldridge, M. and Jennings, N. R. *Agent Theories, Architectures, and Languages: a Survey.* In: Wooldridge and Jennings, editors, Intelligent Agents, Springer-Verlag, (1995), 11–22.

[12] Marsá, I., López, M.A., Velasco, J.R. and Navarro, A. *Mobile Personal Agents for Smart Spaces,* Proceedings of the IEEE International Conference on Pervasive Services (IEEE ICPS 06), Lyon, France, (2006), 299–302.

[13] De la Hoz, E., Marsá, I., López, M.A. and Alarcaos, B. *A Hierarchical, Agent-based Approach to Security in Smart Offices*, Proceedings of the International Conference on Ubiquitous Computing (ICUC 06), Alcalá de Henares, Spain, (2006), 11–19.

[14] Marsá, I. *A Hierarchical, Agent-based Architecture for Smart Spaces*, Technical Report 2006-101, Telematics Services Engineering Group, Univ. of Alcalá, (2006).

[15] FIPA. *FIPA Agent Management Specification, document SC00023K*, (2004). Available at www.fipa.org.

[16] Ilarri, S., Mena, E. and A. Illarramendi, A. *Dealing with Continuous Location-Dependent Queries: Just-in-Time Data Refreshment*. Procs. of the First IEEE Annual Conference on Pervasive Computing and Communications (PerCom), Dallas, (2003), 279–286.

[17] Ilarri, S., Mena, E. and A. Illarramendi, A. *Self-synchronization of Cooperative Agents in a Distributed Environment*. Procs. of Third International/Central and Eastern European Conference on Multi-Agent Systems (CEEMAS), Prague, (2003), 51–60.

[18] Ilarri, S., Mena, E. and A. Illarramendi, A. *Location-Dependent Queries in Mobile Contexts: Distributed Processing Using Mobile Agents*, IEEE Transactions on Mobile Computing 8, 1029–1043, 2006.

[19] Badrinath, B.R., Acharya, A. and Imielinski, T. *Impact of mobility on distributed computations*. CM Operating Systems Review 27, No. 2, 1993.

[20] Burg, B., Tab, R. and Schmitt, A. *Information Services Provisions in a Telecommunications Network*. United States Patent 6512922, (2003).

[21] Fischmeister, S. *Mobile Software Agents for Location-Based Systems*. Procs. of Agent Technologies, Infrastructures, Tools, and Applications for E-Services, NODe 2002 Agent-Related Workshops, Erfurt, Germany, (2002), 226–239.

[22] Liu, G.Y. and Maguire, G.Q. *Efficient Mobility Management Support for Wireless Data Services*. Procs. of 45th IEEE Vehicular Technology Conference (VTC'95), Chicago, (1995).

[23] Terry, D., Goldberg, D., Nichols, D. and Oki, B. *Continuous queries over append-only databases*. Procs. of ACM SIGMOD International Conference on Management of Data (SIGMOD'92), San Diego, (1992), 321–330.

[24] López-Carmona, M.A. and Velasco, J.R. *A Fuzzy Constraint Based Model for Automated Purchase Negotiations*, TADA/AMEC 2006, Lecture Notes in Artificial Intelligence, Vol. 4452, 234–247. Springer Verlag (2007).

[25] López, J.S., Bustos, F.A. and Julián, V. *Tourism Services Using Agent Technology: A MultiAgent Approach* INFOCOMP - Journal of Computer Science - Special Edition pp. 51–57. (2007)

[26] Balabanovic, M., Shoham, Y. *Content-based, collaborative recommendation*. Communications of the ACM 40-3, 66–72, 1997.

[27] Jain, A.K., Dubes, R.C. *Algorithms for clustering data*. Prentice-Hall, (1988).

[28] Chen, H. *An Intelligent Broker Architecture for Pervasive Context-Aware Systems*, PhD Thesis, University of Maryland,(2004).

[29] Román, M., Hess, C.K., Cerqueira, R., Ranganathan, A., Campbell, R. and Nahrstedt, K. *Gaia: A Middleware Infrastructure to Enable Active Spaces*, IEEE Pervasive Computing, 74–83, Oct-Dec (2002).

[30] Johanson, B., Fox, A. and Winograd, T. *The Interactive Workspaces Project: Experiences with Ubiquitous Computing Rooms*, IEEE Pervasive Computing, 67–74, (2002).

Antonio Moreno
Departamento de Ingeniería Informática y Matemáticas,
Universidad Rovira i Virgili,
ETSE, Campus Sescelades,
Av. Països Catalans, 26,
43007 Tarragona,
Spain
e-mail: antonio.moreno@urv.cat

AgentCities.ES Groups

AiA: Applying intelligent Agents

University Jaume I (UJI)

- **Web page:** http://www.aia.uji.es
- **Main researchers:** Dr. Luis A. García Fernández
- **Presentation**

    The Applying intelligent Agents group was founded in 2002 to consolidate, promote research and to apply intelligent agent techonologies to real world problems. AiA group works on two basic theoretical research lines: intelligent agents software architectures and competitive/cooperative behaviours between intelligent agents via communication protocols. AiA research group has a high experience in applying intelligent techniques to road traffic domain and it participates in several EU and National road traffic funded research projects. Another application domain in which we are working is to apply and modify the MOKA methodology to help industrial product designers in Small and Medium Enterprises via ontological engineering and intelligent agents.
- **Research lines**
    - RA1 Micro/agent-level issues in agent technology
        * 1.2.3 Decision making, decision theory, and agency
    - RA2 Macro/society-level issues in agent technology
        * 2.1 Cooperation
        * 2.2 Coordination
        * 2.4 Communication
        * 2.5 Negotiation, bidding and argumentation
- **Application domains**
    - DA2: Information gathering, management and retrieval
    - DA3: Internet and World Wide Web agents
    - DA4: Expert assistants and human computer interfaces
    - DA6: Industrial Control and Scheduling, embbeded systems
    - DA8: Simulation

Engineering and Computer Science Department,
ESTCE, Campus de Riu Sec,
Av. Sos Baynat s/n,
12007 Castellón, Spain
e-mail: garcial@icc.uji.es

ALARCOS

Universidad de Castilla-La Mancha (UCLM)

- **Web page:** http://alarcos.inf-cr.uclm.es/
- **Main researchers:** Dr. Mario Piattini, Dra. Aurora Vizcaino
- **Presentation**

    The ALARCOS research group was created in 1997. Currently, it is formed by 14 PhDs in Computer Science and several PhD students and lecturers. The main goal of the Alarcos Research Group is the investigation of different issues related to the Quality of Information Systems (methodologies, tools, metrics,etc). Related to Agents and multi-agents systems this group is researching in how to use multi-agent systems in order to improve knowledge management systems in software engineering.

- **Research lines**
    - RA1 Micro/agent-level issues in agent technology
        * 1.2.1 Practical reasoning/planning and acting
    - RA2 Macro/society-level issues in agent technology
        * 2.1 Cooperation
        * 2.2 Coordination
        * 2.4 Communication
        * 2.5 Negotiation, bidding and argumentation

- **Application domains**
    - DA2: Information gathering, management and retrieval
    - DA4: Expert assistants and human computer interfaces
    - DA8: Simulation
    - DA10: Education
    - Others: Software Engineering

ESCUELA SUPERIOR DE INFORMATICA,
Campus de Ciudad Real,
Paseo de la Universidad, 4,
13071 Ciudad Real, Spain
e-mail: aurora.vizcaino@uclm.es

ARLab: Agents Research Lab

Universitat de Girona (UdG)

- **Web page:** http://eia.udg.es/arlab
- **Main researchers:** Dr. Josep Lluis de la Rosa, Esteve del Acebo
- **Presentation**

    Agents Research Laboratory (ARLab) of the Universitat de Girona (UdG) is one of the laboratories of the CIDEM's EASY center. At present the research work of the group is financed by different institutions such like 6FP European Comission, Spanish MEC, AGAUR, ICREA, and CIDEM of the Generalitat de Catalunya and the UdG itself, as well as for the researchers in formation of the PROMEP (Mexico). It develops a PhD Program in Information Technologies at the EADS research group of the UdG.

    Agents Research Lab is concerned with the development and analysis of AI techniques and control architectures for both agents and multi-agent systems. The origin of our group lies in the application of Artificial Intelligence to control and supervision problems. Currently, the group is exploiting the particular properties of physical agents in the personalized software agents domain. This involves research on multi-agent architectures for user modeling and recommender systems, trust mechanisms for agent collaboration, integration information frameworks and social networks.

- **Research lines**
    - RA1 Micro/agent-level issues in agent technology
        * 1.1.3 Hybrid agent control architectures
    - RA2 Macro/society-level issues in agent technology
        * 2.1.5 Coalitions and coalition formation
    - RA3 Agent systems implementation issues
        * 3.1 Environments and testbeds for agent system development
- **Application domains**
    - DA1: Electronic commerce information gathering, management and retrieval
    - DA3: Internet and World Wide Web agents
    - DA8: Simulation

EASY Center of the CIDEM IT Network,
Campus de Montilivi,
E17071, Girona,
Catalonia, Spain
e-mail: peplluis@eia.udg.es

BDI: Interoperable Database Group

University of the Basque Country (EHU/UPV)

- **Web page:** http://siul02.si.ehu.es/
- **Main researchers:** Dra. Arantza Illarramendi, Dr. Jesús Bermúdez, Dr. Alfredo Goñi
- **Presentation**

    The Interoperable Database Group is interested in all the areas related to data management and information systems. Specifically, the following areas of interest can be highlighted: heterogeneous, distributed information systems, query processing on global information systems, terminological systems, description logics, mobile computing, and agent based data systems. Regarding the topic of this book, the group has experience in the development of several projects, based on mobile agent technology, for the mobile computing field. It has published around 130 papers at international conferences and in journals. The group cooperates actively with the Distributed Information Systems Group at the University of Zaragoza.

- **Research lines**
    - RA3 Agent systems implementation issues
        * 3.1 Environments and testbeds for agent system development
        * 3.4 Evaluating agent systems
    - RA5 Overview / Review Articles
- **Application domains**
    - DA2: Information gathering, management and retrieval
    - DA3: Internet and World Wide Web agents
    - DA8: Simulation
    - DA12: Mobile computing
    - DA15: Health

Department of Languages and Computer Systems,
Facultad de Informtica de San Sebastián,
University of the Basque Country,
Apdo. 649
20080 Donostia/San Sebastin
e-mail: a.illarramendi@ehu.es

eXiT:
Control Engineering and Intelligent Systems

University of Girona (UdG)

- **Web page:** http://exit.udg.es/
- **Main researchers:** PhD. Dídac Busquets (**contact**), PhD. Joan Colomer, PhD. Sergio Herraiz, PhD. Beatriz López, PhD Joaquim Meléndez, PhD. Carles Pous
- **Presentation**

    eXiT laboratory develops an active research in the field of process supervision with emphasis on the integration of methods and techniques to assess process behaviour from measurements and experience reuse based on the following main points: Case-based Diagnosis, Multivariate statistical process control, Qualitative representation of trends, Knowledge discovering in data bases for situation assessment, Scheduling based on auctions.

- **Research lines on agent and multi-agent systems**
    - RA1 Micro/agent-level issues in agent technology
        * 1.1 Agent control architecture (real time)
        * 1.2.3 Decision making, decision theory, and agency
        * Case-based reasoning
    - RA2 Macro/society-level issues in agent technology
        * 2.1.3 Game/economic theoretic models of cooperation
        * 2.2.1 Coordination techniques and protocols
        * Multi-agent learning

- **Application domains**
    - DA6 Industrial control & scheduling, embedded systems (chemical and petrochemical processes, waste water treatment plants, electric distribution systems)
    - DA11 Robotics (Pioneer)
    - DA17 Bioinformatics (breast cancer, diabetes)
    - DA15 Health (ambulance coordination)

Institute of Informatics and Applications,
Universitat de Girona,
Building P.IV - Campus Montilivi,
17071 Girona, Spain
e-mail: busquets@eia.udg.es

GIA: Artificial Intelligence Group

University Rey Juan Carlos (URJC)

- **Web page:** http://www.ia.urjc.es
- **Main researchers:** Dr. Sascha Ossowski
- **Presentation**

    The Artificial Intelligence Group was founded in 1999 to consolidate and promote research in the field within University Rey Juan Carlos. Group activities comprise a variety of research lines that are tied together by the intelligent agent paradigm, and have given rise to numerous publications in both national and international conferences and journals. The group has also participated in several european and national projects, as well as in various scientific networks such as AgentLink and AgentCities.ES.

- **Research lines**
    - RA1 Micro/agent-level issues in agent technology
        * Agent Control Architecture
        * Foundations of Agency
    - RA2 Macro/society-level issues in agent technology
        * 2.1 Cooperation
        * 2.2 Coordination
        * 2.6.1 Emergence of cooperation and social action
        * 2.6.4 Semantics of multi-agent systems and logics of multi-agent systems
    - RA3 Agent systems implementation issues
        * 3.1 Environments and testbeds for agent system development
- **Application domains**
    - DA2 Information gathering, management and retrieval
    - DA4 Expert assistants and human computer interfaces
    - DA6 Industrial control & scheduling, embedded systems
    - DA12 Mobile computing
    - DA15 Health

DATCCCIA - School of Computer Engineering
C/Tulipán, s/n,
28933 Móstoles, Spain
e-mail: gia@ia.urjc.es

GIAA: Group of Applied Artificial Intelligence

University Carlos III de Madrid (UC3M)

- **Web page:** http://www.giaa.inf.uc3m.es/
- **Main researchers:** Dr. Jose Manuel Molina, Dr. Javier Carbo, Dr. Jesus Garcia, Dr. Miguel Angel Patricio, Dr. Antonio Berlanga.
- **Presentation** The Applied Artificial Intelligence Group (GIAA) at the Carlos III University of Madrid has members with PhD and Bachelor's degrees in Computer Science, Physics and Telecommunications Engineering. GIAA is a leading group of Professors, Senior Lecturers, Lecturers, associates and PhD students known by their ability to solve engineering problems with the newest Artificial Intelligence techniques: Machine Learning, Evolutionary Computation, Data Mining, Multi-Objective Optimization, Fuzzy Systems and Intelligent Agents. GIAA provides support and engineering consulting services to several companies, giving customized training courses and cooperating in national and international research and development projects, cooperating with INDRA, AENA, ISDEFE, GENASYS II SPAIN, THOMSON AYRSYS, BAE SYSTEMS
- **Research lines**
  - RA2 Macro/society-level issues in agent technology
    * 2.1 Cooperation
    * 2.2 Coordination
    * 2.5 Negotiation, bidding and argumentation
  - RA3 Agent systems implementation issues
    * 3.1 Environments and testbeds for agent system development
- **Application domains**
  - DA1 Electronic Commerce Information gathering, management and retrieval
  - DA13 Intelligent home and office
  - DA7 Telecomms network management and control
  - DA8 Simulation

Department of Computer Science,
EPS, Campus Leganes,
Av. Universidad, 30,
Leganes 28911 Madrid, Spain
e-mail: molina@ia.uc3m.es

Grasia!: Research Group on Software Agents: Engineering and Applications

Universidad Complutense Madrid (UCM)

- **Web page:** http://grasia.fdi.ucm.es
- **Main researchers:** Dr. Juan Pavón, Dr. Jorge Gómez-Sanz, Dr. Rubén Fuentes, Dr. Millán Arroyo, Dr. Manuel Ortega.
- **Presentation**

    The *Grasia!* research group is mainly involved in the development of applications and services with multi-agent systems (MAS). We have a pragmatic view of the application of agent technology, so we focus on its software engineering issues. As a result of our experience, we have defined a methodology for the development and deployment of MAS, *INGENIAS*. This methodology is supported by a set of tools that facilitate a component-based and model driven engineering approach to build multi-agent systems.
- **Research lines**
    - RA1 Micro/agent-level issues in agent technology
        * 1.1 Agent control architectures
    - RA2 Macro/society-level issues in agent technology
        * 2.1 Cooperation - 2.2 Coordination
        * 2.6 Foundations of multi-agent systems
            · 2.6.1 Emergence of cooperation and social action
            · 2.6.2. Sociology, ethology, and their relationship to MAS
            · 2.6.3 Emergent functionality and swarm behaviour in MAS
    - RA3 Agent systems implementation issues
    - RA4 Best practice in agent system development
        * 4.1 Standards for (multi-) Agent Systems
        * 4.2 Analysis, specification, design and verification techniques
- **Application domains**
    - DA2: Information gathering, management and retrieval
    - DA4: Expert assistants and human-computer interfaces
    - DA6: Industrial control and scheduling (resource planning)
    - DA12: Mobile computing (ubiquitous computing)- DA5: Workflow
    - DA8: Simulation (social) - Others: Web site personalization

Dep. Ingeniera del Software e Inteligencia Artificial,
Facultad de Informtica, Ciudad Universitaria s/n,
28040 Madrid, Spain
e-mail: jpavon@fdi.ucm.es

GSI: Intelligent Systems Group

Universidad de Murcia (UMU)

- **Web page:** http://www.um.es/gsi
- **Main researchers:** Juan A. Botía, Antonio F. G. Skarmeta
- **Presentation**

     This research group is the basis which constituted the Computer Science Faculty in the University of Murcia. We have offers of collaboration in domains related with data mining, telematics, intelligent techniques applied to agriculture, medicine, etc. We have five different research lines: sensor information procesing, optimization and intelligent decision making, inference and machine learning with uncertainty, intelligent cooperative systems and e-learning. At the moment, the group is composed by more than 10 professors and more than 30 collaborators through grants and contracts from european, national and local research projects.

- **Research lines**
    - RA2 Macro/society-level issues in agent technology
        * 2.1 Cooperation
        * 2.2 Coordination
    - RA4 Best practice in agent system development
        * 4.2. Analysis, specification, design and verification techniques for agent systems
- **Application domains**
    - DA12: Mobile computing
    - DA13: Intelligent home and office
    - DA14: Advances services
    - DA7: Telecomms network management and control
    - DA9: Entertainment and virtual environments

Departamento de Ingeniera de la Informacin y las Comunicaciones,
Fac. Informtica, Campus Espinardo,
Espinardo, Murcia,
30071, Murcia, Spain
e-mail: jcadenas@um.es

GSI-ISYS Intelligent systems research group

Universidad Politécnica de Madrid (UPM)

- **Web page:** http://www.gsi.dit.upm.es
- **Main researchers:** Dr. G. Fernández, Dra. M. Garijo-Ayestarán, Dra. Ana García-Serrano
- **Presentation**

    The GSI-ISYS research group started around 1983 and currently has members from the ETSI Telecomunicación and from the Facultad de Informática. Current research projects are funded by EU funds, by Spanish funding agencies, or by Spanish regional organisations and companies. Its members are interested in applying AI techniques (expert systems, fuzzy models, CBR) in order to solve complex problems. More than 100 students have completed their BSc, MSc or PhD degrees within the group. The members of the group have generated more than 200 papers in national and international conferences and journals.

- **Research lines**
    - RA1 Micro/agent-level issues in agent technology
        * 1.1 Agent Control Architecture
        * 1.2.3 Decision making, decision theory, and agency
    - RA2 Macro/society-level issues in agent technology
        * 2.1 Cooperation - 2.2 Coordination - 2.4 Communication
        * 2.6.3 Emergent functionality and swarm behaviour in MAS
        * 2.6.4 Semantics of multi-agent systems and logics of MAS
    - RA3 Agent systems implementation issues
        * 3.1 Environments and testbeds for agent system development
        * 3.2 Programming languages, tools, and libraries
        * 3.3 Relationship of agents to objects and other paradigms

- **Application domains**
    - DA2: Information gathering, management and retrieval - DA15: Health
    - DA3: Internet and WWW agents - DA13: Intelligent home and office
    - DA4: Expert assistants and human computer interfaces
    - DA12: Mobile computing - DA16: Grid computing - DA8: Simulation
    - DA7: Telecomms network management and control - DA10: Education

DIT
ETSI Telecomunicación - Ciudad Universitaria,
28040 Madrid, Spain
e-mail: gfer@dit.upm.es, mga@dit.upm.es, agarcia@dia.fi.upm.es

GTI-IA: Grupo de Tecnología Informática - Inteligencia Artificial

University Politécnica de Valencia (UPV)

- **Web page:** http://www.dsic.upv.es/users/ia/ia.html
- **Main researchers:** Dr. Vicente J. Botti
- **Presentation**
    This is a multi-disciplinar group dating from the beginning of 1985. It is composed of 30 teachers (27 PhD), 25 Technicians and Scholarship holders. The group is organised into three specialised groups: Artificial Intelligence, Multi-Agent Systems and Real-Time systems. We have experience in the transference of results to local, national and international industry.
- **Research lines**
    - RA1 Micro/agent-level issues in agent technology
        * 1.1.3 Hybrid agent control architectures
        * 1.2.4 Agent representation and specification formalisms
    - RA2 Macro/society-level issues in agent technology
        * 2.2 Coordination
        * 2.4 Communication
        * 2.6 Foundations of multi-agent systems
    - RA3 Agent systems implementation issues
        * 3.1 Environments and testbeds for agent system development
        * 3.2 Programming languages, tools, and libraries for agent system development
        * 3.4 Evaluating agent systems
    - RA4 Best practice in agent system development
        * 4.2 Analysis, specification, design and verification techniques
    - Others: Real-Time AI/Rule-based systems, autonomous vehicles
- **Application domains**
    - DA3: Internet and World Wide Web agents
    - DA6: Industrial control & scheduling, embedded systems
    - DA8: Simulation
    - DA9: Entertainment and Virtual Environments
    - DA11: Robotics

Departamento de Sistemas Informticos y Computacin,
Universidad Politcnica de Valencia,
Camino de Vera, s/n,
43022 Valencia, Spain
e-mail: vbotti@dsic.upv.es

GWAI: Intelligent Agents Web Group

University of Vigo (UVigo)

- **Web page:** http://gwai.ei.uvigo.es
- **Main researchers:** Dr. Juan Carlos Gonzlez Moreno
- **Presentation**

    The Intelligent Agents Web Group, belonging to the Computer Science Department, was founded on January 1999 due to the members' interest on Agents and Multi-agent Systems. The group participates in and leads several projects in the Agent Oriented Software Engineering field. These projects are mainly centered in evaluation of existing methodologies and definition of new ones, paying special attention to the development process. Jointly several multi-agent systems have been developed in domains which range from e-learning to information retrieval. The work has generated contributions in conference proceedings, papers in journals and books.
- **Research lines**
    - RA1 Micro/agent-level issues in agent technology
        * 1.2.4 Agent representation and specification formalisms
    - RA3 Agent systems implementation issues
        * 3.2 Programming languages, tools, and libraries for agent system development
    - RA4 Best practice in agent system development
        * 4.2 Analysis, specification, design and verification techniques for agent systems
- **Application domains**
    - DA2: Information gathering, management and retrieval
    - DA3: Internet and World Wide Web agents
    - DA4 Expert assistants and human-computer interfaces
    - DA5 Business process control, workflow, emergency management
    - DA9 Entertainment and virtual environments
    - DA10: Education
    - DA12: Mobile computing
    - DA14 Advanced services

Department of Computer Science,
ESEI: Escola Superior de Enxeera Informtica,
Campus As Lagoas,s/n
32004 Ourense, Spain
e-mail: jcmoreno@uvigo.es

IIIA: Artificial Intelligence Research Institute

Artificial Intelligence Research Institute (CSIC)

- **Web page:** http://www.iiia.csic.es
- **Main researchers:** Dr. Carles Sierra (head of the group), Dr. Josep Lluis Arcos, Dr. Marc Esteva, Dr. Pere Garcia, Dr. Pablo Noriega, Dr. Enric Plaza, Dr. J.Antonio Rodriguez-Aguilar, Dr. Jordi Sabater, Dr. Marco Schorlemmer.
- **Presentation**

    The Multiagent Systems Group is one of the leading groups world wide. The group has acquired prestige in the area of regulated agent environments due to the theoretical proposals and the methodologies and software tools it has developed around them. The group developed one of the first successful working applications of MAS in the world to date. The group has developed the Electronic Institutions Development Environment (EIDE), a set of tools aimed at supporting the engineering of intelligent distributed applications as electronic institutions. Electronic institutions are appropriate in complex domains where multiple partners are involved, and high degree of coordination and collaboration is required.
- **Research lines**
    - RA1 Micro/agent-level issues in agent technology
        * 1.2.3 Decision making, decision theory, and agency
    - RA2 Macro/society-level issues in agent technology
        * 2.1 Cooperation, 2.2 Coordination, Computational Market Systems, 2.5 Negotiation, bidding and argumentation, 2.6 Foundations of Multi-Agent systems
    - RA3 Agent systems implementation issues
        * 3.2 Programming languages, tools, and libraries for agent system development
- **Application domains**
    - DA1: E-Commerce Information gathering, management and retrieval
    - DA3: Internet and World Wide Web agents
    - DA4: Expert assistants and human computer interfaces
    - DA5: Business process control, workflow, emergency management
    - DA8: Simulation

Campus UAB,
08193 Bellaterra, Spain
e-mail: sierra@iiia.csic.es

ITAKA: Intelligent Technologies for Advanced Knowledge Acquisition

University Rovira i Virgili (URV)

- **Web page:** http://deim.urv.cat/~itaka
- **Main researchers:** Dr. Antonio Moreno, Dr. Aida Valls
- **Presentation**

    The ITAKA research group was officially created in January 2007, building on the success of the former GruSMA working group. It provides a framework in which undergraduate/graduate Computer Science students who are interested in the latest Artificial Intelligence techniques may share their knowledge and experiences in fields like Intelligent Decision Support Systems, Multi-Agent Systems, Ontology Learning and Advanced Knowledge Management. Until summer 2007 around 37 students have completed their BSc or MSc degrees within the group. These works have generated more than 60 papers in national and international conferences and journals. The group has also been awarded some relevant international prizes (two at the AgentCities Agent Technology Competition and the Cooperative Information Agents 2005 System Innovation Award).

- **Research lines**
    - RA1 Micro/agent-level issues in agent technology
        * 1.2.3 Decision making, decision theory, and agency
    - RA2 Macro/society-level issues in agent technology
        * 2.1 Cooperation
        * 2.2 Coordination
        * 2.6.4 Semantics of Multi-Agent systems and logics of Multi-Agent systems
- **Application domains**
    - DA2: Information gathering, management and retrieval
    - DA3: Internet and World Wide Web agents
    - DA4: Expert assistants and human computer interfaces
    - DA8: Simulation
    - DA12: Mobile computing
    - DA15: Health

Department of Computer Science and Mathematics,
ETSE, Campus Sescelades,
Av. Països Catalans, 26,
43007 Tarragona, Spain
e-mail: antonio.moreno@urv.cat

KEMLg: Knowledge engineering and machine learning group

Technical University of Catalonia (UPC)

- **Web page:** http://www.lsi.upc.edu/~webia/KEMLG/
- **Main researchers:** Dr. Miquel Sànchez, Dr. Javier Béjar, Dr. Luigi Ceccaroni, Dr. Ulises Cortés, Dr. Karina Gibert, Dr. Mario Martín, Dr. Josep M. Pujol, Dr. Ton Sales, Dr. Ramon Sangüesa, Dr. Javier Vázquez, Dr. Steven Willmott
- **Presentation**

    The Knowledge engineering and machine learning group (KEMLg) is part of the public Technical University of Catalonia (UPC) whose main goals are the analysis, design, implementation and application of various artificial intelligence techniques in relation to complex real-world systems and domains, such as collaboration environments for strategic innovation, wastewater management, health, environmental processes, cultural heritage, education and tourism. The artificial intelligence techniques involved, in which the KEMLg is expert, are: knowledge representation, ontologies, the semantic Web and Web services; software agents, electronic institutions and Multi-Agent systems; intelligent decision support systems; data mining; supervised and unsupervised machine learning; Bayesian networks; case-based reasoning; knowledge-based systems; knowledge acquisition and knowledge discovery from structural analysis; simulation and analytical models. The KEMLg is currently involved in four EU funded projects: the IP project "Laboranova: a collaboration environment for strategic innovation", to change existing technological and social infrastructures for collaboration and support knowledge workers in sharing, improving and evaluating ideas systematically across teams, companies and networks (IST-5-035262-IP), with a total budget of 10M; WINDS; ENGAGE; and ASPIC, focused on knowledge-based services for the information society.
- **Research lines**
    - RA1 Micro/agent-level issues in agent technology
    - RA2 Macro/society-level issues in agent technology
    - RA3 Agent systems implementation issues
    - RA4 Best practice in agent system development

UPC - Campus Nord
Omega building
C. Jordi Girona Salgado, 1-3
08034 Barcelona, Spain
e-mail: miquel@lsi.upc.edu

SeNDA: Security of Networks and Distributed Systems

Universitat Autònoma de Barcelona (UAB)

- **Web page:** http://senda.uab.es
- **Main researchers:** Dr. Sergi Robles, Dr. Joan Borrell, Dr. Ramon Martí, Dr. Guillermo Navarro, Carles Garrigues, Jordi Cucurull
- **Presentation**

    The Security of Networks and Distributed Applications group is a research and teaching group within the Department of Information and Communications Engineering of the Universitat Autònoma de Barcelona. Its aim is to research in the areas of applied network security and secure distributed applications. During the last years the group has been focusing on mobile agent technology, where it has produced a large number of journal papers, conference contributions and book chapters. The group has leaded and participated in several projects related to agents, and has designed several protocols and environments for the development of secure mobile agent applications.

- **Research lines**
    - RA3 Agent systems implementation issues
        * 3.1 Environments and testbeds for agent system development
        * 3.2 Programming languages, tools, and libraries for agent system development
    - RA4 Best practice in agent system development
        * 4.1 Standards for Multi-Agent Systems
        * 4.2 Analysis, specification,design and verification techniques for agent systems
    - Others: Security. Agent inter-operability.
- **Application domains**
    - DA2 Information gathering, management and retrieval
    - DA5 Business process control, workflow, emergency management
    - DA7 Telecomms network management and control
    - DA12 Mobile computing
    - DA15 Health

Department of Information and Communication Engineering
ETSE, Edifici Q, Campus UAB,
08193 Bellaterra, Spain
e-mail: sergi.robles@uab.cat

SID: Distributed Information Systems

University of Zaragoza (UZ)

- **Web page:** http://sid.cps.unizar.es/
- **Main researchers:** Dr. Eduardo Mena
- **Presentation**

  The Distributed Information Systems Group is interested in all the areas related to databases and information systems: semantic web, mobile computing, mobile agents, wireless data services, distributed and heterogeneous information systems and databases, and simulation environments. Regarding the topic of this book, the group has experience in the development of several projects, based on mobile agent technology, for the mobile computing field. It has also experience researching in the field of mobile agents; thus, for example, the mobile agent platform SPRINGS has been developed within the group. The group has published around 130 papers at international conferences and in journals. The group members are also members of the Interoperable Database Group.

- **Research lines**
  - RA3 Agent systems implementation issues
    * 3.1 Environments and testbeds for agent system development
    * 3.2 Programming languages, tools, and libraries for agent system development
    * 3.4 Evaluating agent systems
  - RA5 Overview / Review Articles
- **Application domains**
  - DA2: Information gathering, management and retrieval
  - DA3: Internet and World Wide Web agents
  - DA8: Simulation
  - DA12: Mobile computing

Department of Computer Science and Systems Engineering,
Edificio Ada Byron,
Maria de Luna, 1,
50018 Zaragoza
e-mail: emena@unizar.es

TDG: The Distributed Group

University of Seville (US)

- **Web page:** www.tdg-seville.info and www.macmas.org
- **Main researchers:** Dr. Rafael Corchuelo and Dr. Antonio Ruiz-Cortés and Dr. Joaquin Peña
- **Presentation**

    Since late 1997, our effort focuses on developing description languages and tools for dealing with the complexity of Internet-based applications, chiefly in the field of e-businesses. The group focuses on AOSE and web wrappers. Regarding AOSE, we apply novel techniques to deal with complexity such as MAS Product Lines, Model-Driven Development, and Autonomic Computing. We are developing extensions of the MaCMAS AOSE methodology that cover these topics. Regarding wrapping web sites, we are working on a framework called IntegraWeb that helps agent developers to extract information with semantics from the web; it can also deal with changes to the structure of a web page, which improves adaptability; furthermore, it achieves a complete separation between the data extraction procedure and the logic or base functionality an agent encapsulates.

- **Research lines**
    - RA1 Micro/agent-level issues in agent technology:
        * 1.2.6 Computational/complexity issues of agency
    - RA2 Macro/society level issues in agent technology:
        * 2.1 Cooperation - 2.2 Coordination
        * 2.5 Negotiation, bidding and argumentation
    - RA4 Best-practice in agent system development:
        * 4.1 Standards for Multi-Agent systems
        * 4.2 Analysis, specification, design and verification techniques

- **Application domains**
    - DA1 E-Commerce Information gathering, management and retrieval
    - DA2 Information gathering, management and retrieval
    - DA3 Internet and World Wide Web agents- DA14 Advanced services
    - DA5 Business process control, workflow, emergency management
    - DA6 Industrial control and scheduling, embedded systems

Department Lenguajes y Sistemas Informaticos,
ETSI Informatica,
Av. Reina Mercedes, sn,
41012 Seville, Spain
e-mail: corchu, aruiz, joaquinp@us.es

TSERG: Telematics Services Engineering Research Group

University of Alcalá (UAH)

- **Web page:** http://www.it.aut.uah.es/ist
- **Main researchers:** Dr. Juan R. Velasco, Dr. Bernardo Alarcos, Dr. Miguel A. López-Carmona, Antonio J. de Vicente, Enrique de la Hoz, Andrés Navarro, Iván Marsá-Maestre, Álvaro Paricio.
- **Presentation**

    TSERG is formed by 8 members of the Department of Computer Engineering staff, and around 12 latest course students from the *Escuela Politecnica Superior* and *ETS de Ingenieria Informatica* of the University of Alcala. Our work is centered on five research lines which provide a framework where different research projects are being developed: Agent architectures for digital environments, negotiation systems, communication strategies in ad-hoc networks, physical architectures, and security in agent environments. The group has generated more than 40 papers in national and international conferences and journals.
- **Research lines**
    - RA1 Micro/agent-level issues in agent technology
        * 1.2.3 Decision making, decision theory, and agency
    - RA2 Macro/society-level issues in agent technology
        * 2.2 Coordination
        * 2.3 Computational Market Systems
        * 2.4 Communication
        * 2.5 Negotiation, bidding and argumentation
- **Application domains**
    - DA1: Electronic Commerce Information gathering, management and retrieval
    - DA5: Business process control, workflow, emergency management
    - DA7: Telecomms network management and control
    - DA12: Mobile computing
    - DA13: Intelligent home and office
    - DA14: Advanced services

Departamento de Automatica, Area of Telematics Engineering,
Escuela Politecnica, Campus Universitario,
Ctra. Madrid-Barcelona, km. 31.600
28871 Alcala de Henares (Madrid), Spain
e-mail: juanramon.velasco@uah.es

Book contributors

- Instituto de Investigación en Intel.ligencia Artificial - CSIC: Josep Lluís Arcos, Jordi Sabater.
- Universidad Autónoma de Barcelona: Sergi Robles.
- Universidad Carlos III de Madrid: Javier Carbó, Susana Fernández, Virginia Fuentes, Raquel Fuentetaja, Manuel González, Sergio Jiménez, José M. Molina, Nayat Sánchez.
- Universidad Complutense de Madrid: Rubén Fuentes, Jorge Gómez, Juan Pavón.
- Universidad de Alcalá de Henares: Bernardo Alarcos, Enrique de la Hoz, Miguel A. López Carmona, Iván Marsá.
- Universidad de Burgos: Emilio S. Corchado.
- Universidad de Castilla-La Mancha: Mario Piattini, Javier Portillo-Rodríguez, Oscar M. Rodríguez, Juan Pablo Soto, Aurora Vizcaíno.
- Universidad de Girona: Esteve del Acebo, Bianca Innocenti, Beatriz López, J.L. Marzo, E.Muntaner.
- Universidad de Murcia: Juan A. Botia, Guillermo Vigueras.
- Universidad del País Vasco: Arantza Illarramendi.
- Universidad de Salamanca: Juan M. Corchado.
- Universidad de Sevilla: Joaquín Peña, Antonio Ruiz-Cortés.
- Universidad de Vigo: Pedro Cuesta, Alma M. Gómez, Juan C. González.
- Universidad de Zaragoza: Sergio Ilarri, Eduardo Mena.
- Universidad Politécnica de Valencia: Estefanía Argente, Vicente Botti, Carlos Carrascosa, Adriana Giret, Vicente Julián.
- Universidad Pontificia de Salamanca: Javier Bajo.
- Universidad Rey Juan Carlos: Ramón Hermoso.
- Universidad Rovira i Virgili: David Isern, Antonio Moreno, Aida Valls.
- IOWA State University, USA: J. Dehlinger, R.R.Lutz.
- NASA Goddard Space Flight Center, USA: M. G. Hinchey.

Whitestein Series in Software Agent Technologies and Autonomic Computing

Edited by

Marius Walliser, Stefan Brantschen, Monique Calisti and Stefan Schinkinger

This series reports new developments in agent-based software technologies and agent-oriented software engineering methodologies, with particular emphasis on applications in the area of autonomic computing and communications.
The spectrum of the series includes research monographs, high quality notes resulting from research and industrial projects, outstanding Ph.D. theses, and the proceedings of carefully selected conferences. The series is targeted at promoting advanced research and facilitating know-how transfer to industrial use.

BIRKHÄUSER